Scenic North Alabama

By Robert Schuffert

ISBN 0-9744781-0-5
Second Printing, June, 2004
Copies of this book and photographic
enlargements of images can be ordered on-line at:
Http://Www.SchuffertStudios.Com
Robert Schuffert Studios
Huntsville, Alabama 35803
Cover Photo: Peavine Falls, Oak Mountain State Park

Introduction

The natural beauty of North Alabama is often found hidden in its backcountry. This book is intended to familiarize the traveler with North Alabama's most scenic locations and routes. The northeast quadrant of the state contains beautiful mountainous landscapes. These mountains are the southwest extremity of the Appalachian Mountain Range, which extends through Georgia, Tennessee and northeast into the New England states. Further westward across North Alabama, the flatlands surrounding the Tennessee River Valley have a beauty all their own with swamplands, marshes and backwaters. Traveling southward, you'll find additional mountains and rolling hills. Get off the Interstate highways! Along Alabama's back roads, you'll find many scenic barns and houses remaining from the early to mid 1900's, and a few from the 1800's. Some of Alabama's original covered bridges are still in light use today. Scenic Drives across North Alabama reveal varied landscapes to the traveler. Fields and meadows where farmers raise cotton, corn and soybean cover the terrain. During the off-season, these fields are planted with beautiful golden grasses swaying with the breeze. Other prominent land uses in North Alabama are dairy and tree farms and horse and cattle ranches. Alabama elevation rises from sea level at the Gulf of Mexico to 2,407 feet at Mount Cheaha in North Alabama.

Many parks have been established around the abundant Indian culture, which flourished in this area until the middle nineteenth century. General Andrew Jackson's forces defeated the Upper Creek Indians at the Battle of Horseshoe Bend on the Tallapoosa River in 1814, paving the way for Alabama's entry into the Union in 1819. Many of the lodges, cabins and supporting structures within Alabama's State Parks were constructed by members of the *Civilian Conservation Corp* (CCC) during the 1930's. President Franklin D. Roosevelt promoted the CCC during the Great Depression to provide work for thousands of unemployed veterans and young men.

Most people are familiar with the beauty within the Great Smokey Mountain National Park, but not so familiar with the beauty found in surrounding areas such as North Alabama. I hope this book will relay that beauty. Northern Alabama's State Parks, National Forests and National Preserve provide many activities for people of all ages and cultures. Most parks have accommodations for the physically disabled, and some have Americans with Disabilities Act (ADA) Boardwalks leading to scenic overlooks specially designed to accommodate wheelchairs.

About the Author

The author, Robert Schuffert, has lived in northeast Alabama for 18 years after growing up in south central Alabama. Born in Montgomery, he moved to Huntsville in 1984 pursuing his computer career. Interested in photography since 1964, and in awe of nature's beauty, he started *Robert Schuffert Studios, Outdoor Photography*, in 1999. Photographing frequently around the USA, he realized the natural beauty to be found right here in Alabama. The author took all photographs in this book (except this one of himself) during his travels around the state. Robert's photographs have been published in numerous books and calendars, and he was the 2002 Landscape Category and Grand-Prize winner of a local photography contest sponsored by the *Decatur Daily* newspaper. Robert's images were accepted and displayed by the Guntersville Museum and Cultural Center, Guntersville, Alabama in *Winterfest 2003*, and by the Tennessee Valley Art Center in Tuscumbia, Alabama in *Photography 2003*. He is a member of the *Huntsville Photographic Society* where he serves as newsletter editor. Robert's photographs have placed in several of the Society's monthly photo competitions. Robert also has a web site at www.SchuffertStudios.Com where he displays some of his images and posts screen savers

Dedication

This book is dedicated to my late wife Kathy with whom I was fortunate to share 24 years. Mary Katherine Davis Schuffert, or Kathy, was loved by all that knew her. Suddenly, in November 1998, Kathy suffered a massive brain aneurysm and passed away the next morning, at the peak of her career as a financial advisor. She never realized the rewards of her life-long efforts. During the last months of our lives together, I vividly remember her saying to me, "I can't believe you've never done anything with your photography". I thank her for the opportunity to try.

TABLE OF CONTENTS

Caution!

- Cell phone service is not provided in most areas listed in this book. Remember, if you become injured, it is a long way to get medical attention.

- There are dangerous ledges and cliffs near waterfalls and overlooks. The rocks can be slippery, even when dry, due to moss and algae, which grows abundantly in this moist environment. When hiking rocky terrain, place your feet on dry, bare, stable and level rock surfaces. Rocks covered with leaves, pine straw, moss or water become very slippery under weight. Be careful and watch your children.

- Be aware that poisonous snakes are present in Alabama forests. They are most often found near fallen trees, rocks and near creeks, streams and rivers. Since they hibernate during the colder months, this is the best time for hiking. Experienced hikers know to step *on* the log, then over, instead of just stepping *over* the log. This places your leg further away in case a snake is lurking under. In all my hiking experience, I have only seen two snakes. Both snakes sensed my presence and departed the area quickly.
  So did I!

Poison ivy in spring.

- Poison ivy, oak and sumac are often found in Alabama forests. Most people are allergic to at least one of these plants. Rashes usually appear a few days after contact with the plant's oil. One remedy is to wash infected areas immediately with water and alcohol to remove the oil. Wear long pants when trekking through underbrush. Poison ivy and oak both have three leaves and usually grow as small shrubs up to 30 inches high covering the ground. Poison oak may grow into a vine and climb tree trunks. Poison sumac has 7 to 13 leaves on each stem and grows as high as a small tree. All three plants have oval shaped serrated leaves, green in summer, turning yellow or red in fall.

- Alabama was home to four Indian cultures during the nineteenth century: the Creek, Cherokee, Choctaw and Chickasaw. Alabama's soft limestone and sandstone holds many Indian hieroglyphics. All Indian artifacts are protected by law; do not dig, destroy, or remove artifacts from the lands.

- Some areas listed in this book are located on private property. Please be respectful of the owner's privacy and property. Do not trespass without permission and please don't litter or damage trees or shrubbery.

- Always lock unattended vehicles and store valuables out of sight.

Map Information

All direction maps are color-coded for ease of identification. Major cities are outlined in yellow with black text. Lakes, creeks and rivers are light blue, while Interstates are a darker blue. National Forests, parks and scenic routes are highlighted in green. Hiking trails are a medium gray. All other points of interests are highlighted in red.

Direction maps are drawn to scale. North is up on all maps unless otherwise noted. All County Roads (CR#) shown on the direction maps are paved unless marked as "*dirt*". Most National Forest Roads (FR#) are dirt or gravel but usually passable in any smaller vehicle. Although not marked as such, most of the county roads are very scenic alternative routes. If you have the time, travel these as much as possible.

Additional Information

This mountainous terrain is home to many beautiful waterfalls, big and small, tall and wide. Most waterfalls are seasonal, generally flowing September through May. Some will stop completely during the summer months. Even the larger waterfalls slow to a trickle June through August. In years of drought, their flow may also diminish September through May. The best time to view waterfalls is a week or two after heavy rainstorms. This period allows the sediment to subside, providing clear whitewater around the falls and rapids. Waterfall dimensions in this book are close estimates. Most of these falls have not been measured. *Twin falls* are side-by-side while *double falls* are near but at different levels.

The different seasons change the face of the landscape. Fall brings a burst of color to the forests beginning in October and lasting through November. During winter months when trees are bare, waterfalls are more easily seen and the higher elevations often covered with snow. Springtime, as early as mid-March, color is added to forests once again when dogwood, redbud, wisteria, mountain laurel and rhododendron bloom. Summer restores its lush, green fullness to the terrain.

The most common trees in North Alabama include hardwoods, such as oak, hickory, maple, tupelo, elm, ash, walnut, sycamore and magnolia; and conifers such as white and yellow pine, cypress, eastern hemlock and cedar. Smaller flowering trees often found under the shelter of the larger trees include dogwood, redbud, cherry and wisteria (actually a vine, but will grow into a tree). With such a diverse variety of foliage, the forests are sprinkled with color during spring and fall seasons.

North Alabama geology is composed mainly of limestone and sandstone, both soft and easily eroded. Over the centuries, underground water erosion has created many natural caverns, attracting spelunkers from afar to explore. The soft stone also contains many Indian hieroglyphics, protected by law.

North Alabama temperatures normally range from a frigid 25 degrees, to a warm, humid 95 degrees. A comfortable year round climate for outdoor recreation. Activities include fishing, boating, sailing, canoeing, kayaking, swimming, whitewater rafting, hiking, camping, golfing, hunting, horse back riding, repelling and yes, even *snow skiing* during the winter months!

There are numerous overlooks along the roadways; many scenes can be viewed right from your vehicle. Others require a short trek, some along paved walkways or boardwalks. For the dedicated hiker, many other natural treasures can be found. Some of Alabama's most untouched areas require longer hikes, but the scenes obtained are well worth the effort. Alabama State Parks provide trail maps and Nature Centers generally located at their Country Stores. Many State Parks provide lodges, restaurants, cabins, chalets and campgrounds. For reservations or information on any of Alabama's State Parks, call 1-800 ALA-PARK.

Wildlife is abundant along the trails and even near most State Park facilities at dawn and dusk. Deer, coyote, bobcat, rabbit, wild turkey and many other animals inhabit North Alabama forests. Several State Parks are home to rare and endangered species of plants and wildlife, some which exist nowhere else in the world.

Lord, let me see the light in a unique perspective and photograph it so others may see the beauty of your work.

About this book

This book is organized as a travel guide to North Alabama's most scenic locations. It lists **National Parks, Preserves and Forests, State Parks, Private Parks, Canyons, Caverns, Covered Bridges, Natural Bridges, Scenic Routes and Waterfalls.**

The **Suggested Scenic Routes** section lists official scenic drives and other scenic routes. This section also suggests how much time should be allotted. The **Quick Reference Guide** (QRG) contains a list of State, National and private parks, followed by an alphabetical listing of the different scenes and drives, along with a brief description and scenic rating. The QRG should help you easily locate the scenes that match your interests. Once you have found an item of intrigue, you are referred to a specific page for detailed information concerning that location. Example:

Little River Canyon National Preserve - (Page 121) ★★★★★

In the **Detailed Information Section**, maps and directions are provided for each location, along with color photographs, descriptions of facilities and nearby points of interest.

Star Rating:
A star system (1-5) is used to rate items, where 5 stars indicate a "must-see" location as rated by the author. The stars indicate only the scenic quality of the site. Some private locations have a low rating due to lack of public access.

Trail Rating:

Easy –	A paved or well maintained pathway or boardwalk with no major inclines or obstacles.
Easy to Moderate –	A well maintained pathway with a few short inclines or obstacles.
Moderate –	A maintained pathway with several steep inclines, tree roots, loose rocks, shallow stream crossings or small obstacles.
Hard –	A frequently traveled path with some major obstacles such as stream crossings or steep inclines.
Tough –	A less traveled path with major obstacles such as fallen trees, streams, boulders or steep inclines.

Abbreviations used throughout this book:

ADA—Americans with Disabilities Act
CCC—Civilian Conservation Corp.
CB –Covered Bridge
CR – County Road
FR or FS – Forest Road or Service
NM – National Monument
NMP – National Military Park
NP – National Preserve
NWA – National Wildlife Area
NWR – National Wildlife Refuge
RV – Recreational Vehicle
SP – State Park

North Alabama Scenic Locations

This map of the northern half of Alabama denotes the location of most sites covered by this book. As you read through the different chapters, you may find additional small scenic areas not shown here. The next three maps are rotated to enlarge their size. On these maps, light gray lines denote major highways.

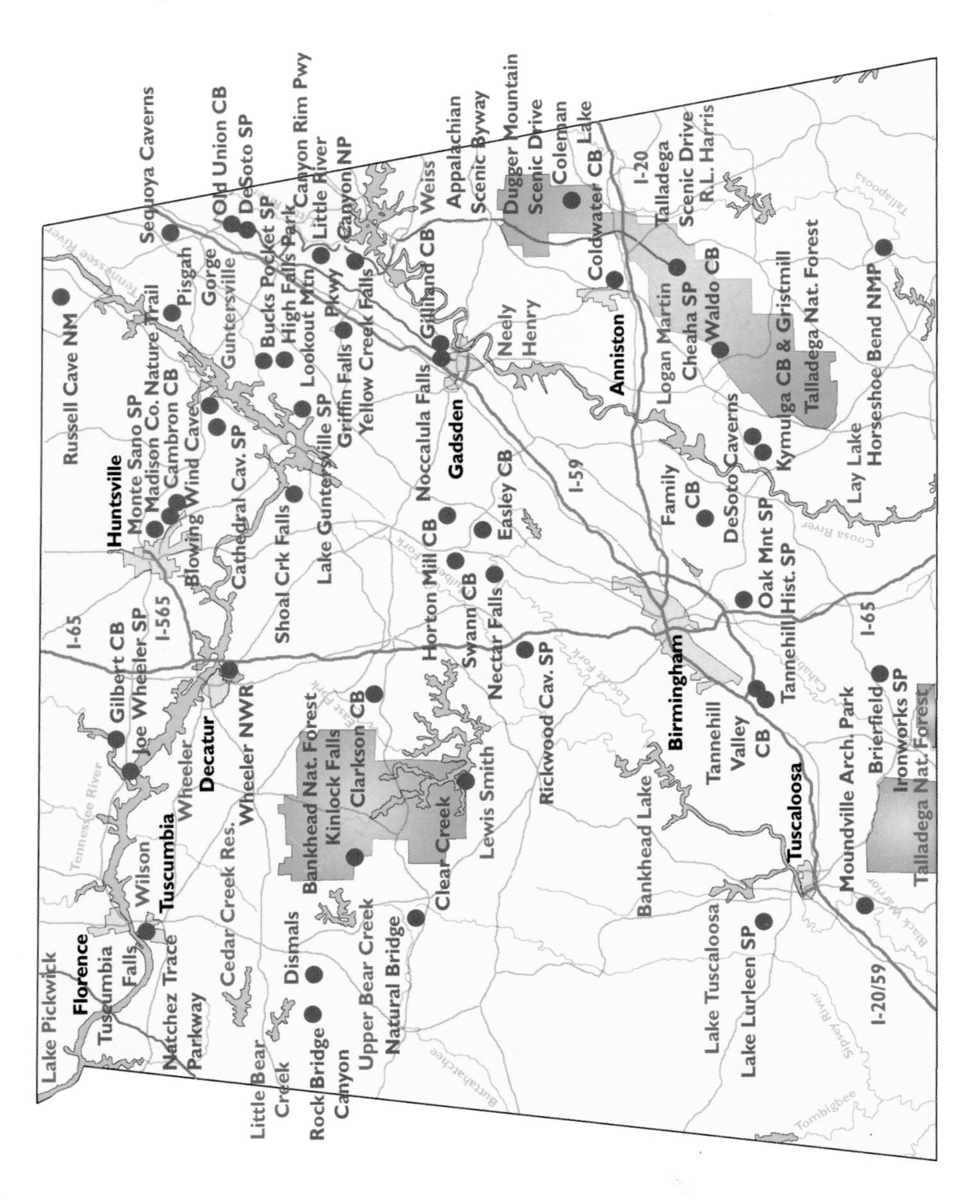

Suggested Scenic Routes

Golden grasses surround this old barn hidden in a hollow on Ala. 46 just south of I-20.

Wildflowers in front of a beautiful old barn on CR 1 in Maud near the southern end of the Natchez Trace Parkway.

Reminiscence of an old homestead on CR 57 near Oneonta.

Scenic Routes

This map shows Official Scenic Drives and other routes to follow when traveling between the locations covered in this book. Most of these routes bypass major cities and the associated heavy traffic. Most are also very scenic. The scenic routes are highlighted in green, while the continuing highways are light gray. Interstates are blue. Many of the other highways are scenic also; I tried to limit the number to avoid confusion. Depending upon your starting location, you should be able to find a road to reach any of these drives to continue on to your destination, whether it is a day trip or week long vacation.

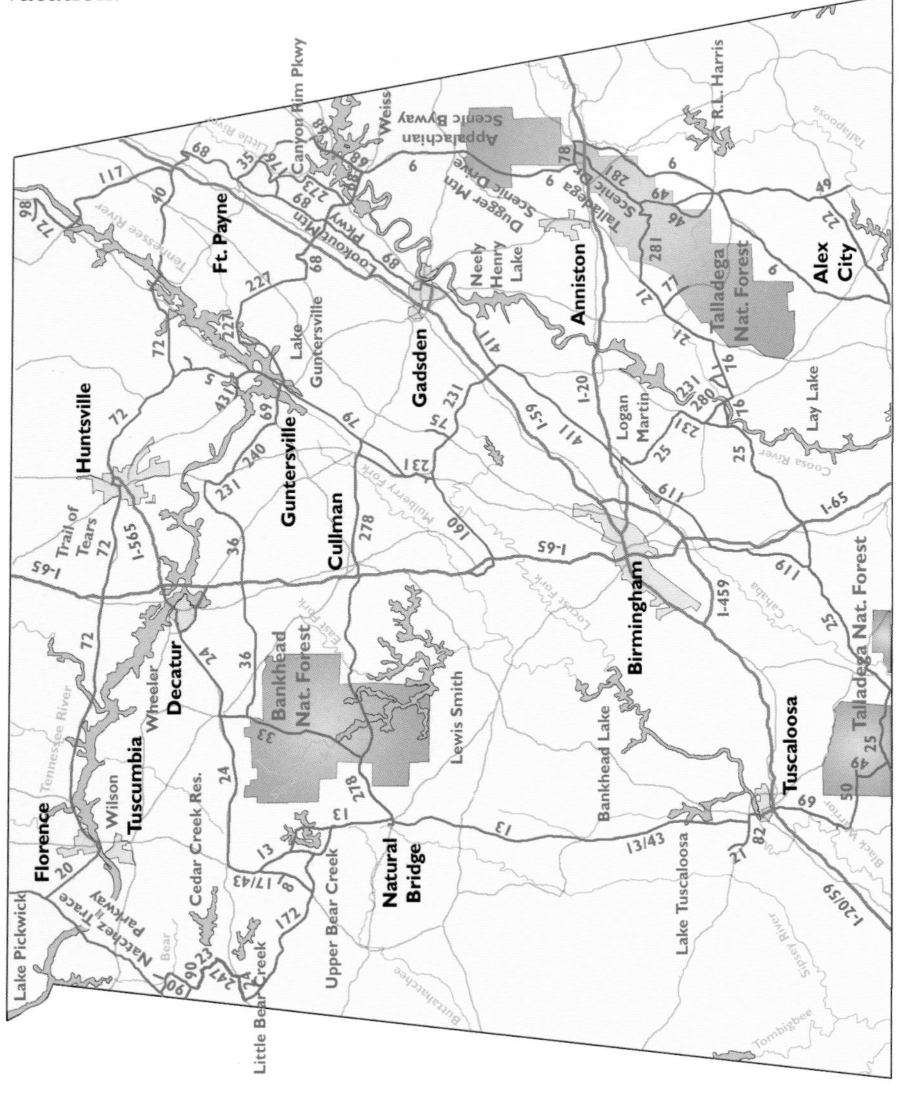

Day Trips

On this map, I've divided North Alabama into 10 sections: Guntersville, Ft. Payne, Oneonta, Talladega, Childersburg, Birmingham, Tuscaloosa, Bankhead, Florence and Huntsville. The destinations in these sections are reachable in one day if you are only planning a day trip. In most sections, one day will require eight to nine hours if you want to visit all sites. Remember to add the travel time from your starting location. If you can spend more time, combine sections and establish a route plan. Of course, many of these destinations will be more enjoyable if you spend more than one day. Many of the State Parks offer lodges, restaurants and campgrounds for longer, overnight journeys. The circles are about 50 miles across: an easy drive for one day. The following pages in this section document each of these areas.

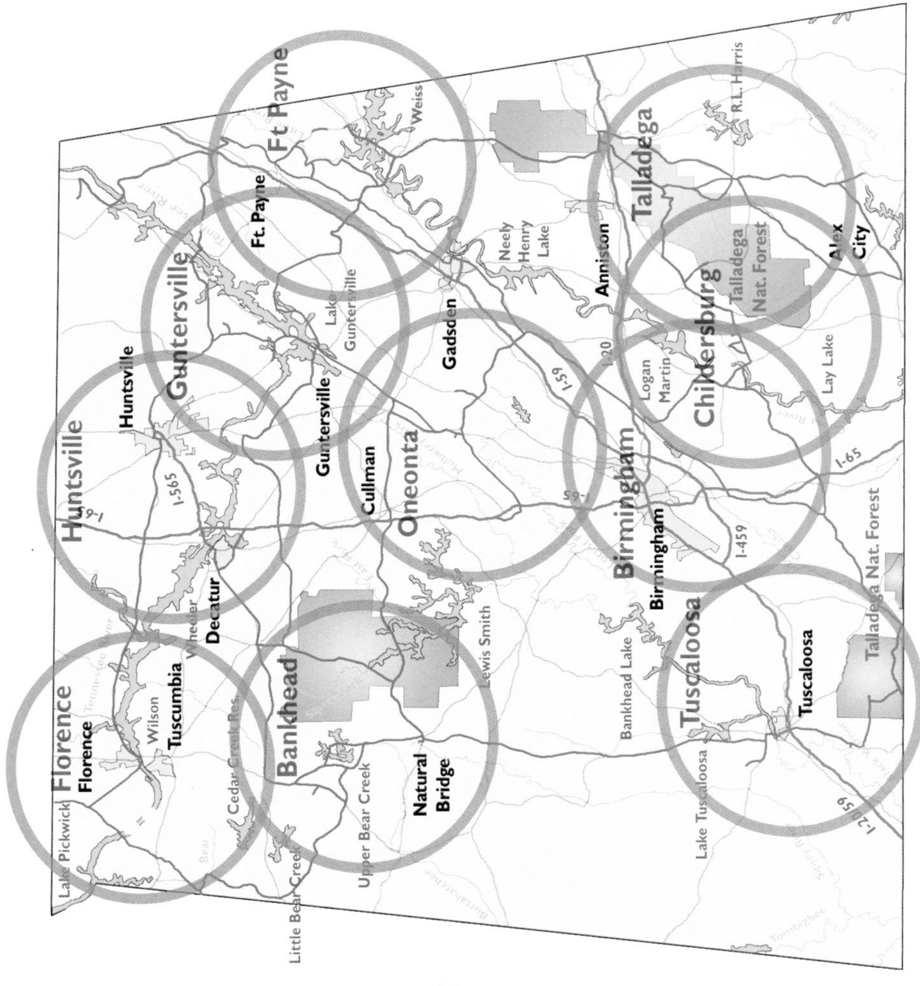

Bankhead Section

This section can be driven in one day. Travel time between these three sites will require about one-and-a-half hours, depending on traffic. Hiking through all three parks will take about the same amount of time each, for a total time of six hours. This may leave you with time to visit Clarkson Covered Bridge east of Natural Bridge along US 278. Bankhead National Forest is also included in this section, just east of this map. Most activities in this area require hiking, horseback riding, kayaking or canoeing and need to be planned separately. The exception is Kinlock Falls beside FS 210 in the National Forest. See the Direction Map for Dismals Wonder Garden (page 86) for more points of interest.

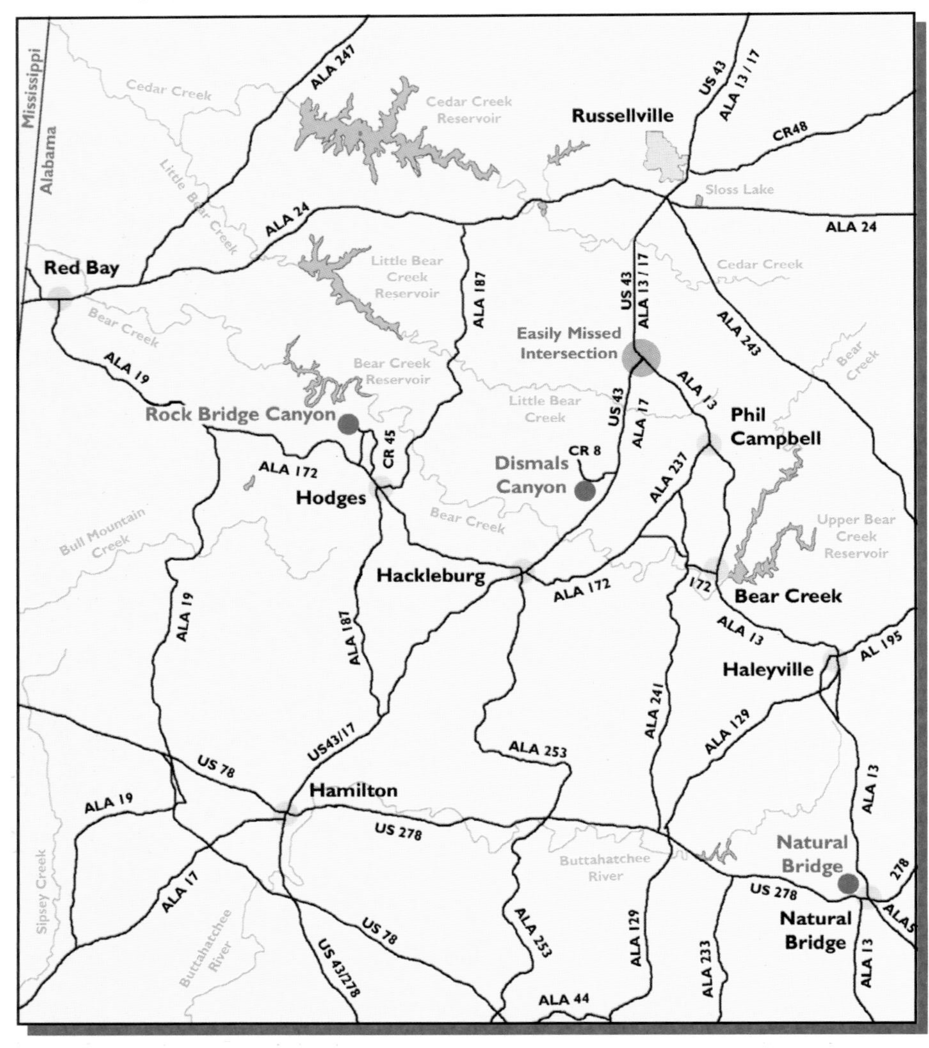

Birmingham Section

It is easy to spend a full day at Oak Mountain State Park with its hiking, boating and horse riding facilities. If possible take time to travel the Montevallo-Ashville Stage Route north, then Ala. 25 south. Despite being so close to Birmingham, this route has many scenic areas and the traffic is surprisingly light. This route will also lead you to Childersburg, where you will find Kymulga Covered Bridge and Gristmill and DeSoto Caverns Park.

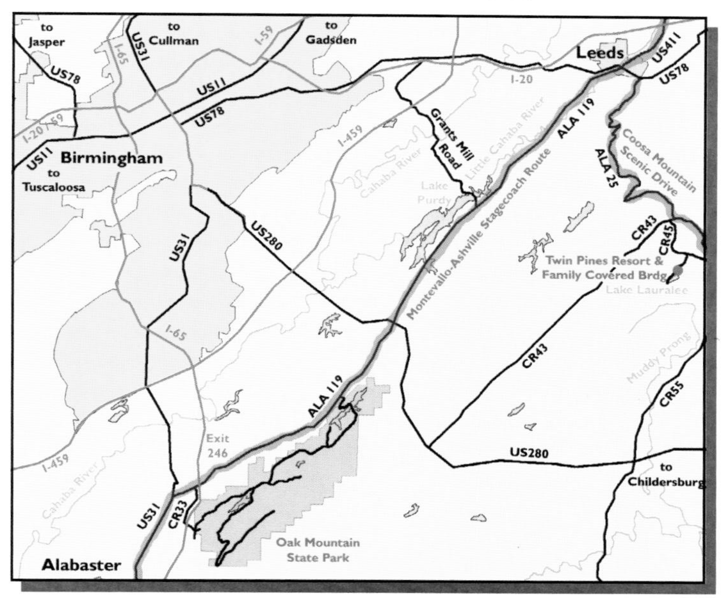

Tannehill Historical State Park is located 18 miles southwest of Birmingham along I-20/59. The many historical and scenic attractions here could easily require a full day. Tannehill Valley Covered Bridge is only two miles away. Brierfield Ironworks Historical State Park is just southeast of Tannehill.

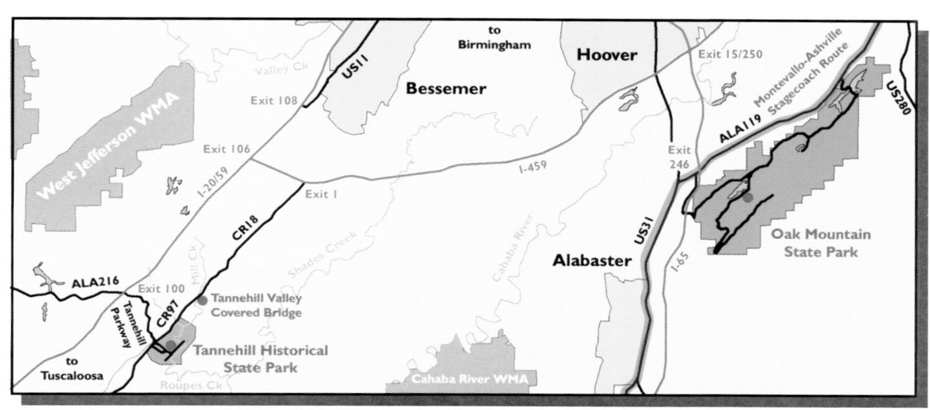

Childersburg Section

These three sites are within 25 miles of each other so this is an easy one-day trip. The main concern is tour times at DeSoto Caverns. If you have extra time, take the scenic drive northwest following US 231 then Ala. 25 to Leeds. From here, Ala. 119 south follows the scenic Montevallo-Ashville Stagecoach Route.

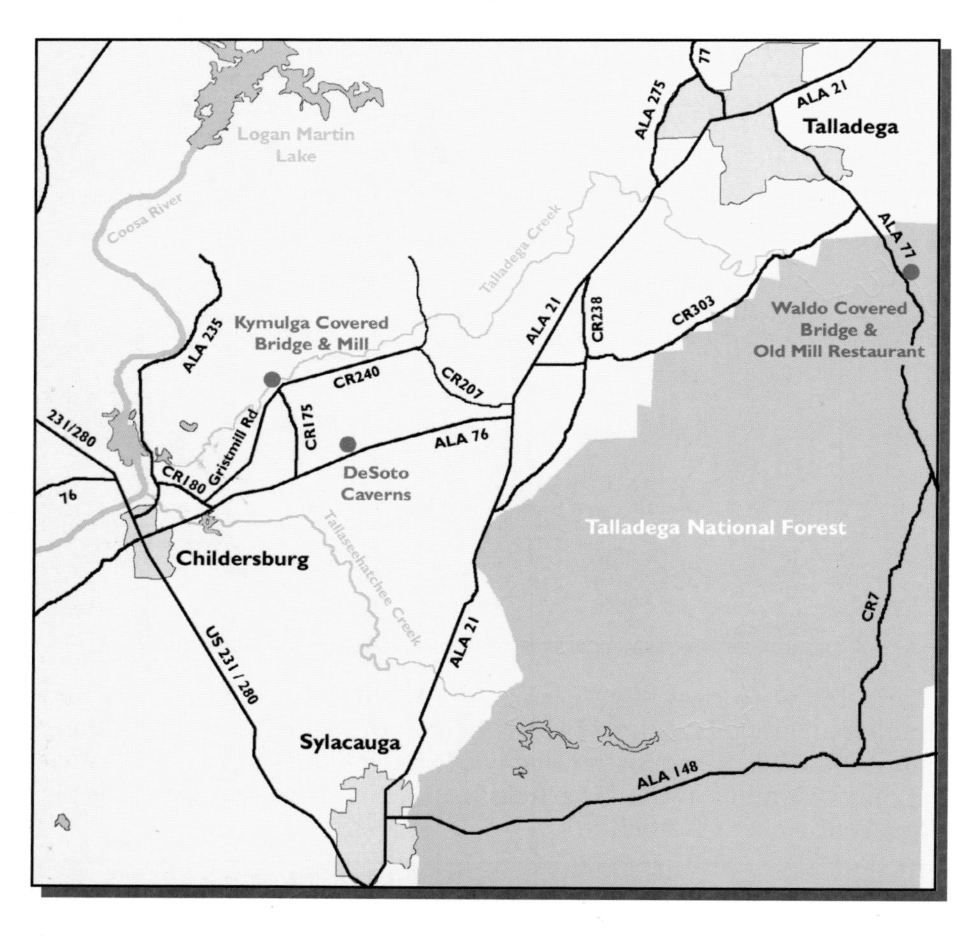

Florence Section

The Florence section consists of two one-day excursions. One day can be spent touring the Natchez Trace and a second day at Joe Wheeler State Park.

The Natchez Trace, west of Florence, extends 33 miles through the northwest corner of Alabama. Joe Wheeler State Park, east of Florence, provides all sorts of water activities, plus golf, camping, hiking and picnicking. Further east of Florence is Gilbert Covered Bridge near Athens.

Natchez Trace

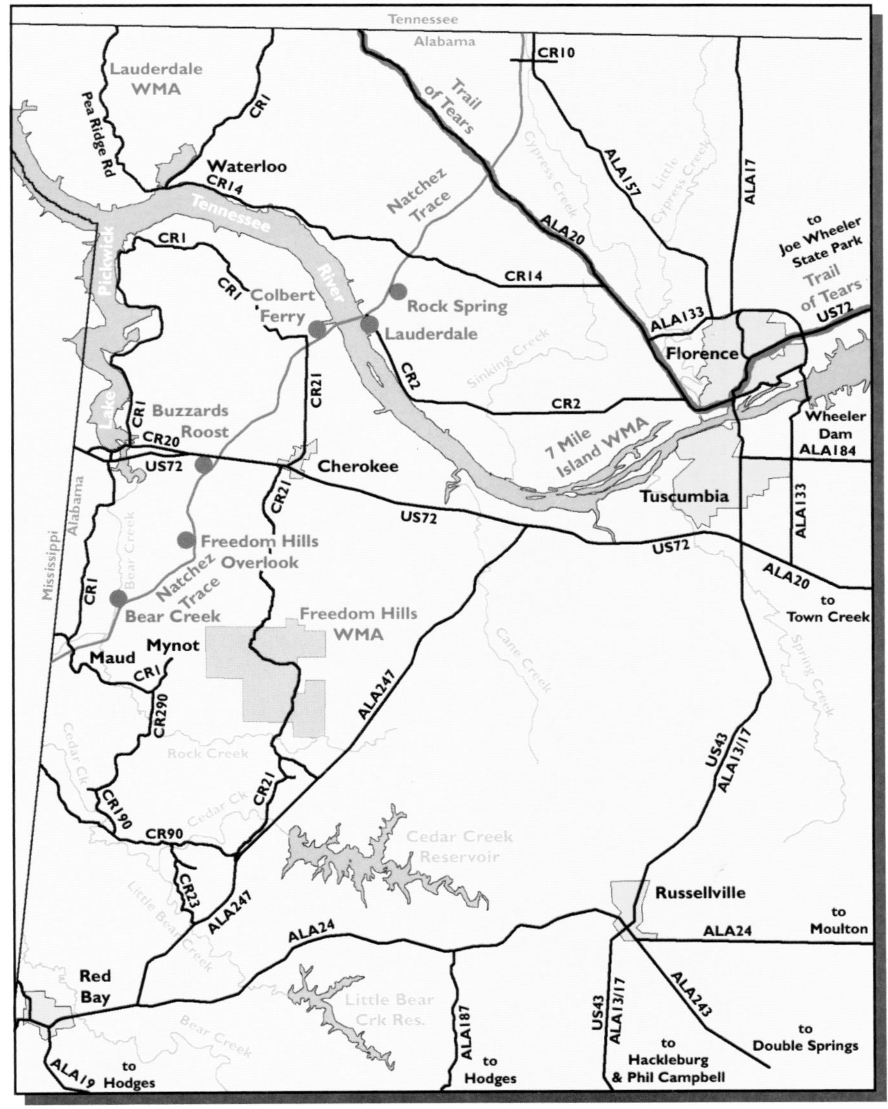

Ft. Payne Section

Within this section is some of North Alabama's most beautiful scenery. From tremendous waterfalls to breathtaking canyon overlooks, this section should be #1 on your planned destination list. DeSoto State Park provides full lodging, restaurant and camping facilities. Little River Canyon National Preserve begins only 10 miles southeast of the park and contains one of the most extensive canyon systems east of the Mississippi River, up to 700 feet deep.

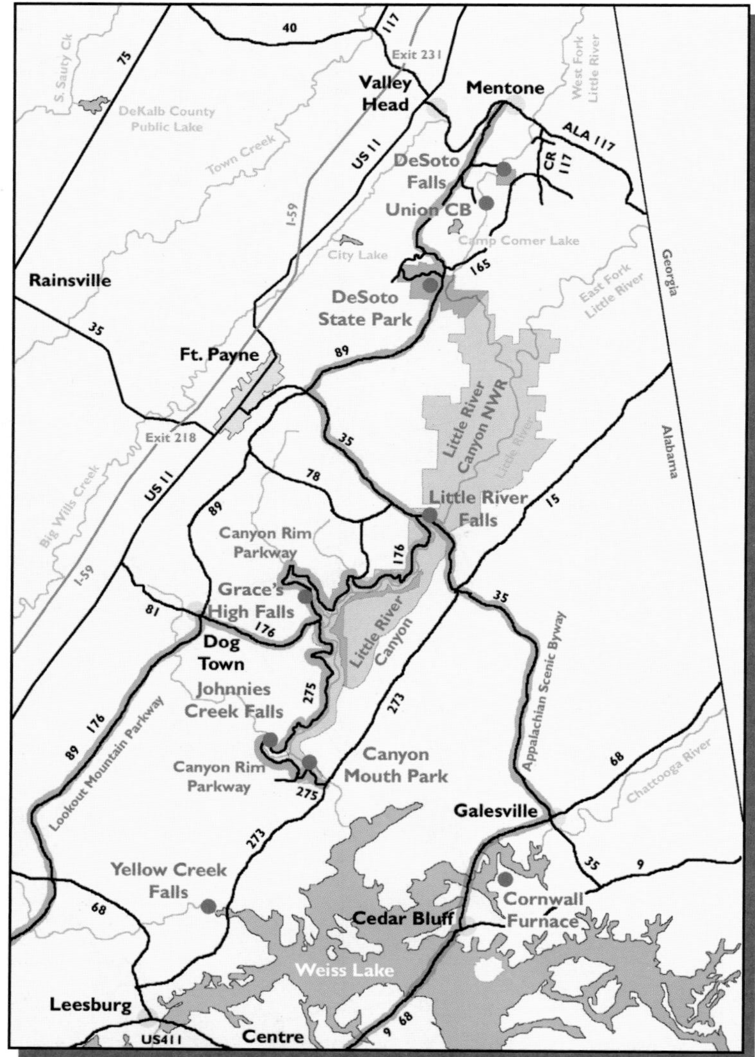

This entire tour can be traveled in one day if necessary, but to fully experience the wonders exposed here requires at least two days, preferably three, if your schedule allows. see DeSoto State Park or Little River Canyon National Preserve for details.

Major highlights in this section are Mentone, Cloudmont Resort, DeSoto Falls, DeSoto State Park, Lost Falls, Little River Falls, Grace's High Falls, Yellow Creek Falls, Little River

Canyon Rim Parkway, Lookout Mountain Parkway and Old Union Covered Bridge. Almost every road on these maps affords outstanding scenery for travelers and traffic is light. Cherokee Rock Village and Griffin Falls are just outside this area to the southwest. Russell Cave National Monument and Sequoyah Caverns Park are northwest of this area.

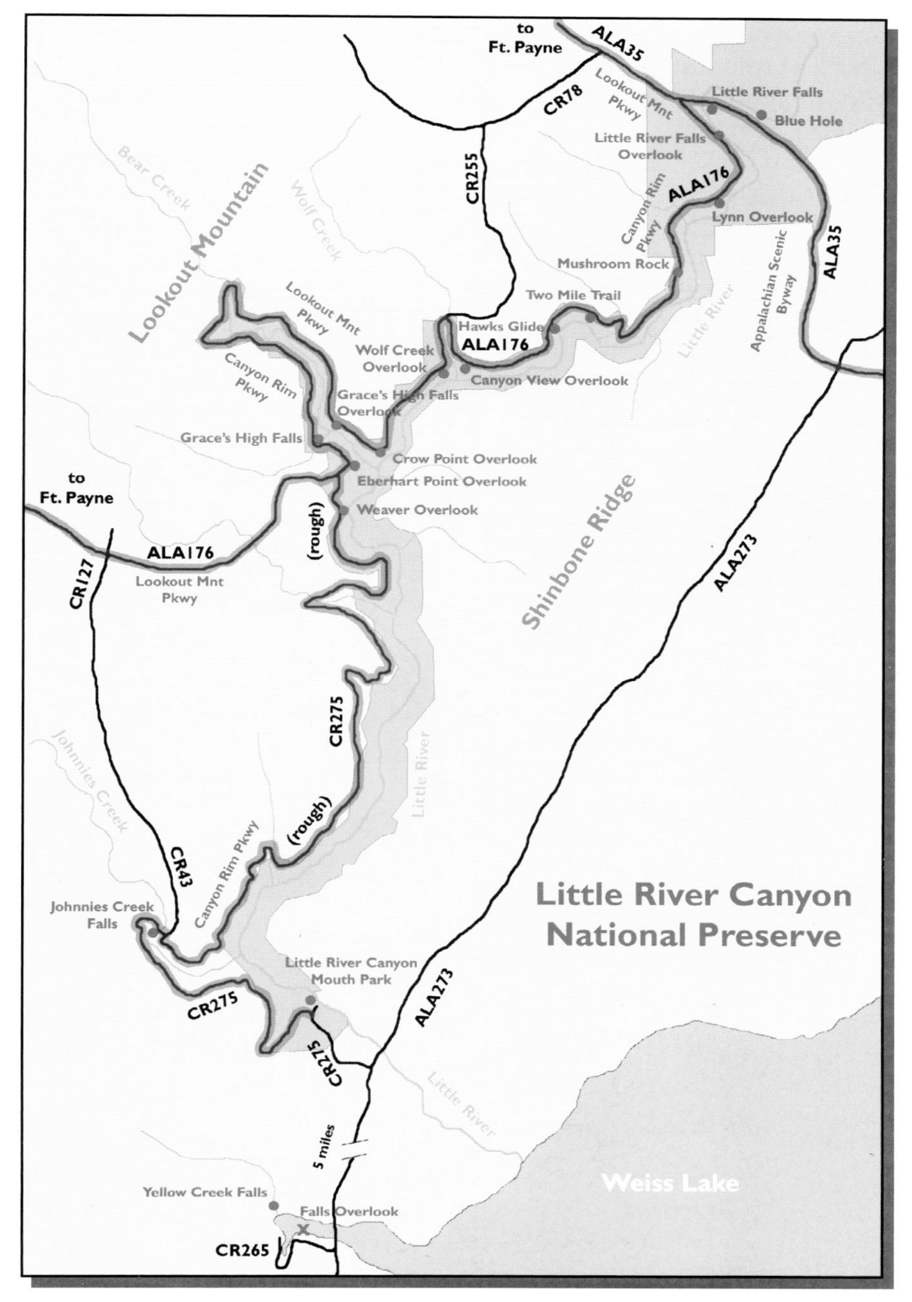

Guntersville Section

The area surrounding Guntersville holds many Alabama natural treasures. This area has so many destinations, it's difficult to see them all in one day. Guntersville State Park has full lodging facilities: Buck's Pocket State Park has campgrounds only. If you want to tour everything shown on the map below, plan on at least a two-day visit. See Guntersville State Park Details.

Major highlights in this area are High Falls and Natural Bridge, Cathedral Caverns, Ghost Creek Falls and Natural Bridge, Buck's Pocket and Lake Guntersville State Parks. Pisgah Gorge is just north of this map. Almost every road shown provides outstanding scenery and traffic is usually light. To the southeast are Cherokee Rock Village and Griffin Falls.

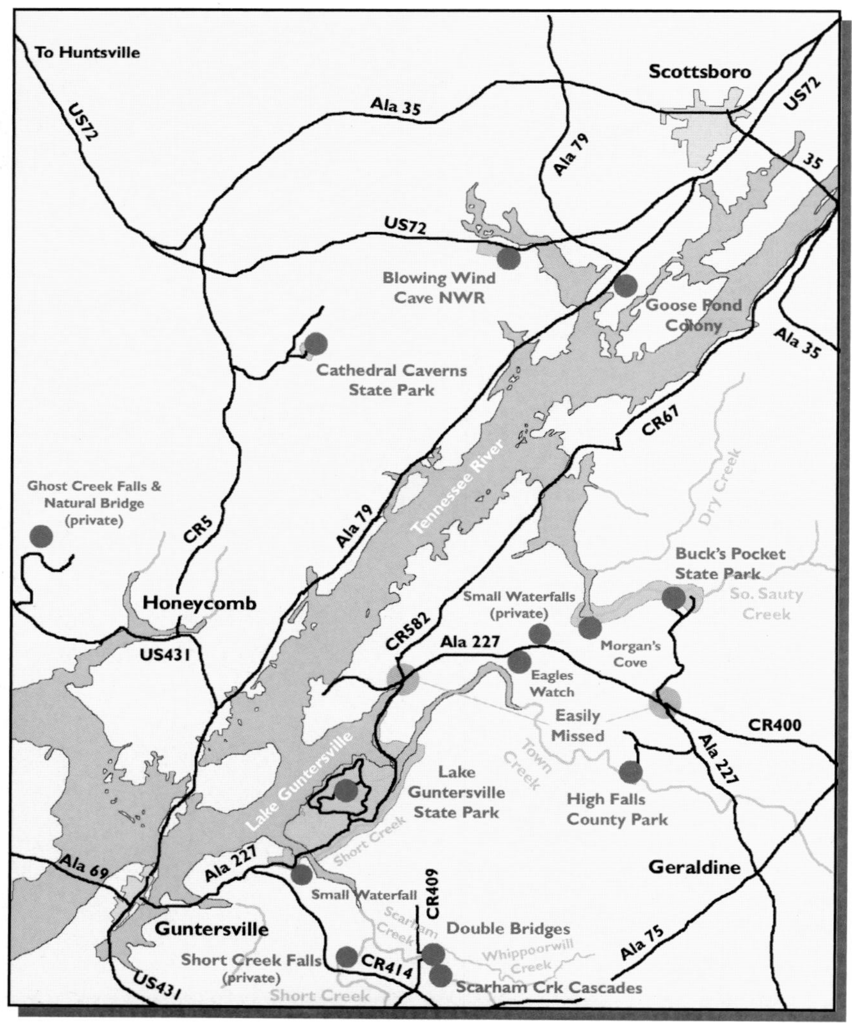

Huntsville Section

Monte Sano State Park and Madison County Nature Trail are the major scenic features around Huntsville. Start with a two-mile hike around Skye Lake at the Nature Trail, then explore the trails and Tavern Ruins at Monte Sano. This is easily a day excursion. There are many other attractions in Huntsville, such as various museums and the Space & Rocket Center. Also in this section is Wheeler NWR west toward Decatur. From Huntsville, the scenic route follows US 231 south to Lacey's Spring, where you turn right onto Ala. 36. Follow Ala. 36 west to Pence and turn right onto Ala. 67. Three miles beyond I-65, the Visitor's Center and Wildlife Viewing Observatory are on the left. This route takes a little more time, but is much more scenic than the Interstates.

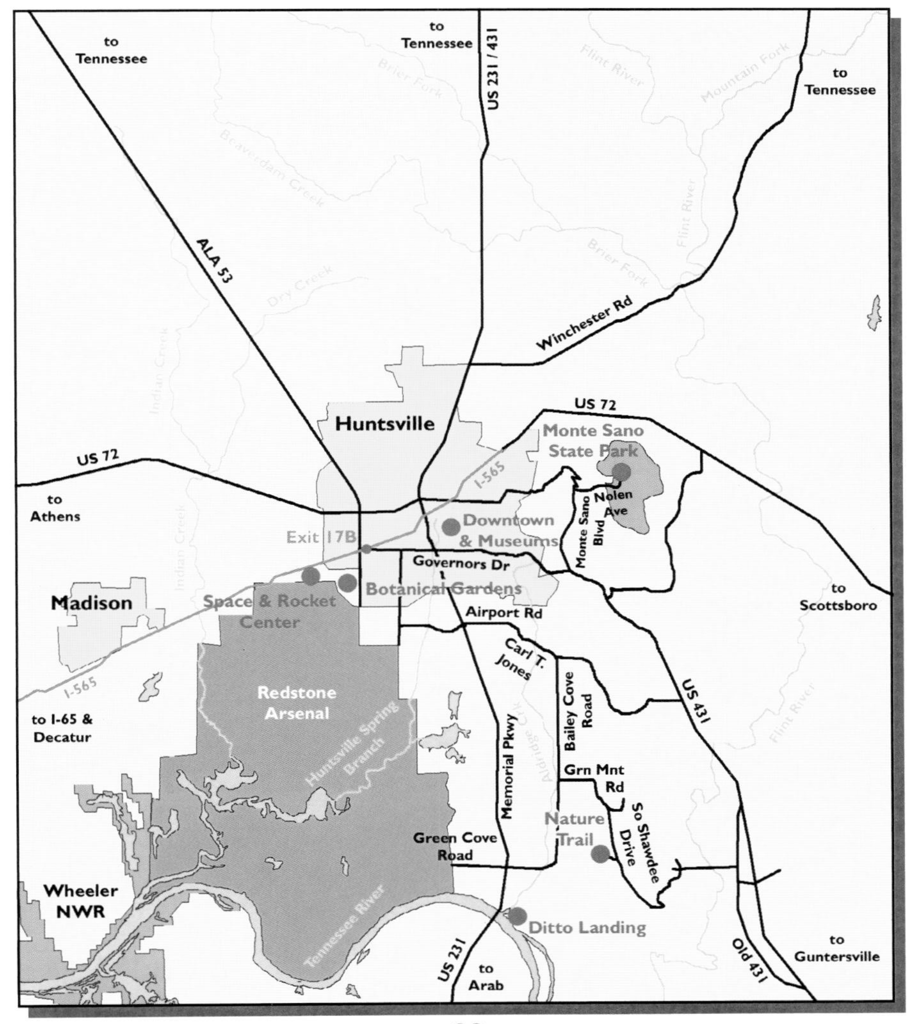

Oneonta Section

All destinations in this section can be toured in one day. If you plan to kayak or canoe the Mulberry or Locust Forks, you may decide to camp at Rickwood Caverns State Park. Driving between all of the sites shown below will require about two hours. If you also hike to Locust Fork Falls, add two more hours. Nectar Falls and all three covered bridges require only the time you want to spend at each, since they are all roadside features. The one-mile underground tour through Rickwood Caverns will take at least two hours. Be sure to check tour times prior to planning your visit. Call 1-800-ALA-PARK for information.

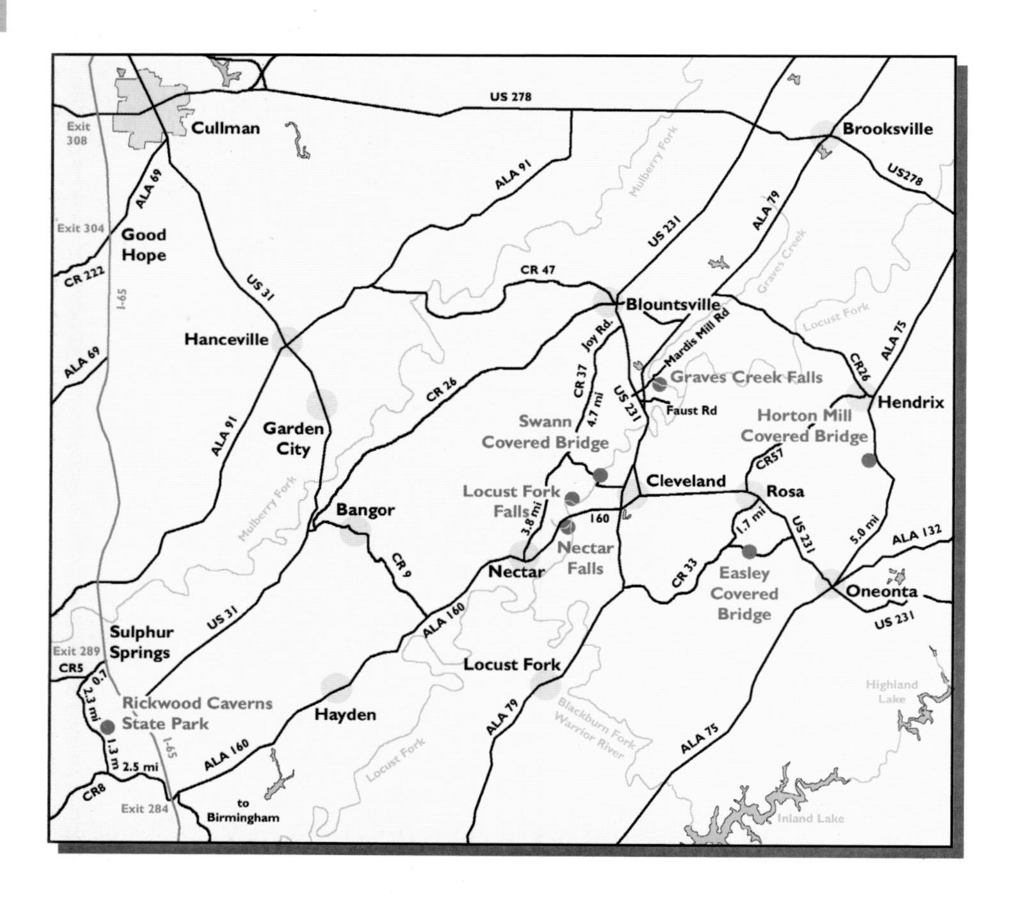

Talladega Section

All sites in this section can be driven in one day, including traveling to Waldo Covered Bridge. Beginning at Coldwater Covered Bridge, follow US 78 to the Talladega Scenic Drive. Tour the Scenic Drive 20 miles to Cheaha State Park, the highest point in Alabama. If you hike to all waterfalls shown below and to Bald Rock and Pulpit Rock Overlooks, there may not be time to see Waldo Covered Bridge unless you bypass High Falls. Coleman Lake Recreation Area is just north of Heflin in the National Forest.

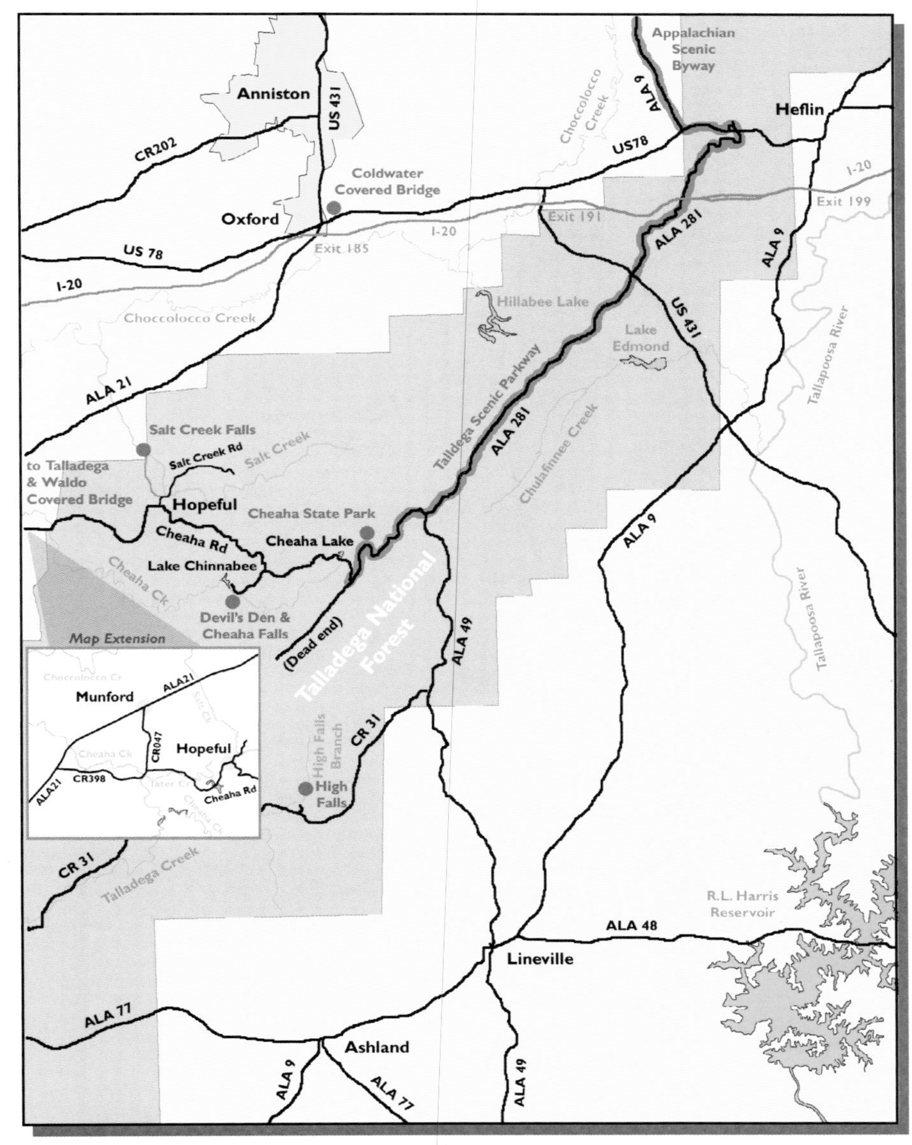

Tuscaloosa Section

Moundville and Lake Lurleen State Park can be seen in one day, depending upon your planned activities. Since the route between them goes through Tuscaloosa and Northport, time your travel with regard to rush hour. Moundville is an interesting park that may require more time than allotted.

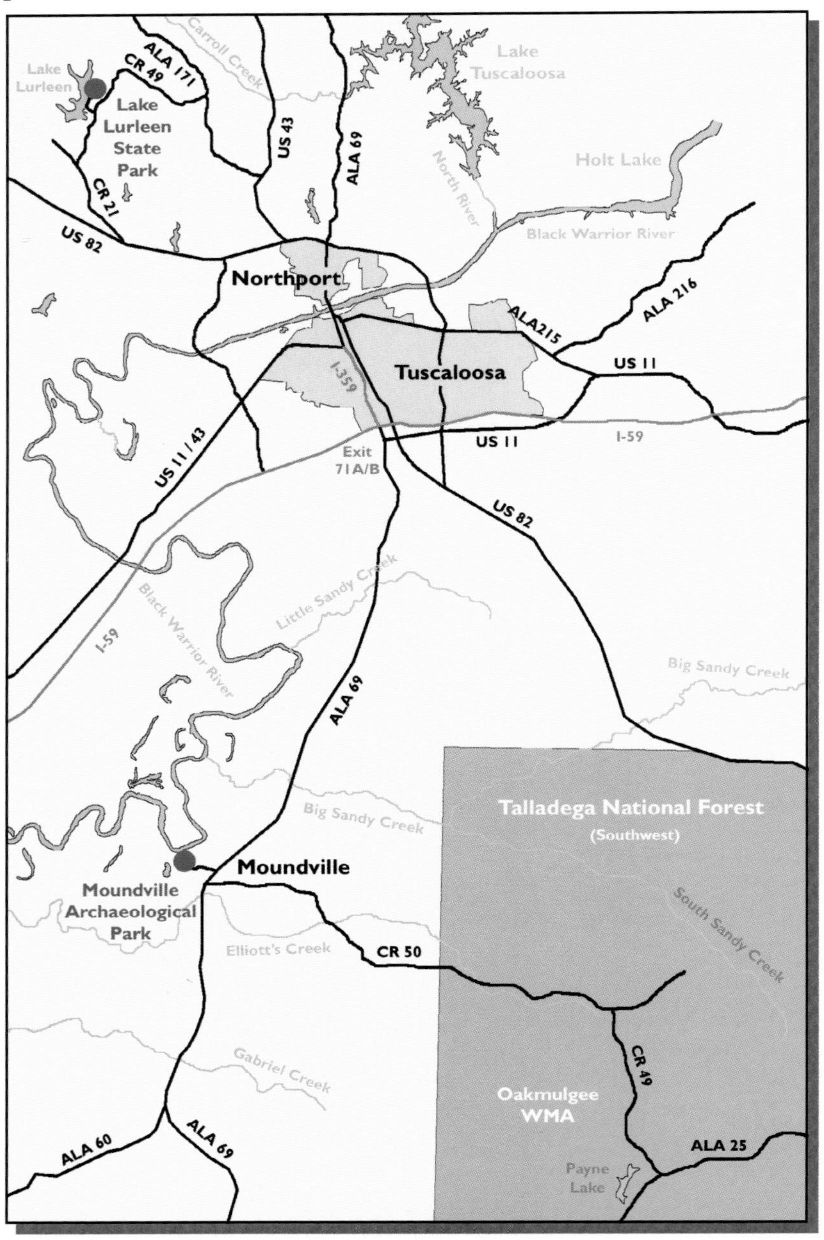

Quick Reference Guide

An early morning November sun casts long shadows across this old Henagar barn on CR 40.

Dawning sunlight illuminates a fine mist over the Flint River southeast of Huntsville on an early October morning.

National Forests

Talladega Nat. Forest (Northeast section) – (Page 186) ★★★★

Encompassing the highest point in Alabama at 2,407 feet elevation, this area provides scenic overlooks, streams and waterfalls. Fully developed Cheaha State Park and the Talladega Scenic Drive along the Horseblock Mountain ridge are within forest boundaries. Most acreage is natural forest with many hiking trails. The Pinhoti Trail leads north by the Coleman Lake Recreation Area then continues to the Chief Ladiga Trail at Piedmont.

William B. Bankhead Nat. Forest – (Page 199) ★★★★★

Preserved in its natural state, this National Forest is a retreat with many beautiful waterfalls, miles of hiking trails and streams, the Sipsey River (listed as a *National Wild and Scenic River)* and Lewis Smith Lake. There are very few facilities inside the forest boundaries. This area is rich with Indian artifacts (protected by law). Being almost totally untouched by development, this area is the experienced hiker's paradise. Alabama's largest tree is within forest borders.

National Preserve & Parks

Blowing Wind Cave National Wildlife Refuge – (Page 53) ★
This cave is home to 250,000 endangered bats. Near dusk, view the bats exiting the cave in search of insects around the backwaters of Lake Guntersville on the Tennessee River. The cave is named after the cool breeze that emanates from its mouth during summer months.

Horseshoe Bend National Military Mon. – (Page 100) ★★★
Drive around or hike across lands surrounding the Indian village Tohopeka, Alabama's only National Park. Horseshoe Bend is an historic location where a bend in the Tallapoosa River forms a natural defensive boundary. The Upper Creek Indians called this area home until defeated by General Andrew Jackson in the early 1800's.

Little River Canyon National Preserve – (Page 121) ★★★★★
The Preserve features one of the deepest gorges east of the Mississippi River. Canyon Rim Parkway winds 22 miles along the western canyon rim. Breathtaking canyon overlooks and outstanding scenic waterfalls in nearby DeSoto State Park.

Natchez Trace Parkway – (Page 146) ★★★
Established in 1938, Natchez Trace follows an historic Indian trail 445 miles from Natchez, Mississippi to Nashville, Tennessee, with 33 miles extending through the northwest corner of Alabama. Part of the National Scenic Byways Program, the National Park Service preserves historic sites along this excursion.

Russell Cave National Monument – (Page 175) ★★★
First opened in 1953, this cave contained one of the longest and most complete archaeological records in eastern America, which indicated habitation over an 8,000-year period.

Wheeler National Wildlife Refuge – (Page 196) ★★★
This area contains 34,500 acres of land set aside to provide habitat for birds, fish, reptiles and amphibians. The Refuge includes 18,000 surface acres of water and is a popular location for fishing. Several highways intersect the waters, providing scenic drives.

State Parks

Brierfield Ironworks Historical State Park – (Page 55) ★★

A furnace constructed during the Civil War period to produce iron for the Confederate Army, at its peak produced 25 tons per day. Delivered to the Selma Arsenal, this iron was used for plates in gunboats and other naval ordnance. Several historical structures have been restored in the park.

Bucks Pocket State Park – (Page 59) ★★★★

Buck's Pocket is located on Sand Mountain near Lake Guntersville. On the canyon's south ridge adjacent to the picnic areas, a boardwalk leads to Point Rock, which overlooks the canyon and campground below. The campground is situated on the canyon floor beside South Sauty Creek. Located not far from High Falls County Park and Lake Guntersville State Park, Buck's Pocket is a secluded location for camping and hiking. Gain access to Lake Guntersville at nearby Morgan's Cove, which is an extension of the park.

Cathedral Caverns State Park – (Page 62) ★★★★

Located on the side of 1,100 foot Gunters Mountain near Grant, Cathedral Caverns has the largest cave entrance in America with a 128-foot span in limestone. The cavern also features the world's largest stalagmite, the world's largest stalagmite forest and the world's largest frozen waterfall. Since the property's recent purchase by the state, construction has just been completed on the visitor's center. A guided tour along the 3,500-foot concrete path leads visitors over an underground stream.

Cheaha State Park – (Page 65) ★★★★

The highest point in Alabama, Mount Cheaha rises 2,407 feet above sea level. It features panoramic views from overlooks, the swimming pool, lodge and restaurant. Cheaha State Park is completely within the Talladega National Forest boundaries.

DeSoto State Park – (Page 78) ★★★★★

DeSoto State Park, located in northeast Alabama near Fort Payne on Lookout Mountain, includes all necessary facilities. This is *the* destination for scenic waterfalls! Nearby *Little River Canyon National Preserve* provides numerous overlooks along its scenic Canyon Rim Parkway.

Joe Wheeler State Park – (Page 105) ★★★★

Joe Wheeler has all the finer amenities of a park. With an outstanding lodge and marina on Wheeler Lake, recreational activities abound. A par 72 golf course adds to its attractiveness.

Lake Guntersville State Park – (Page 112) ★★★★

Straddling 1,140-foot Taylor Mountain on a peninsula at Lake Guntersville, this park has all facilities, including a par 72 golf course and beach area. Wildlife is abundant all around the park.

The lodge, chalets and overlooks provide outstanding views of the Tennessee River and Lake Guntersville below, especially at sunset. Located nearby are Buck's Pocket State Park, High Falls County Park and Ghost Creek Falls and Natural Bridge.

Lake Lurleen State Park- (Page 117) ★★

Located just west of Tuscaloosa, 250-acre Lake Lurleen provides peaceful relaxation while camping or picnicking along its hillside shores or canoeing its waters.

Monte Sano State Park – (Page 135) ★★★

A small limited facility park adjacent to Huntsville with picnic areas and hiking and biking trails. The park has scenic overlooks and small waterfalls after rainstorms. The Monte Sano Planetarium, established by Werner Von Braun, is adjacent the park. Nearby are the Space & Rocket Center, Madison County Nature Trail and several museums.

Oak Mountain State Park – (Page 155) ★★

Alabama's largest State Park, Oak Mountain provides many outdoor activities such as camping, picnicking, fishing, biking, hiking, swimming, horseback riding and boating. The park's most scenic features include mountaintop overlooks, Peavine Falls and miles of trails through mountainous, forested areas.

Rickwood Caverns State Park – (Page 164) ★★

These caverns were carved by underground water 260 million years ago. Seashells and marine fossils line the walls and ceilings. Located in a secluded area north of Birmingham just off I-65, the park has minimal facilities. Several covered bridges and waterfalls are located nearby.

Tannehill Historical State Park – (Page 191) ★★

This park features an historic furnace built in 1860 along the Roupes Creek. During Civil War years, the furnace produced 20 tons of iron per day, used to supply the Confederacy with ordnance.

Other Parks

Cherokee Rock Village – (Page 70) ★★

This 200-acre county park affords magnificent views overlooking Weiss Lake, Leesburg and Centre. Huge sandstone formations at the bluff attract rock climbers and campers.

DeSoto Caverns Park – (Page 76) ★★

Privately owned and operated, DeSoto Caverns has a history dating back to the 1700's. The Cathedral Room is large; over 300 feet by 50 feet and the ceiling is 12 stories above. Many activities are here for the family, including laser light shows.

Dismals Wonder Garden – (Page 85) ★★★★

The Dismals is a small but beautiful privately owned canyon. Two waterfalls are found along the 3/4-mile hike through the canyon, Rainbow and Secret Falls. Huge boulders and rock cliffs are highlighted with bright green moss. The Dismals Branch Stream passes between and under these boulders along the canyon floor. Champion Tree, an Eastern Hemlock, is the largest in Alabama. The National Park Service recognizes the park.

High Falls County Park – (Page 96, photo 97, 99) ★★★★★

As Town Creek rushes across Sand Mountain toward Lake Guntersville on a rocky streambed, it drops 55 feet at High Falls Park. During heavy rains, this fall can be as much as 300 feet wide. Erosion from the waterfall has formed a natural bridge at the north side of the falls. Falling water gushes through the opening. A wooden bridge with native stone supports crosses Town Creek above the falls. Within 20 miles are Lake Guntersville and Buck's Pocket State Parks.

Hurricane Creek Park – (Page 102) ★★★

This 55-acre park north of Cullman includes waterfalls, a natural bridge and unusual rock formations in a small canyon along Hurricane Creek. Two miles of moderate hiking trails meander through the canyon. To ascend or descend the canyon, the park has a small cable car system modeled after The Incline in Chattanooga.

Kymulga Covered Bridge – (Page 75, photo 108, 109) ★★★★

Kymulga Covered Bridge is at its original location near Childersburg. 105 feet in length and 10 feet wide, it is a single span bridge constructed in 1860 over Talladega Creek. Adjacent to the bridge, Kymulga Gristmill is still in operation. Campgrounds, a picnic area and two miles of hiking trails are in the park. Kymulga is listed on the National Register of Historic Places.

Madison County Nature Trail – (Page 133) ★★★★

Atop Green Mountain in Huntsville, this park includes a two mile hiking trail around its lake. The Cambron Covered Bridge and a pioneer homestead are found along the trail.

Moundville Archaeological Park – (Page 142) ★★★★

This park encompasses 26 flat-topped pyramid shaped mounds built by Native American Indians during the Mississippian Period, 1,000 to 1,500 AD. The highest mound towers 60 feet above the plains along the banks of the Black Warrior River. It is rich in Indian culture dating back at least 12,000 years.

Oakville Indian Mounds Park & Museum—(Map 201) ★★★

Hidden between Cullman and Moulton near Ala 157 on CR187 1/2 mile from Jesse Owens Park, this historical area once contained 20 native Indian burial mounds. The remaining ceremonial mound rises 27 feet and covers an area of 1.8 acres. The museum exhibits over 1000 artifacts of Indian habitation as long as 2000 years ago. Artesian wells made this location prime for the Copena Indians of the period and now replenishes a large lake adjacent to picnic areas.

Natural Bridge Park – (Page 149) ★★★★

With a span of 148 feet, this 60-foot high sandstone bridge is one of America's longest. This is a privately owned and operated park with gift shop, picnic areas and hiking trails.

Noccalula Falls – (Page 151, 152, photo 153, 154) ★★★★

90-foot high Noccalula Falls is located at the southern end of Lookout Mountain Parkway which tours northeasterly to Mentone. The park is just two miles from I-59 Exit 188 in Gadsden. The falls are named after an Indian princess who hurdled herself into the canyon when her chieftain father exiled her lover.

Pisgah Gorge (Page 159) ★★★

Being a small narrow canyon in Sand Mountain by the Tennessee River, Pisgah Gorge is another of Alabama's hidden natural wonders. Little Bryant Creek flows through the canyon forming two huge waterfalls. A bluff overlook on a rock outcrop provides a magnificent view of the lower waterfall as it free falls 25 feet then cascades another 75 feet to the canyon floor.

Rock Bridge Canyon – (Page 167) ★★★★

A privately owned park, this is one of Alabama's hidden secret treasures, not found on many roadmaps. The canyon contains many natural formations found in North Alabama such as a huge 50-foot span natural bridge with an adjacent waterfall and two more beautiful waterfalls along the stream below. The canyon remains in a very natural state with 3/4 miles of tough hiking trails through moss covered boulders.

Sequoyah Caverns Park – (Page 178) ★★★★★

The "Looking Glass Caverns" are usually described as one of the country's most outstanding. Crystal clear pools and lakes reflect the beauty of natural underground formations. Buffalo and deer roam the fields adjacent the park. The caverns and campgrounds are privately owned and accommodate the physically disabled.

Canyons

Buck's Pocket State Park – (Page 59) ★★★★

Buck's Pocket is located on Sand Mountain near Lake Guntersville. On the canyon's south ridge adjacent to the picnic areas, a boardwalk leads to Point Rock, which overlooks the canyon and campground below. The campground is situated on the canyon floor beside South Sauty Creek. Located not far from High Falls County Park and Lake Guntersville State Park, Buck's Pocket is a secluded location for camping and hiking. Gain access to Lake Guntersville at nearby Morgan's Cove, which is an extension of the park.

Dismals Wonder Garden – (Page 85) ★★★★

The Dismals is a small but beautiful privately owned canyon. Two waterfalls are found along the 3/4-mile hike through the gorge, Rainbow and Secret Falls. Huge boulders and rock cliffs are highlighted with bright green moss. The Dismals Branch Stream passes between and under these boulders along the canyon floor. Champion Tree, an Eastern Hemlock, is the largest in Alabama. The park is recognized by the National Park Service.

Hurricane Creek Park – (Page 102) ★★★

This 55-acre park north of Cullman includes waterfalls, a natural bridge and unusual rock formations in a small canyon along Hurricane Creek. Two miles of moderate hiking trails meander through the canyon. To ascend or descend the canyon, the park has a small cable car system modeled after The Incline in Chattanooga.

Little River Canyon National Preserve – (Page 121) ★★★★★

Little River Canyon is one of the deepest gorges east of the Mississippi River. Canyon Rim Parkway winds 22 miles along the western canyon rim. Breathtaking canyon overlooks and outstanding scenic waterfalls here and in nearby DeSoto State Park.

Little River Canyon on a foggy winter afternoon.

Noccalula Falls – (Page 151, 152, photo 153, 154) ★★★★

90-foot high Noccalula Falls is located at the southern end of Lookout Mountain Parkway which tours northeasterly to Mentone. The park is just two miles from I-59 Exit 188 in Gadsden. The falls are named after an Indian princess who hurdled herself into the canyon when her chieftain father exiled her lover.

Pisgah Gorge (Page 159) ★★★

Being a small narrow canyon in Sand Mountain by the Tennessee River, Pisgah Gorge is another of Alabama's hidden natural wonders. Little Bryant Creek flows through the canyon forming two huge waterfalls. A bluff overlook on a rock outcrop provides a magnificent view of the lower waterfall as it free falls 25 feet then cascades another 75 feet to the canyon floor.

Rock Bridge Canyon – (Page 167) ★★★★

A privately owned park, this is one of Alabama's hidden secret treasures, not found on many roadmaps. The canyon contains many natural formations found in North Alabama such as a huge 50-foot span natural bridge with an adjacent waterfall and two more beautiful waterfalls along the stream below. The canyon remains in a very natural state with 3/4 miles of tough hiking trails through moss covered boulders.

Swann Covered Bridge – (Page 75, 130, photo 131) ★★★★★

Swann is a three-span bridge built in 1934. At 324 feet, it is the second longest in Alabama. It spans a beautiful small canyon on Locust Fork and is open to local traffic.

Caverns

Blowing Wind Cave NWR – (Page 53) ★

Home to 250,000 bats, you will welcome the cool breeze blowing out during the summer months. Bats can be seen exiting the cave to feed at dusk June through August.

Cathedral Caverns State Park – (Page 62) ★★★★

Located on the side of 1,100 foot Gunters Mountain near Grant, Cathedral Caverns has the largest cave entrance in America with a 128 foot span in limestone. The cavern also features the world's largest stalagmite, the world's largest stalagmite forest and the world's largest frozen waterfall. Since the property's recent purchase by the state, construction has just been completed on the visitor's center. A guided tour along the 3,500-foot concrete path leads visitors over an underground stream.

DeSoto Caverns Park – (Page 76) ★★

Privately owned and operated, DeSoto Caverns history dates back to the 1700's. The Cathedral Room is large; over 300 feet by 50 feet and the ceiling is 12 stories above. Many activities are available for the family, including laser light shows.

Rickwood Caverns State Park – (Page 164) ★★

These caverns were carved by underground water 260 million years ago. Seashells and marine fossils line the walls and ceilings. Located in a secluded area north of Birmingham just off I-65, the park has minimal facilities. Several covered bridges and waterfalls are located nearby.

Russell Cave National Monument – (Page 175) ★★★

First opened in 1953, this cave contained one of the longest and most complete archaeological records in eastern America, which indicated habitation over an 8,000-year period.

Sequoyah Caverns Park- (Page 178) ★★★★★

The "Looking Glass Caverns" are usually described as one of the country's most outstanding. Crystal clear pools and lakes reflect the beauty of natural underground formations. Buffalo and deer roam the fields adjacent to the park. The caverns and campgrounds are privately owned and accommodate the physically disabled.

Covered Bridges

The map on page 73 of the Detailed Information Section shows the general location of covered bridges in North Alabama.

Cambron Covered Bridge – (Page 74, 134, photo 134) ★★★
The Cambron Covered Bridge is a newly constructed replica built across a marsh along the lake edge at the Madison County Nature Trail in Huntsville. The bridge can be seen along the hiking trail.

Clarkson Covered Bridge – (Page 74, photo 50) ★★★★
Twelve feet wide and 250 feet long over Crooked Creek, Clarkson Covered Bridge is one of the longest bridges in the old south. Originally built in 1904, repaired in 1923 and restored in 1976, the bridge is listed on the National Register of Historical Places. An old mill with waterwheel is located in the adjacent picnic area.

Coldwater Covered Bridge – (Page 74) ★★
Coldwater Covered Bridge, 60 feet long and 10 feet wide, was originally built before 1850 in Coldwater and moved to Oxford Lake Park in 1996.

Easley Covered Bridge – (Page 74) ★★★
Originally constructed in 1927, Easley Covered Bridge is a one-span bridge 95 feet long. It is still open to local traffic on a minor roadway.

Gilbert Covered Bridge – (Page 74, photo 39) ★★
Constructed by the Gilbert family in 1997, the bridge has gum and oak framing, pine lathing, elm flooring and cherry siding with a tin roof. The bridge is 40 long, 10.5 feet wide and 12 feet high and is located on private property. (Photo on next page.)

Gilliland Covered Bridge – (Page 74, 151, photo 154) ★★★
Gilliland Covered Bridge was built in 1899 near Reece City and moved to Noccalula Falls Park in 1966.

Horton Mill Covered Bridge – (Page 74) ★★★
Constructed in 1935, this is the highest covered bridge above water in the United States. Horton Mill is 220 feet long, 14 feet wide and rises 70 feet above the Calvert Prong of the Warrior River.

Kymulga Covered Bridge – (Page 75, 108) ★★★★
Kymulga Covered Bridge is at its original location near Childersburg. 105 feet in length and 10 feet wide, it is a single span bridge constructed in 1860 over Talladega Creek. Adjacent the bridge, Kymulga Gristmill is still in operation. Campgrounds, a picnic area and two miles of hiking trails are in the park. Kymulga is listed on the National Register of Historic Places.

Old Union Covered Bridge – (Page 75, 79, photo 50) ★★★★
Located in Cloudmont Resort between DeSoto State Park and Mentone off CR 89, the bridge was purchased and moved here to

span Little River. It is located on private property at Cloudmont Resort; check for directions and permission at the Pro Shop.

Saunders Family Covered Bridge – (Page 75, 140) ★★★

The Saunders Family constructed this bridge in 1987 at Twin Pines Resort east of Birmingham. The bridge spans a small creek at the edge of Lake Lauralee.

Swann Covered Bridge – (Page 75, 130, photo 131) ★★★★★

Swann is a three-span bridge, built in 1934. At 324 feet, it is the second longest in Alabama. It spans a beautiful canyon on Locust Fork and is open to local traffic.

Tannehill Valley Covered Bridge – (Page 75, 191, photo 39) ★★

Now closed to traffic, this covered bridge crosses Mill Creek two miles northeast of Tannehill Historical Park on CR97. Photo below.

Waldo Covered Bridge – (Page 75, see map page 77) ★★★★

Built prior to the Civil War, this single span bridge crosses Talladega Creek behind Waldo Gristmill, recently restored as a restaurant. Part of the elevated roadway leading to the bridge has deteriorated and fallen away.

Gilbert Covered Bridge (above) near Athens was constructed in 1997.

Tannehill Valley Covered Bridge

Natural Bridges

Ghost Creek Falls and Natural Bridge – (Page 93) ★★

Privately owned, this is another of Alabama's hidden wonders. Ghost Creek is a natural spring that emerges from a cave in the mountainside, then plummets into an underground stream below creating Ghost Creek Falls on its exterior journey. Adjacent is another creek and waterfall that flows under a natural bridge to the same underground stream. This natural spring produces water pure enough to drink.

High Falls, County Park – (Page 96, photo 97, 99**)** ★★★★★

As Town Creek rushes across Sand Mountain toward Lake Guntersville on a rocky streambed, it drops 55 feet at High Falls Park. During heavy rains, this fall can be as much as 300 feet wide. Erosion from the waterfall has formed a natural bridge at the north side of the falls. Falling water gushes through the opening. A wooden bridge with native stone supports crosses Town Creek above the falls. Within 20 miles are Lake Guntersville and Buck's Pocket State Parks.

Hurricane Creek Park – (Page 102) ★★★

This 55-acre park north of Cullman includes waterfalls, a natural bridge and unusual rock formations in a small canyon along Hurricane Creek. Two miles of moderate hiking trails meander through the canyon. To ascend or descend the canyon, the park has a small cable car system modeled after The Incline in Chattanooga.

Natural Bridge Park – (Page 149) ★★★★

With a span of 148 feet, this 60-foot high sandstone bridge is one of America's longest. This is a privately owned and operated park with gift shop, picnic areas and hiking trails.

Natural Bridge Recreation Area— (Map page 202) ★★

This medium-size natural bridge is hidden in a small ravine in Bankhead National Forest along CR63, just north of US278. A short paved trail leads to the bridge.

Rock Bridge Canyon – (Page 167) ★★★★

A privately owned park, this is another of Alabama's hidden secret treasures, not found on many roadmaps. The canyon contains many natural formations found in North Alabama such as a huge 50-foot span natural bridge with an adjacent waterfall and two more beautiful waterfalls along the stream below. The canyon remains in a very natural state with 3/4 miles of tough hiking trails through moss covered boulders.

Scenic Routes

Appalachian Scenic Byway – (Page 51) ★★★

This is a newly established Byway extending from Fort Payne to Cheaha State Park in the Talladega National Forest. Along this Byway the traveler will see Little River Falls, Yellow Creek Falls, Weiss Lake, Dugger Mountain and the Talladega Scenic Drive. The route follows Ala. 35 from Ft. Payne, Ala. 68 to Cedar Bluff, Ala. 9 through Piedmont to US 78 near Heflin, then joins with the Talladega Scenic Drive which ends at Cheaha State Park, the highest point in Alabama.

Chief Ladiga Trail – (See map, page 188) ★★

Alabama's first rails-to-trails project, this recently established easy paved trail follows an abandoned railroad corridor from the Georgia State line, through Piedmont to Anniston. The trail is open to non-motorized vehicles only. Thirty-three miles long, the trail passes wetlands, forests and farmlands, providing beautiful views of the Talladega Mountains. The trail will soon connect with Georgia's Silver Comet Trail totaling 90 miles from Anniston to near Atlanta. The Eubanks Welcome Center in Piedmont on Dailey Street is the home of the trail.

Dugger Mountain Scenic Drive – (Page 91) ★★

This scenic drive extends from Piedmont 9 miles south along Ala. 9, passing Dugger Mountain in the Talladega National Forest, the second highest point in the state. At the southern end Rabbittown Road leads through the National Forest.

Little River Canyon Rim Pkwy – (Page 125, map 123) ★★★★★

Little River Canyon is one of the deepest gorges east of the Mississippi River. Canyon Rim Parkway winds 22 miles along the western canyon rim. Breathtaking canyon overlooks and outstanding scenic waterfalls here and in nearby DeSoto State Park.

Lookout Mountain Parkway – (Page 132) ★★★★

Extending 93 miles from Gadsden to Chattanooga, there are many beautiful waterfalls, canyons and bluff overlooks along the way. During August, this route hosts The World's Longest Yard Sale with over 4,000 yard-sale vendors extending along the US 127 corridor 450 miles into Ohio.

Montevallo-Ashville Stagecoach Route – (Page 140) ★★★

This scenic drive follows an old stagecoach route between Montevallo and Ashville, following Ala. 119 and US 411. This is a very scenic route to bypass Birmingham's heavy traffic. Oak Mountain State Park is near the drive just south of Birmingham. Ala. 25 extending from Leeds, east of Birmingham, southeast to Vincent at US 231 is another scenic detour over Coosa Mountain.

Natchez Trace Parkway – (Page 146) ★★★

Established in 1938, Natchez Trace follows an historic Indian trail 445 miles from Natchez, Mississippi to Nashville, Tennessee, with 33 miles extending through the northwest corner of Alabama. Part of the National Scenic Byways Program, the National Park Service preserves historic sites along this excursion.

Talladega Scenic Drive – (Page 65, 186, map 66, 189) ★★★★

The Talladega Scenic Drive extends 20 miles along Horseblock Mountain ridge from Cheaha State Park, the highest point in Alabama at 2,407 feet, northeast to Heflin. Four overlooks provide scenic views over the surrounding lands.

Trail of Tears Corridor – (Page 146, 175, map 147, 176) ★

The Trail of Tears traces the route of 17,000 Cherokee Indians forced by the Indian Removal Act of 1830 to leave their homeland and move west to Oklahoma. The National Park Service recognized this route as an *Official Historic Route* in 1996. The Trail of Tears follows US 72 from Bridgeport in northeast Alabama to Alabama's western border at Waterloo. Today, this route is heavily developed near metropolitan areas. Through the countryside, there are many scenic locations along the course. The annual Commemorative Motorcycle Ride in October follows this path and has grown to over 90,000 participants since its inception in 1994.

Waterfalls

The map on page 195 of the Detailed Information Section shows major waterfall locations in North Alabama.

Azalea Cascades – (Page 82) ★
Located around the deck at the end of DeSoto State Park's ADA accessible boardwalk, Laurel Cascades is a small one-foot high fall that creates a pleasant atmosphere for relaxing.

Cheaha Falls – (Page 68) ★★
Cheaha Falls is a small 10-foot waterfall in Cheaha State Park near Chinnabee Lake along the Chinnabee Silent Trail.

DeSoto Falls – (Page 82) ★★★★★
Falling 100 feet into the canyon below, DeSoto Falls is the site of Alabama's first hydroelectric plant. The dam is the only historic structure remaining, creating a small, peaceful lake for picnics, canoeing, fishing and swimming.

Devil's Den Falls – (Page 68, photo 69) ★★
This is a small waterfall near Chinnabee Lake along the Chinnabee Silent Trail. The pool below the falls is a popular swimming area.

Double Bridges Falls (Red Mill Falls) – (Page 90, photo 89) ★
Scarham and Whippoorwill Creeks join at Double Bridges (the site of an old mill). Both creeks have waterfalls just before joining. A pull-off between the bridges provides a vantage point to view the falls.

Ghost Creek Falls and Natural Bridge – (Page 93, 116) ★★
Privately owned, this is one of Alabama's hidden wonders. Ghost Creek is a natural spring that emerges from a cave in the mountainside, then plummets into an underground stream below creating Ghost Creek Falls on its exterior journey. Adjacent is another creek and waterfall that flows under a natural bridge to the same underground stream. This natural spring produces water pure enough to drink.

Grace's High Falls – (Page 125) ★★★
One of Alabama's highest waterfalls, Grace's High Falls exists only during rainy seasons. Situated along Little River Canyon Rim Parkway with its magnificent viewpoints, it's hard to be disappointed even if the falls aren't flowing during your visit.

Graves Creek Falls (Page 130, map 129) ★★★
This is a beautiful, easily accessible waterfall within 100 yards of the roadway requiring a moderate hike. At the falls, Graves Creek is about 35 feet wide and the water drops 16 feet. Mardis Mill Road crosses Ala. 79 just 0.7 miles north of US 231. Private property.

Griffin Falls – (Page 72, 132) ★
Griffin Falls is another seasonal waterfall. Occasionally, a large

amount of water flows over a rocky outcrop at the bluff on Sand Mountain. Located on private property, it is best viewed while traveling westward on Ala. 68 2.5 miles west of I-59. A tough 1/8-mile uphill hike along the creek will reach the bottom of this 60-foot waterfall.

High Falls County Park – (Page 96, photo 97, 99) ★★★★★

As Town Creek rushes across Sand Mountain toward Lake Guntersville on a rocky streambed, it drops 55 feet at High Falls Park. During heavy rains, this fall can be as much as 300 feet wide. Erosion from the waterfall has formed a natural bridge at the north side of the falls. Falling water gushes through the opening. A wooden bridge with native stone supports crosses Town Creek above the falls. Within 20 miles are Lake Guntersville and Buck's Pocket State Parks.

High Falls, Talladega National Forest (Page 190) ★★

Located near the southern boundary of Talladega National Forest, this waterfall drops about 15 feet. An easy to moderate 1/8 mile hike is required.

Indian Falls – (Page 82, photo 78) ★★★

A small waterfall in DeSoto State Park is only 300 feet from the boardwalk parking area. A hiking trail bridge passes right over the top of the waterfall and a side trail leads below to a nice viewpoint. Laurel Creek's flow varies significantly with rainfall amounts.

Johnnie's Creek Falls – (Page 125) ★★★

Just outside Little River Canyon National Preserve boundaries, Johnnie's Creek creates an impressive 15-foot cascade. This cascade is a popular swimming area during the summer months.

Kinlock Falls – (Page 203, photo below) ★★★★

Located in Bankhead National Forest, Kinlock Falls is a 15-foot cascade adjacent to the roadway. Located on FS 210 at Hubbard Creek, this is another popular swimming area.

***Kinlock Falls*, Bankhead National Forest.**

Laurel Falls – (Page 82) ★

1/8 mile beyond the ADA Boardwalk in DeSoto State Park, Laurel Falls is a small 1-foot drop under rhododendrons and mountain laurel.

Little River Falls – (Page 83, 125, photo 124) ★★★★★

Falling 45 feet and as much as 300 feet wide, the pure waters of Little River create a remarkable waterfall. Easily accessible along a paved, inclined path from the parking area, stop here before touring Little River Canyon Rim Parkway. The rocky riverbed above the falls is a popular swimming area.

Locust Fork Falls – (Page 129, photo 130, 131) ★★★

Also known as Powell Falls. A 1.2-mile hard southwesterly hike along the northwest edge of the Locust Fork from Swann Covered Bridge near Cleveland leads to the falls. A twin waterfall dropping about 6 feet, one fall is 20 feet wide while the other is 35 feet wide. Kayakers practice frequently here. It is located on private property.

Lost Falls – (Page 82, photo 81) ★★★★

A small but beautiful fall hidden in DeSoto State Park 3/8 mile beyond the end of the boardwalk. Laurel Creek flows over a rocky streambed above the falls then plummets 12 feet over Lost Falls. Access requires a moderate hike.

Lower Pisgah Falls (Page 159, 162, photo 160) ★★★

Located at Pisgah Gorge, this is a combination waterfall. As Little Bryant Creek plummets over the top, it free-falls 25 feet, then cascades down the rocks for another 75 feet before reaching the pool below. The point overlook is on a ledge 200 feet above the canyon floor with no safety barriers.

Lower Rock Bridge Falls – (Page 167, 172, photo 171) ★★★★

A small, beautiful waterfall hidden in Rock Bridge Canyon, this fall is situated next to the lower parking area. Reaching it requires a short but moderate hike. With a 6-foot free-fall below, the cascades above create a combination waterfall height of 18 feet. It is an outstanding waterfall for photography.

Nectar Falls – (Map 129, 165, photo 47) ★

Nectar Falls forms a very nice cascade beside CR 160 at the Locust Fork of the Black Warrior River near Nectar, Alabama. From a small pull-off on the south side of CR 160 and west of the bridge, a moderate walk 100 feet around the hillside leads to the cascades. The cascades are on a small side creek adjacent the pull-off. Located 1.75 miles west of Ala. 79 on Ala. 160.

Noccalula Falls – (Page 151, 152, photo 153, 154) ★★★★

Black Creek falls over 90 feet into the canyon below. Noccalula is a private park with campgrounds and hiking trails around the canyon and under the falls. Gilliland Covered Bridge was recently moved to the gardens overlooking the ravine.

Peavine Falls – (Page 155, 157, photo 48, front cover) ★★★★
This is a beautiful 20-foot waterfall hidden on top of Double Oak Mountain in Oak Mountain State Park. A hard trail leads to the top.

Rainbow Falls – (Page 85, 88, photo 87) ★★
Rainbow Falls, located at the head of Dismals Canyon, falls 15 feet. A small dam and footings of an old mill remain near the top. From the falls, Dismals Branch Stream continues through the canyon.

Red Mill Falls (Double Bridges Falls) – (Page 89, 90) ★
The falls were named after the red mill standing above Scarham Creek by the falls. A small dam at the top of the falls was constructed for the mill. Located at Double Bridges, Whippoorwill Falls is nearby.

Salt Creek Falls—(Page 190, map 189) ★★
A tough 1/4-mile trail leads to the top of Salt Creek Falls. The falls are impressive, but there is no trail leading below for a better view.

Secret Falls – (Page 85, 88, photo 85) ★★
With a drop of about 6 feet, this waterfall is found along a side trail in Dismals Canyon.

Scarham Creek Cascades – (Page 90) ★
A one-quarter mile hard hike leads to Scarham Cascades. Falling about 6 feet and 30 feet wide, it is hidden upstream from Double Bridges and difficult to reach. There is no trail. It is located on private property.

Shoal Creek Falls – (Page 181, 182, photo 183) ★
This fall is located near Guntersville Dam on the south side of the Tennessee River along Shoal Creek. About 40 feet wide and dropping 10 feet, this double waterfall is hidden behind a country store. It is owned by Marshall County, but is not developed as a park.

Short Creek Falls – (Page 116, 184, photo 194) ★
If this waterfall were accessible to the public, it would be rated a 4-star. The view from the highway is limited, but the falls at times can be as much as 150 feet wide with a 15-foot drop. It is located on private property.

So. Caney Ck Falls – (Page 199, 203, photo 194, 200) ★★★★★
This is a beautiful 25-foot waterfall great for photography. Actually, two creeks flow over the bluff side by side. The larger creek flows almost year-round. The sandy bottom pool below usually casts a yellow-green tint. Reaching it requires a tough 3/4-mile hike in Bankhead National Forest. If the trail has been cleared of fallen trees, the hike would be then rated hard.

Tuscumbia Falls – (Page 107, 146) ★★★
This is a manmade waterfall in downtown Tuscumbia, but is so naturally constructed, it deserves recognition. About 25 feet high, the waters form several cascades and free-falls as the water tumbles into the park's lake.

Upper & Lower Factory Falls (Page 88) ★★

Found along Bear Creek, Upper Factory Falls drops about 6 feet, while Lower Factory Falls drops about 18 feet. The flow of both waterfalls is dependent upon the Tennessee Valley Authority's (TVA) power requirements. The flow is usually substantial during weekends. Bear Creek is a popular location for kayak runs. By water only.

Upper Pisgah Falls - (Page 159, 162, photo 163) ★★★

Located at Pisgah Gorge, this waterfall drops about 100 feet. It is difficult to view from its overlook because of thick overgrown foliage at the ridge. The trail leads to the top of the falls providing a magnificent view over the falls into the canyon below.

Upper Rock Bridge Falls – (Page 167, 172, photo 169) ★★★★

Another small but beautiful waterfall with a 35-foot drop hidden in Rock Bridge Canyon, it requires a tough hike to reach. The totally natural surroundings add to its splendor.

Whippoorwill Creek Falls – (Page 89, 90) ★

As Whippoorwill Creek joins Scarham Creek, you will find a 10 foot high waterfall. Small interesting rapids are upstream beyond the bridge. Located at Double Bridges, you'll find Red Mill Falls nearby on Scarham Creek.

Yellow Creek Falls–(Page 72, map 122, 123, 132) ★★

A massive amount of water drops about 50 feet over this waterfall. Since the adjacent property is privately owned and access is limited to boats or a distant viewpoint across the lake, this waterfall is rated lower. If access were easier, it would be rated four-stars.

***Nectar Falls* between Nectar and Cleveland on Ala. 160 is hidden less than 100 feet from the roadway.**

Hidden in a secluded ravine within Bankhead National Forest, this unnamed waterfall is representative of many found along the hiking trails. Taken during May, this image is enhanced by the humid environment mildly fogging the camera lens.

DETAILED INFORMATION

Old Union Covered Bridge was moved here to span Little River at Cloudmont Resort.

Clarkson Covered Bridge spans 250 feet across Crooked Creek near Cullman.

Appalachian Scenic Byway

Description ★★★

This newly designated scenic byway tours near by many of North Alabama's natural treasures. Beginning at Ft. Payne, the route follows Ala. 35 south to Little River Canyon at Ala. 176. Near this intersection, you'll see the impressive Little River Falls. The Byway then continues south on Ala. 35 to Ala. 68 in Gaylesville. At Cedar Bluff, follow Ala. 9 south across Weiss Lake. Near Piedmont, it passes Dugger Mountain, the second highest point in Alabama. Continuing south on Ala. 9, the Byway then follows US 78 east to the Talladega Scenic Drive, which leads 20 miles south to Cheaha State Park, the highest point in Alabama.

Nearby Points of Interest

Just beyond the north end of the Byway are DeSoto State Park and DeSoto Falls. The Canyon Rim Parkway follows Ala. 176 south from Little River Falls. Near Cedar Bluff is Cornwall Furnace. Remaining from 1862, it is a Confederate Ironworks similar to Brierfield and Tannehill. Just north of Leesburg you'll find Yellow Creek Falls and Little River Canyon Mouth Park. Also, just northwest of Leesburg is Cherokee Rock Village and Griffin Falls. Coldwater Covered Bridge is in Oxford near I-20, while Waldo Covered Bridge is near Talladega. Coleman Lake Recreation Area is in the Talladega National Forest north of Heflin.

Location and Directions

This drive is too long to reflect on one map. These four maps (next page) show portions of the Byway. It can be reached from I-59, Exit 218 near Ft. Payne at the north end and from I-20, Exit 199 near Heflin at the south end.

Scenes

Waterfalls:

This Byway passes near many of Alabama's largest waterfalls. Six waterfalls in nearby DeSoto State Park, including DeSoto Falls and Little River Falls. Grace's High Falls, Johnnies Creek Falls, and Yellow Creek Falls are near Little River Canyon.

Creeks:

Wolf Creek and **Bear Creek** form tributary canyons to Little River Canyon. Both provide magnificent canyon overlooks.

Terrapin Creek and **Choccolocco Creek** are popular canoeing and kayaking locations near the Talladega National Forest.

North

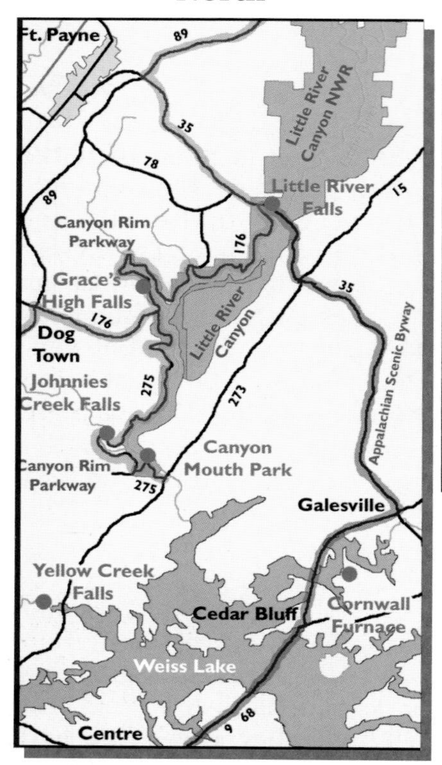

Cedar Bluff/Centre area

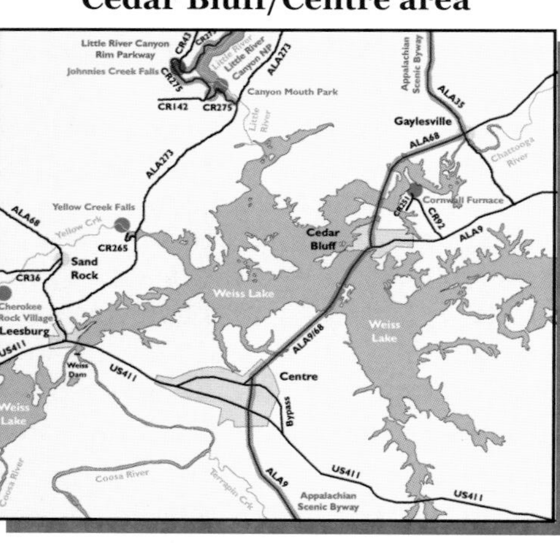

Central

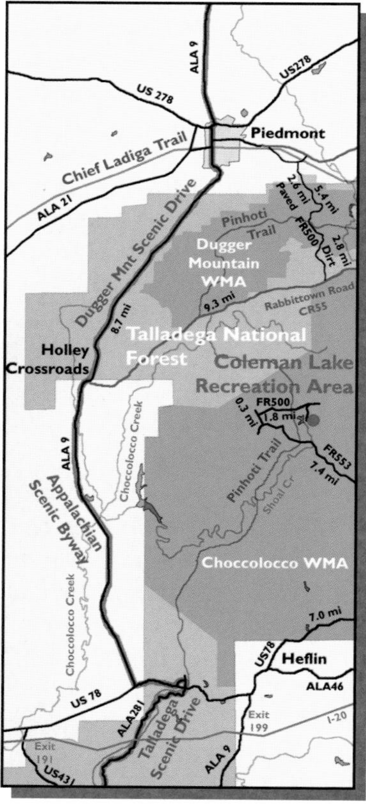

South

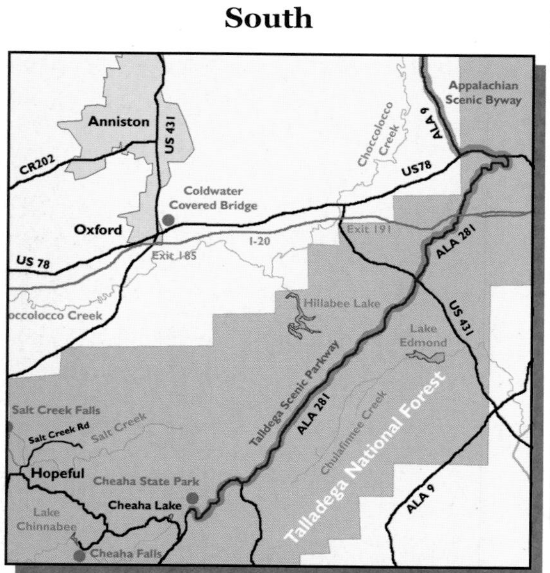

Blowing Wind Cave NWR

Park Description ★

Blowing Wind (Sauta) Cave is named for the cool breeze emanating from the cave opening during summer months. The cave has two entrances; one is accessible from the side, while the other is hidden on top of the mountain. This difference in elevation creates an air current through the cave, which changes direction during the year as the outside temperature varies. During the summer months, the cool breeze emanating from the entrance is very welcomed! The cave contains 250,000 endangered Gray and Indian bats, so access is by permit only. At dusk in June, July and August, view the bats exiting the cave to feed on insects at the surrounding backwaters of the Tennessee River. A small stream flows from the mouth of the cave toward the lake. While the Refuge includes 264 acres, there are no facilities or improvements in the area. Park at the gate on US 72, then walk 250 yards beyond the gate to the cave path on the right.

Blowing Wind Cave.

Nearby Points of Interest

Cathedral Caverns is 13 miles to the southwest. Scottsboro is eight miles east. Huntsville is 34 miles west along US 72, the Trail of

Tears Corridor. Lake Guntersville State Park, Buck's Pocket State Park and High Falls County Park are located to the south across the Tennessee River.

Location and Directions

From Huntsville, it is 34 miles to Blowing Wind Cave. Take I-565 east; I-565 terminates and becomes US 72 east. Continue east on US 72. Go 8.7 miles past the CR5 turnoff to Cathedral Caverns State Park. When you see the lake on your left, begin checking the turnoffs on the right (south) side of US 72. The paved turnoff has a steel bar gate blocking the roadway just west of the 131 mile marker. There are no facilities. During early summer, Lake Guntersville's shores are lined with blooming water lilies.

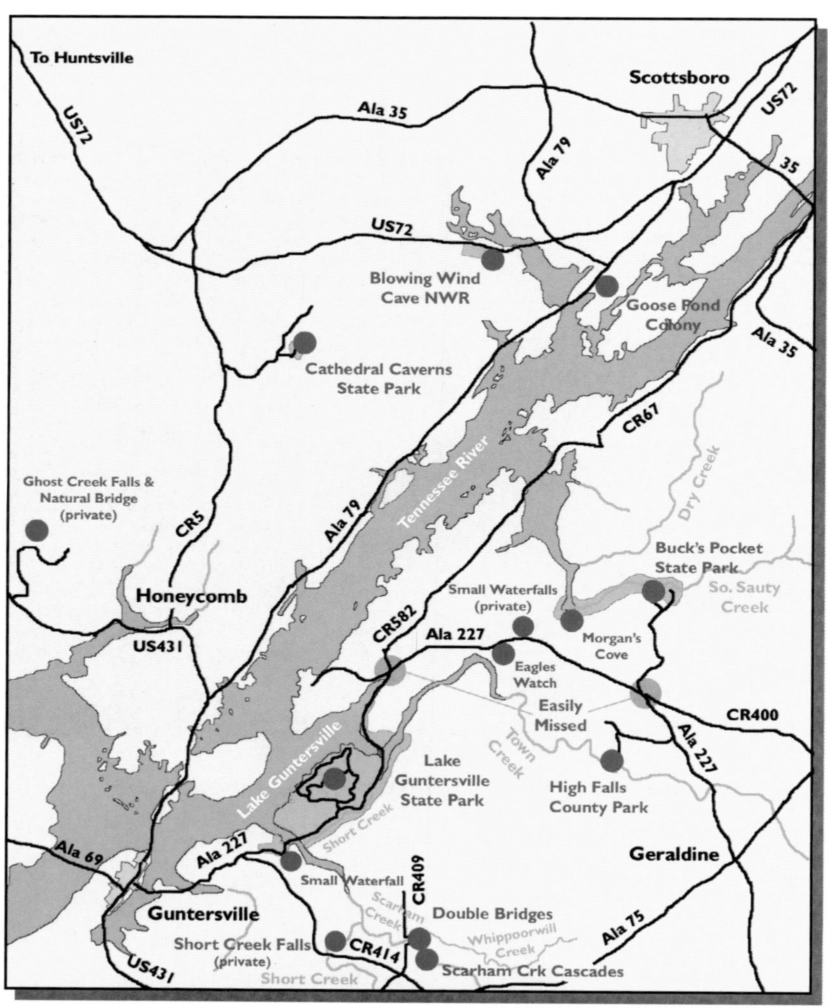

Brierfield Ironworks Historical SP

Park Description ★★

Built in 1862 by the Bibb County Iron Company to provide high-grade ore for weapons of the Confederacy, the furnace originally stood 60 feet tall. The Confederate government forcibly purchased the facility in 1863 and constructed a second furnace, raising production to 25 tons per day. This output was destined for Confederate naval ordinance in Selma. Union troops under General James Wilson destroyed the facility in 1865 along with the nearby Tannehill facility. The brick furnace is in ruins today. Efforts are under way to protect and restore the furnace to its original condition. Today, the park provides a peaceful setting for campers and tourists. Many old structures from the 1800's and early 1900's have been reconstructed in the park.

Deteriorating brickwork of Brierfield Furnace.

Nearby Points of Interest

The lands between Montevallo and Brierfield consist of beautiful grass covered rolling hills contributing pastures for horse and llama ranches. The scenic Montevallo-Ashville Stagecoach Route begins just seven miles east of the park and goes northeast to Ashville. Tannehill Historical State Park is only 28 miles to the north. Tannehill is another Ironworks Historical Park similar to Brierfield. Tannehill Valley Covered Bridge is near Tannehill Park. Oak Mountain State Park is northeast near I-65 south of Birmingham.

Location and Directions

From the southern end of the scenic Montevallo-Ashville Stagecoach Route (Ala. 119) in Montevallo, take Ala. 25 south seven miles to CR 62 and turn left. The park entrance is just ahead on the left. Brierfield is 15 miles west of I-65 Exit 228 following Ala. 25 south.

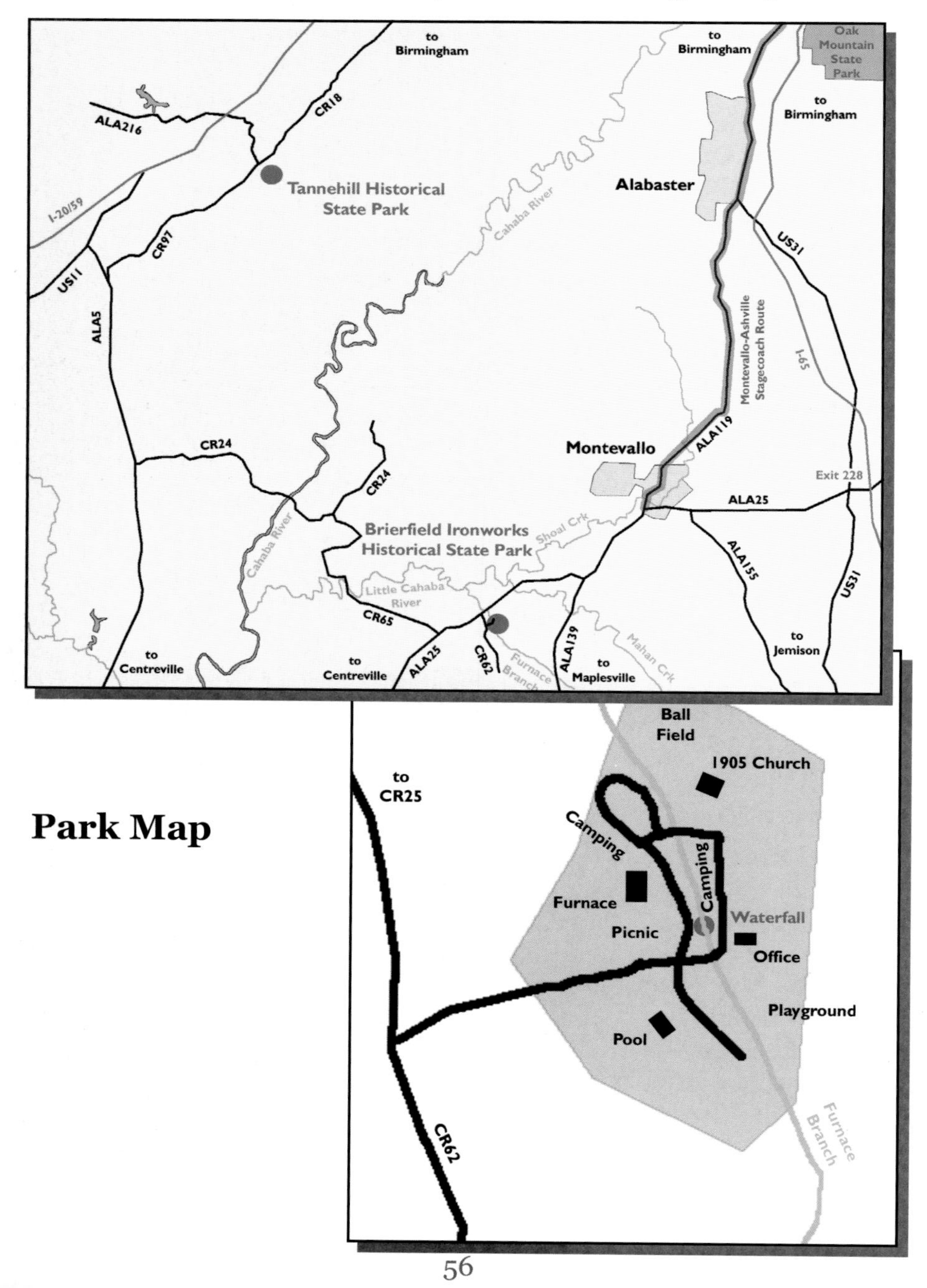

Park Map

Park Facilities

Cabins:

The park maintains several restored rustic cabins furnished for light housekeeping.

Campgrounds:

There are 25 fully developed campsites with water and electrical connections for tents or RV's situated beside Furnace Branch. An overflow area can handle another 15 campers if necessary. These sites also have access to water and electrical connections. A dump station is available.

Country Store:

The country store and registration office provides minimal picnic and camping supplies.

Swimming Pool:

A large pool and bathhouse is open to visitors Memorial Day through Labor Day.

Picnic Areas:

The picnic area includes a pavilion and an amphitheater adjacent the furnace ruins. Playgrounds are just a short walk away.

Hiking trails:

Being a fairly small park, a one-half mile easy walk leads to all points in the park.

Scenes

Waterfalls:

A small 2-foot high waterfall on Furnace Branch is situated in the middle of the park.

Creeks:

Furnace Branch flows through the center of the park near the furnace ruins.

Foliage:

Most trees in the area were felled to provide charcoal to fuel the furnaces. Today, tall pines and a few hardwoods stand. Wild hydrangea can be found throughout the park.

A small waterfall along Furnace Branch at the center of the park.

The turquoise waters of South Sauty Creek transgress huge boulders before reaching Lake Guntersville.

Buck's Pocket State Park

Park Description ★★★★

Buck's Pocket State Park encompasses 2,000 acres secluded in a small canyon near Lake Guntersville. The campground is alongside South Sauty Creek in the bottom of the canyon. Towering over 450 feet above is Point Rock Overlook and the adjacent picnic area. Morgan's Cove, seven miles away in park boundaries, provides a boat ramp and fishing piers. The park's seclusion makes it an attractive weekend get-a-way.

A foggy late afternoon at Morgan's Cove boat ramp.

Nearby Points of Interest

High Falls County Park with its wide 55-foot high waterfall and Natural Bridge is only eight miles south. Along Ala. 227 three miles southeast of the turnoff for Buck's Pocket where Town Creek crosses, you'll find major rapids where kayakers practice. Here you'll also find remnants of stone walls remaining from an old mill. 1.5 miles west of Morgan's Cove turnoff on Ala. 227, you'll find a small creek and waterfall on the north side of the road. The waterfall is viewable from your car but is easily missed due to surrounding foliage. Just west of this waterfall is a popular Bald Eagle watch point overlooking Town Creek Valley. Lake Guntersville State Park with full facilities is 18 miles southwest following Ala. 227. Pisgah Gorge and its two large waterfalls are to the northeast.

Location and Directions

From US 431 in Guntersville, take Ala. 227 east 20 miles. Turn left on CR 402. The stop sign 3/4-mile ahead is at Grove Oak. Go straight onto CR 19. Follow CR 19 for 2.2 miles to the State Park entrance on the left.

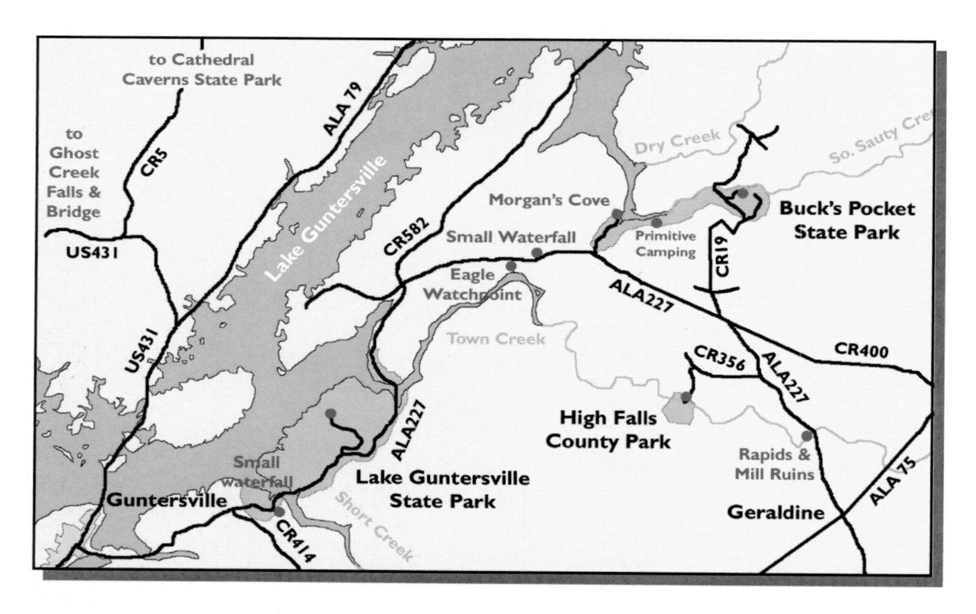

Park Map

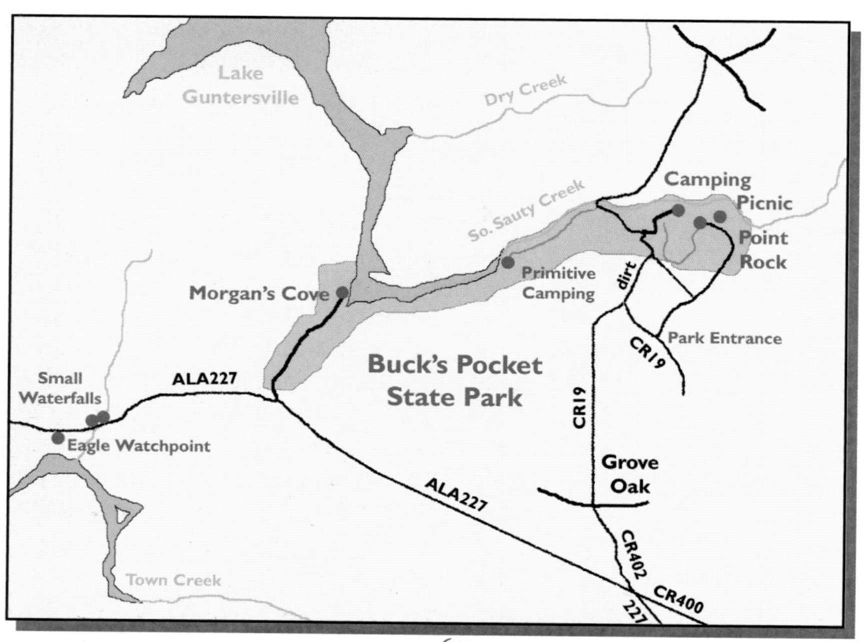

Vines and moss covered trees along a dry creek bed.

Park Facilities

Visitor's Center:

The registration office includes a bathhouse and laundry for registered campers. The office has limited picnic and camping supplies.

Picnic Areas:

The picnic area is located on top of the bluff overlooking the canyon adjacent Point Rock Boardwalk.

Hiking trails:

There are six miles of hiking trails and six miles of horse riding trails in the park. One trail leads from the campground area to Point Rock above (hard) and another follows South Sauty Creek (moderate, 2 miles) to the primitive camping area.

Scenes

Waterfalls:

Hiking westward along South Sauty Creek toward the primitive camping area are several large cascades. There are no large waterfalls in the park boundaries, although there are several in the area (see map).

Point Rock:

A 1/8-mile boardwalk with steps leads from the picnic parking area along a ridge to Point Rock. From here, you'll have magnificent views of the canyon's rocky outcrops and the campground below.

Creeks:

South Sauty Creek flows through the canyon beside the main campground area. A small, unpaved road leading to the primitive camping area follows South Sauty Creek for two miles to Lake Guntersville backwaters, not far from Morgan's Cove.

Foliage:

Dogwood and redbud trees are sheltered under huge pines. Short needle pines are most abundant. Mountain laurel are also abundant, blooming in May and June.

Cathedral Caverns State Park

Park Description ★★★★

With an entrance 128 feet wide, Cathedral Caverns has the largest entrance opening of any cave in America. When reaching the first gate inside the caverns, turn around and view the sunlight bouncing from the limestone walls and ceiling for a sense of the cave's enormity. The cavern was privately owned and undeveloped until recently when the state purchased the property and developed the pathways and lighting systems. The cave extends 6,500 feet into the mountain, but is opened to the public for only 3,500 feet along a concrete pathway. The pathway traverses an underground stream where you will see an old bridge constructed by early explorers. Archeologist digs during the 1950's and 1980's are seen at the cave opening. Creek and Cherokee Indians inhabited the area until the middle 1800's and used these caverns as shelter.

The park is a day use area, open daily from 10 am to 4 pm. During winter months, tours begin every two hours starting at 10 am. Summer months are busier, so tours run hourly from 10 to 4.

Nearby Points of Interest

Located in the country 21 miles from Scottsboro and the Tennessee River, there are not many major scenic attractions nearby. Blowing Wind Cave National Wildlife Reserve is 13 miles towards Scottsboro on US 72. Pisgah Gorge with two huge waterfalls is just east of Scottsboro. Lake Guntersville's backwaters in this area are outlined with blooming water lilies during early summer. Ghost Creek Falls and Natural Bridge is located south following CR 5 then US 231 north. This is a very scenic

The entrance to Cathedral Caverns spans 128 feet.

drive through Grant and Honeycomb. Huntsville is 29 miles west along US 72. The mountains, fields and streams surrounding the area are very scenic all through the year.

Location and Directions

From Huntsville, it is 29 miles to Cathedral Caverns State Park. Take I-565 east; I-565 terminates and becomes US 72 east. Continue east on US 72. Turn right onto CR 5 to Cathedral Caverns State Park. Turn left onto Cathedral Caverns Road, go two miles to Cave Road and turn right. Cave Road terminates in the State Park parking area.

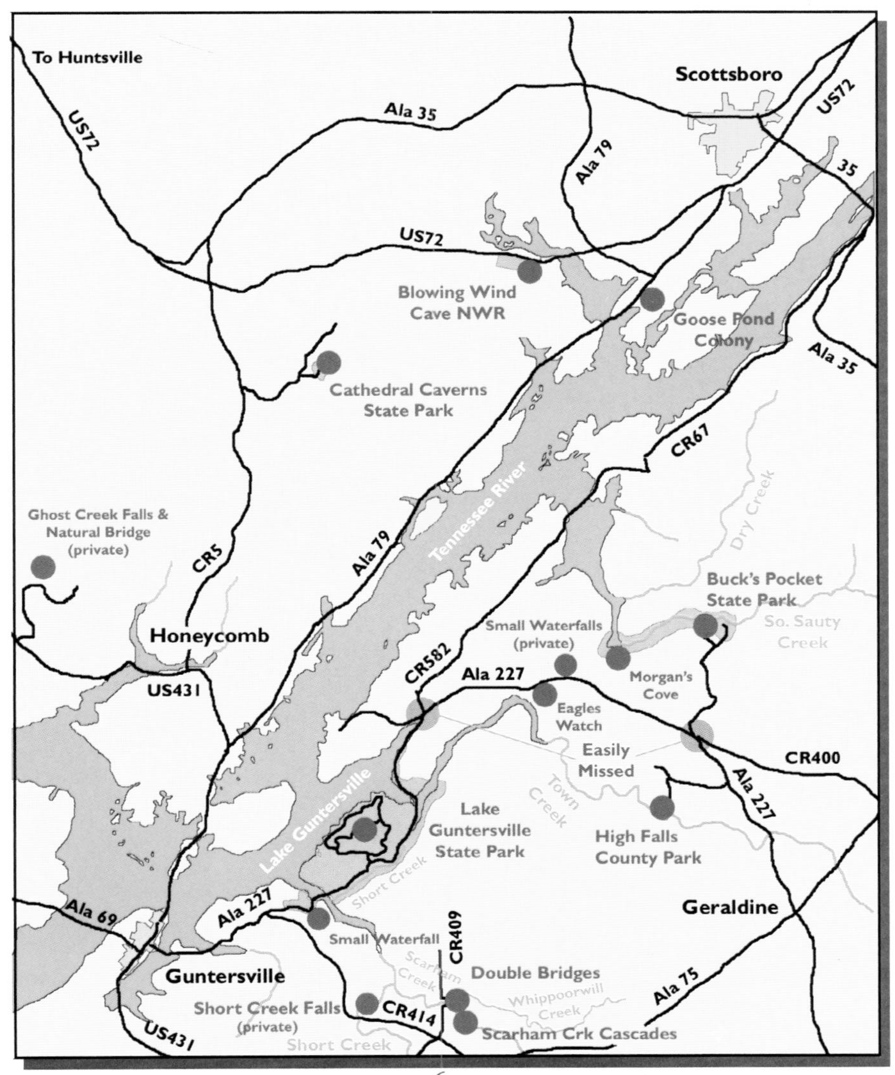

Park Facilities

Visitor's Center:

The newly constructed stone and timber Visitor's Center has concessions and restrooms. The park has no other structural facilities; more are in planning stages.

Picnic Areas:

A picnic area is adjacent the parking lot. Camping and hiking trails are not available, but are planned for the future.

Scenes

Waterfalls:

Other than the water seeping through rock and dripping into the caverns, the park's only waterfall is manmade in front of the Visitor's Center.

Creeks:

The underground stream in the caverns flows below the pathway. During heavy rains, this creek fills and nears the bottom of the path. Creeks nearby the park are small, but their rapids through the rocky beds are very appealing.

Foliage:

Around the park and surrounding lands, cedar trees and long and short needle pines grow abundantly amongst this rocky terrain. Dogwood, redbud and maples begin adding their color to forests in early spring. This could be as early as February, depending on the weather.

Stalagmite forest in the cavern's depths.

Inside looking out: the actual view is much more beautiful than can be captured on film.

Cheaha State Park

Sunset at Pulpit Rock.

Park Description 

One of Alabama's oldest State Parks, Cheaha opened in 1939 following its construction by the CCC. Sitting atop Cheaha Mountain, the highest point in Alabama at 2,407 feet above sea level, the park contains 2,719 acres in the Talladega National Forest. The restaurant, deck, lodge and swimming pool overlook Cheaha Lake 1,000 feet below at the foot of Mount Cheaha. Seventeen acre Lake Chinnabee, also below Mount Cheaha, maintains additional camping and picnic areas and is near two of the park's four waterfalls, Devil's Den and Cheaha Falls. Touring, swimming, fishing, camping, mountain biking and hiking are the Park's most popular activities. The scenic overlooks and the ADA accessible Boardwalk leading to Bald Rock Overlook make this a popular stop for everyone.

Nearby Points of Interest

Talladega Scenic Drive extends 20 miles northeast along Horseblock Mountain from the Park entrance to Heflin near Interstate I-20. Coldwater and Waldo Covered Bridges are nearby in the towns of Oxford and Talladega. The Kymulga Covered Bridge and Gristmill, still in operation, is 45 miles west near Childersburg. Three other covered bridges are near Oneonta, 70 miles northwest. The Talladega Speedway is just north of Talladega off Interstate I-20. The R.L. Harris Reservoir is located southeast following Ala. 49 and 48 through Lineville. Horseshoe Bend National Military Monument is just 50 miles south of Cheaha State Park, while DeSoto Caverns Park is 40 miles southwest. Silver Lakes, between Anniston and Gadsden, is on the Robert Trent Jones Golf Trail.

Location and Directions

From Interstate I-20, take Exit 191 to US 431 south. Follow US 431 south 3 miles to Ala. 281. Follow Ala. 281 south 12 miles to Cheaha State Park.

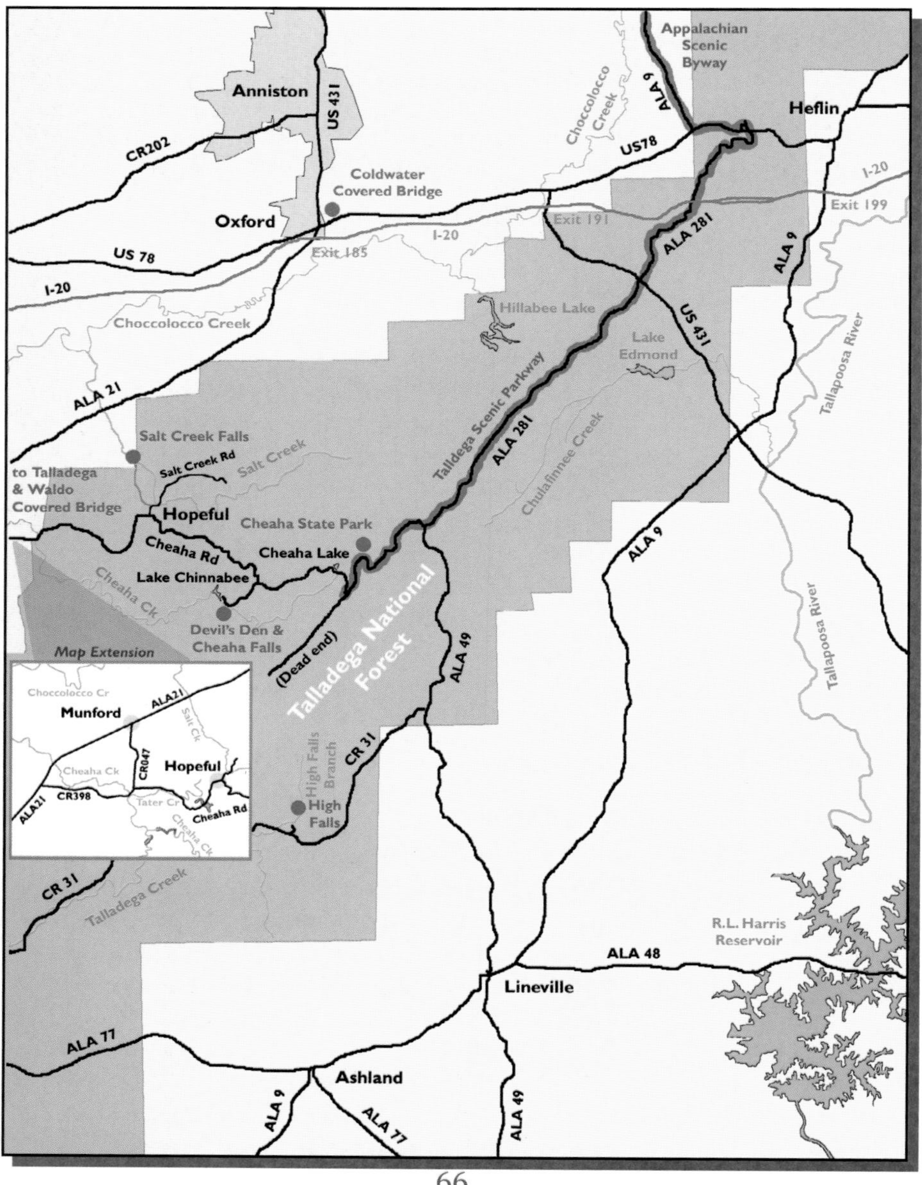

Park Map

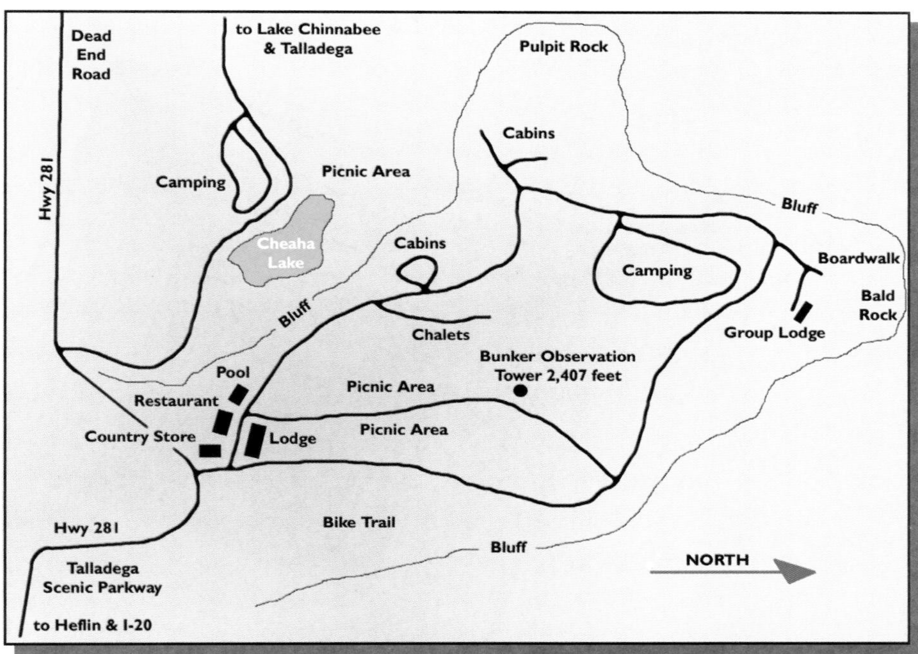

Cheaha Falls.

Views from the restaurant and pool. Cheaha Lake is below the mountain.

Park Facilities

Lodge and Restaurant:

Featuring the newly remodeled 30-unit lodge and 75-seat restaurant, this facility includes meeting rooms and a bluff swimming pool. Overlooking Cheaha Lake and the Talladega National Forest 1,000 feet below, the restaurant and deck provide majestic views, especially at sunset. A separate 50-person group lodge is also available at Bald Rock.

Cabins and Chalets:

Situated in forested areas atop Mount Cheaha, the park's five chalets and 10 rustic cabins are furnished for light housekeeping with linens and kitchen utensils.

Campgrounds:

Cheaha State Park maintains two camping areas with a total of 73 improved sites. The mountaintop area has 43 sites with two comfort stations, while campground #2 near Cheaha Lake includes 30 sites with one comfort station. Both areas have 24 hour gated access. Primitive and semi-primitive sites are available.

Country Store & Information Center:

Located at the park entrance, the store includes a gift shop, furnishes camping and picnic supplies and provides camper registration.

Swimming Pool:

Conveniently located adjacent the lodge and restaurant, relish the magnificent views as you enjoy relaxing beside this pool situated on the bluff overlooking the forest and Cheaha Lake 1,000 feet below. Swimming is a major activity at Cheaha Lake.

Picnic Areas:

There are three picnic areas with pavilions, grills and playgrounds.

Scenes

Waterfalls:

Devil's Den Falls is an easy 1/2-mile hike from the parking and picnic area at Lake Chinnabee, along the Chinnabee Silent Trail. Devil's Den is a small waterfall and pool.

Cheaha Falls, a popular swimming area, is just beyond Devil's Den Falls. This waterfall drops about 10 feet and is very scenic. There are five waterfalls here within 200 yards of each other.

High Falls with a 15-foot drop, is located 15 miles south of the main park, requiring an easy 1/2-mile hike. Follow Ala. 281 north to Ala. 49 south to CR31 South.

Salt Creek Falls is outside Cheaha State Park, but inside the boundaries of Talladega National Forest. As far as I can tell, it is a beautiful waterfall dropping about 40 feet. The trail leads to the top of the falls and there is no easy way down to view them from below. However there is another small 3-foot waterfall just above the main waterfall that is worth the hike to view. BEWARE: the trail nearing the falls is very tough and dangerous. Steep inclines over rocks; be very careful. People have fallen here before resulting in drastic consequences. Refer to the Cautions Section in this book.

Creeks:

Cheaha Creek is the largest creek in the Park. Beginning near Cheaha Lake and flowing westward over Cheaha Falls and Devil's Den Falls, it streams into Lake Chinnabee.

Foliage:

Long needle pine and hardwoods are most abundant. Dogwood and redbud trees bloom during spring months.

Devil's Den Falls.

The mountaintop area, adjacent Bunker Observation Tower positioned at Alabama's highest point, has two pavilions, a large playground and a comfort station. The Cheaha Lake area provides two pavilions, a comfort station/bathhouse, laundry and playground. The Lake Chinnabee area has picnic tables and a small pavilion but no facilities.

Hiking trails:

Cheaha State Park maintains six hiking trails totaling seven miles and eight miles of mountain biking.

Chinnabee Silent Trail passes Devil's Den Falls and Cheaha Falls.

Cheaha Mountain Express Bike Trail is a popular mountain biking trail.

Pulpit Rock Trail is a moderate 1/2-mile path leading to the western bluff for magnificent sunset views.

Bald Rock Boardwalk leads 1,520 feet along an ADA accessible boardwalk to Bald Rock, which overlooks the northern landscape. Wheelchair accessible, this overlook also provides great sunset views.

The **Pinhoti Trail** system extends 100 miles from Sylacauga, through Cheaha State Park, northward to Piedmont where it meets with Chief Ladiga Trail.

Other park trails include the **Cheaha**, **Odum**, and **Cave Creek Trails**.

Cheaha Lake. The beach area is on the left, with Pulpit Rock looming overhead. The lodge is on the right on top of Mount Cheaha.

Cherokee Rock Village

Park Description ★★

A 200-acre County Park on top of Shinbone Ridge of Lookout Mountain, Cherokee Rock Village provides magnificent views overlooking Weiss Lake near Leesburg over 800 feet below. The area has many unusual rock formations along the bluff, attracting sports enthusiasts to practice their climbing techniques in a safer, downscale environment. Tremendous sandstone and quartz outcrops rise as much as 150 feet in the village. Trails lead through narrow passages between huge boulders along the ridge.

Nearby Points of Interest

Griffin Falls is northwest along Ala. 68 just beyond I-59. Yellow Creek Falls is northeast at the edge of Weiss Lake. Little River Canyon Mouth Park is five miles further northeast along Ala. 273. The Canyon Mouth Park is the southern extremity of the Canyon Rim Parkway. Noccalula Falls Park is southwest in Gadsden. Lookout Mountain Parkway passes just to the northwest of Cherokee Rock Village. Cornwall Furnace is near Cedar Bluff on Ala. 9.

Location and Directions

From US 411 in Leesburg, follow Ala. 68 west (north) 2.6 miles

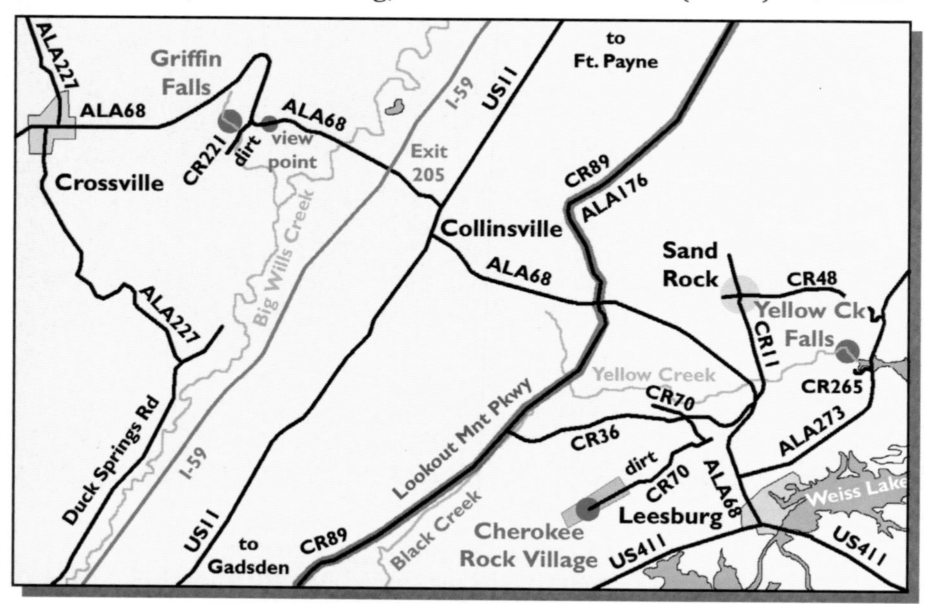

A harsh bluff environment, but this lone short-needle pine thrives on the rocky outcrop. A portion of Weiss Lake can be seen in the distance. Hiking trails meander through the huge boulders 100 feet below. These easy to moderate trails lead visitors by many unusual rock formations, including natural arches. Many people come here to practice their climbing techniques on these vertical sandstone walls.

and turn left onto CR 36 (Valley Street) at the top of Shinbone Ridge. Go 1.5 miles to CR 70 (Indian Creek Ave.) and turn left. Follow CR 70 3.4 miles until it ends at Cherokee Rock Village. Most of CR 70 is dirt and in places rough. CR 36 is 8.7 miles from I-59 along Ala. 68 east.

This twin peaked boulder is one of the many unusual formations found along the bluff.

Park Facilities

Facilities:

There are no facilities available.

Campgrounds:

Primitive camping is allowed in the park.

Hiking trails:

At least 1/2 miles of trails wind through the boulders along the bluff, providing outstanding views of Weiss Lake below. Along the trails, you'll likely see many people scaling the vertical rock walls.

Scenes

Overlooks:

At several places along the trails, open areas in the trees are good viewpoints for the valley over 800 feet below. In the valley are Leesburg, Centre and Weiss Lake and Dam.

Waterfalls:

The flow of **Griffin Falls** (located on private property), is dependent upon the landowner on top of Sand Mountain. Occasionally, a large amount of water is released over the bluff. It can be viewed while traveling westward on Ala. 68 about 2.5 miles west of I-59. At this point, start looking at the rocky bluff in front of your vehicle as you descend the hill going into a right curve. If you miss it, turn left at 2.9 miles onto a dirt road (CR 221) in the curve (before ascending Sand Mountain) and drive 0.4 miles. Pull off on the right at the first bridge and creek. A tough 1/8-mile uphill hike along the creek will reach the bottom of this 60-foot waterfall.

Yellow Creek Falls, hidden in a small ravine, drops 50 feet before reaching Weiss Lake. The adjacent property is privately owned, so access is limited to boats or a distant viewpoint across the lake. On Ala. 273 just south of the bridge and causeway crossing Weiss Lake, turn west onto CR 265. Drive to the last pull-off before the first sharp curve and look northwest into the ravine to view the waterfall across the lake. During summer months when trees are full, the lake front viewpoint is severely hindered.

Covered Bridge Locations & Directions

These are North Alabama's covered bridges. Most are historic bridges remaining from the early 1900's, with a few from the 1800's. The exceptions are the Saunders Family Covered Bridge built in 1987 at Twin Pines Resort (a very scenic convention center and overnight resort), Cambron Covered Bridge at Madison County Nature Trail, Tannehill Covered Bridge near Tannehill Historical State Park and Gilbert Covered Bridge built in 1997 near the Elk River west of Athens.

Covered Bridge Locations

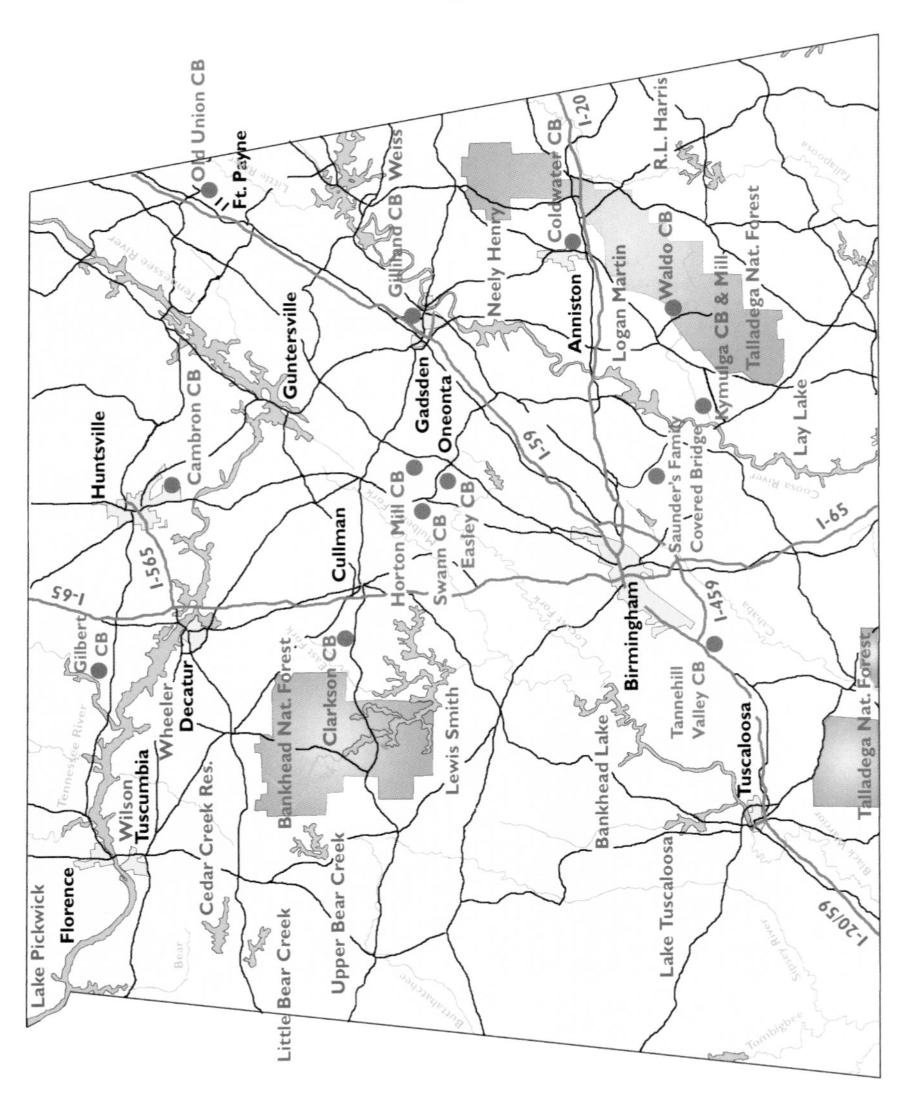

Covered Bridge Directions

Cambron Covered Bridge

From Memorial Pkwy (US 231) in Huntsville, drive east on Airport Road six miles. Airport Road changes to Carl T. Jones Dr., then to Bailey Cove Road southbound. Turn left on Green Mountain Road (at the flashing yellow traffic signal). Drive 1.7 miles up Green Mountain and turn right at the top onto South Shawdee Drive. The Nature Trail is 1.5 miles on the right.

Clarkson Covered Bridge

From I-65 near Cullman, take Exit 308 onto Ala. 278 west. Drive west eight miles and turn right on CR 1117. Go north 1 mile, turn left on CR 1043. Clarkson Covered Bridge is 1 mile on the right.

Coldwater Covered Bridge

From I-20 in Oxford, take Exit 185 onto Ala. 21 north. Turn right at the first traffic light beyond the Interstate onto Recreation Drive and go 1 mile to the stop sign. Turn left, go 200 feet to the parking area on the right. The bridge will be on your right beside the lake at Oxford Lake Park.

Map of Coldwater Covered Bridge.

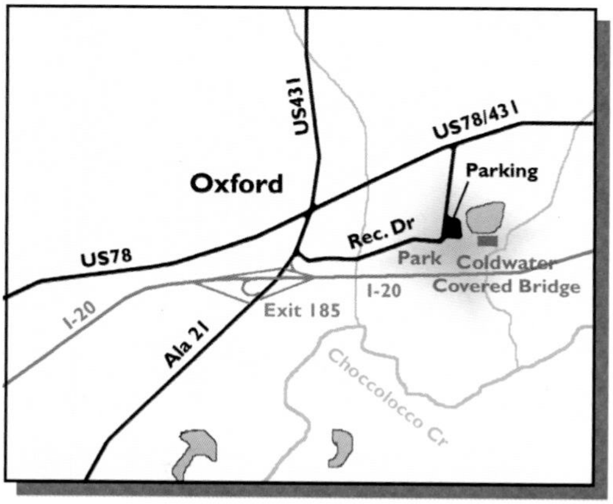

Easley Covered Bridge

From US 231 between Oneonta and Cleveland, turn southwest onto CR 33 in Rosa. Go 1.7 miles to the first paved road and turn left. One-half mile ahead you'll cross the bridge. See map for Swann Covered Bridge on next page. Nectar Falls and Locust Fork Falls are nearby. Swann and Horton Mill Covered Bridges are also nearby.

Gilbert Covered Bridge

From downtown Athens, take Ala. 99 north 5.8 miles and turn left onto CR 26. Drive 3.9 miles west on CR 26 and turn left onto CR 31, Baker Hill Road. The bridge is 1/4 mile ahead on the right.

Gilliland Covered Bridge

From I-59 Exit 188 near Gadsden, take Ala. 211 south for 1.5 miles. Noccalula Falls Park is on the right.

Horton Mill Covered Bridge

From US 231 in Oneonta, follow Ala. 75 north five miles to the bridge on the left. See map for Swann Covered Bridge on next page. Nectar Falls and Locust Fork Falls are west near Cleveland. Swann and Easley Covered Bridges are nearby.

Kymulga Covered Bridge

From US 231/280 in Childersburg, travel east 4.5 miles on Ala. 76. Turn left onto CR 175 north. Kymulga is 2.5 miles straight ahead.

Old Union Covered Bridge

Located between DeSoto State Park and Mentone off CR 89 on private property at Cloudmont Resort. Check for directions and permission at the Pro Shop.

Saunder's Family Covered Bridge

From Leeds, follow Ala. 25 south and turn right onto CR 45 at Sterrett. Drive one mile west to the Twin Pines Resort entrance on the left. Located on private property.

Swann Covered Bridge

From US 231 in Cleveland, take Ala. 160 west 0.8 mile to Ala. 79 north. Travel north one mile to Swann Bridge Road and turn left (west). Swann Bridge is one mile ahead. Nectar Falls and Locust Fork Falls are near the covered bridge. Easley and Horton Mill Covered Bridges are nearby.

Map of Swann, Easley and Horton Mill Covered Bridges.

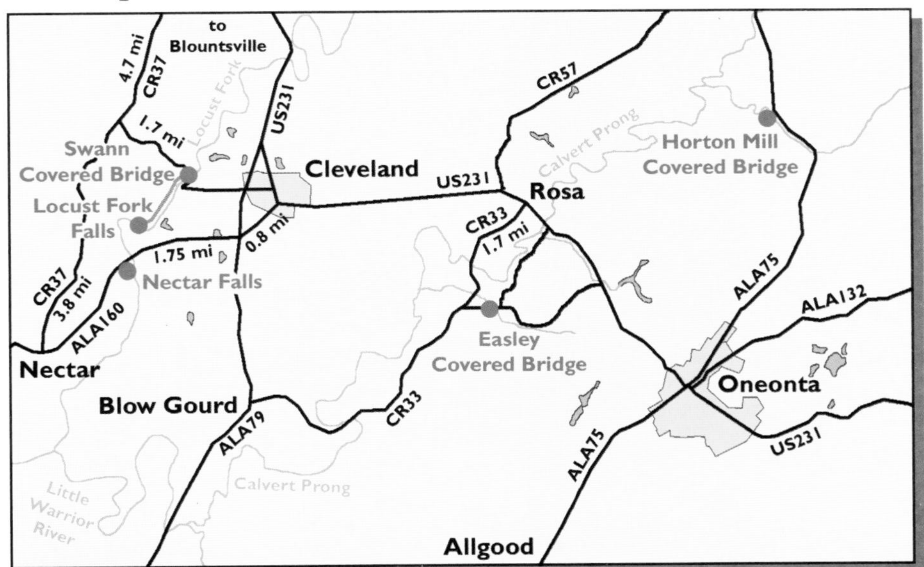

Tannehill Valley Covered Bridge

From Exit 100 on I-20/59 southwest of Birmingham, take Tannehill Parkway south toward Tannehill Historical State Park. Turn left onto CR 97 near the park entrance. Go two miles to Tannehill Valley Covered Bridge on the right.

Waldo Covered Bridge

From Ala. 21 in Talladega, take Ala. 77 south six miles to Waldo Covered Bridge on the left.

DeSoto Caverns Park

Park Description

Originally named Kymulga Cave by the Coosa Indians, in 1975 the cave was renamed to honor Hernando DeSoto for his travels through the area in 1540. DeSoto's army destroyed the Coosa Indian empire during this period. A privately owned and operated park, and an Alabama Historical Site, DeSoto Caverns became America's first officially recorded cave in 1796. The cave's oldest graffiti dates back to 1723. Archaeological excavations reveal native American Indian habitation 2,000 years ago during the Woodland Period.

Here, Confederate soldiers mined saltpeter for gunpowder during the Civil War in the 1860's. During the Prohibition years of the early 1900's, the cave was used as a "speak easy" (honky-tonk). The caverns contain some of the most concentrated Onyx-marble stalactites and stalagmites in the United States. Recognized as one of the largest show caves in the southeastern U.S., its largest room is bigger than a football field and 12 stories high.

Nearby Points of Interest

Kymulga Covered Bridge and Gristmill is only 3.5 miles northwest of the cave. Childersburg is four miles west along Ala. 76. Oak Mountain State Park is 42 miles west. Waldo Covered Bridge and Old Mill Restaurant are 19 miles east following Ala. 76, 21 and 77 through Talladega. The Talladega Speedway and Museum is located just north of Talladega. Horseshoe Bend National Military Monument is southeast following US 280.

Location and Directions

From US 231/280 in Childersburg, follow Ala. 76 east four miles to DeSoto Caverns Park on the left.

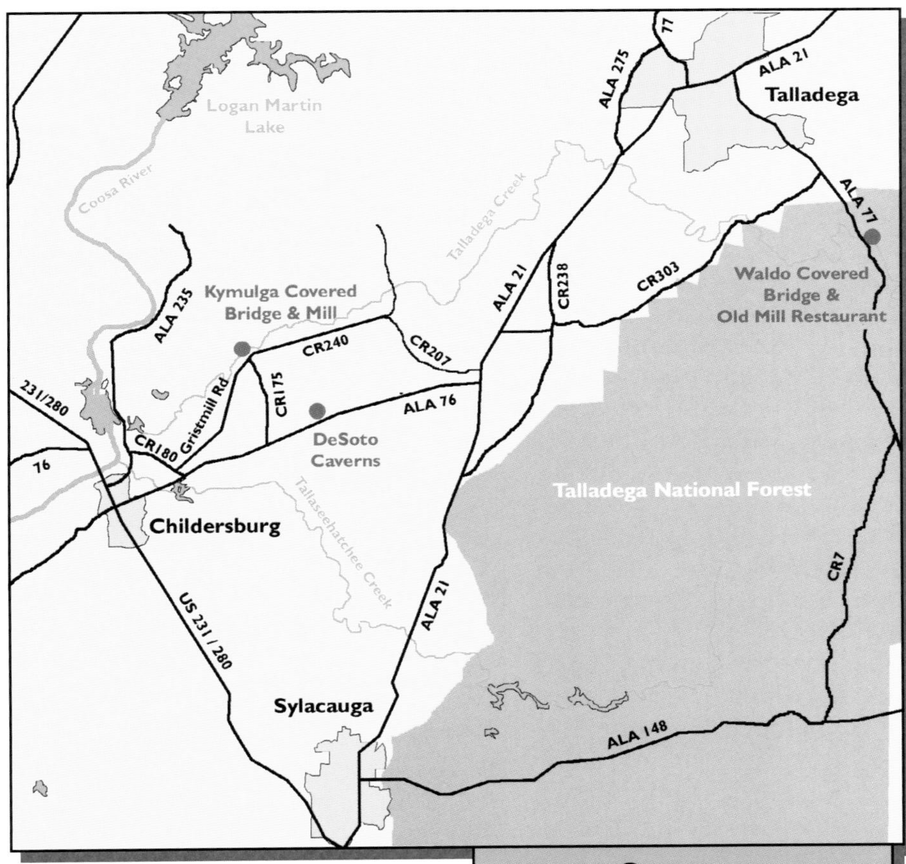

Park Facilities

Gift Shop:

The gift shop is the main visitor center for the park and includes camper registration and supplies. Tickets for the different rides and attractions are purchased here.

Campgrounds:

The adjacent campground has 16 improved sites with connections for RV's.

Picnic Areas:

A picnic area and large pavilion are adjacent the park.

Scenes

Caverns:

DeSoto Caverns has a long and interesting history. Its largest room is over 300 feet by 50 feet and the ceiling towers 12 stories above.

Waterfalls:

The park's only waterfall is manmade. The water flows over several waterwheels and through gem mining troughs.

Foliage:

Long-needle pines are found throughout the park.

DeSoto State Park

Park Description ★★★★★

In the mid 1930's, DeSoto State Park was developed by members of the CCC using native stones and logs. Some of the original furniture in the cabins and country store were assembled by the CCC.

Indian Falls **near the boardwalk.**

The park encompasses over 5,060 acres atop Lookout Mountain along Little River, with the highest point being 1,835 above sea level. Snow accumulates frequently during the winter months. Rhododendron and mountain laurel are abundant throughout the park, with their blooms at peak during May and June, creating a burst of color and fragrance around the trails and streams. The park maintains 8 miles of hiking trails, highlighted by the ADA accessible boardwalk along Laurel Creek. Many nearby attractions include swimming, canoeing, rafting, hiking, golfing, horseback riding, snow skiing (when weather permits) and repelling (by permit). DeSoto State Park is enclosed within the boundaries of the 14,000 acre Little River Canyon National Preserve. Together, these areas provide some of Alabama's most scenic landscapes.

For the waterfall lover, this is *the* park to visit! The park encompasses two of Alabama's largest waterfalls, DeSoto Falls and Little River Falls. While DeSoto Falls is high, at 100 feet, Little River Falls is wide, at 250 feet with a 45-foot drop. Both are impressive waterfalls and easily accessible. Four waterfalls are near the country store in the park, along Laurel Creek. The boardwalk follows Laurel Creek to Laurel Cascades. Laurel Falls and Lost Falls require a short hike beyond the boardwalk. Indian Falls is just a few steps across the road from the boardwalk parking area. A short downhill hike beyond Indian Falls leads to Little River, one of the few rivers in America flowing almost its entire length on top of a mountain. Several more beautiful waterfalls are found in the Little River Canyon area. With the canyon's close proximity, this park should be top on your list of places to visit.

Rhododendron (pink) and mountain laurel (white).

Nearby Points of Interest

Near DeSoto State Park, the visitor finds many popular attractions. Little River Canyon National Preserve forms one of the deepest gorges east of the Mississippi River. Cloudmont Resort, which maintains a 9-hole golf course and snow skiing facilities, is privately owned and operated. Beyond the golf course spanning Little River, the owners relocated *Old Union Covered Bridge.* Mentone is a small town with many antique and craft shops, a few cafes and a bed and breakfast. Fort Payne is the *Official Sock Capital of the World* and home to the country music band, *Alabama* and their *Fan Club Museum.* Howard's Chapel is one mile north of the country store. This church was constructed around part of a huge boulder, which forms part of its altar. Pisgah Gorge is to the west. Sequoyah Caverns is just north of Mentone, with its many subterranean pools and lakes of clear water, reflect the cave's natural rock formations.

Cragsmere Manna Restaurant, located on CR 89 just north of the park provides an excellent atmosphere for dinner.

Location and Directions

DeSoto State Park is located in DeKalb County on Lookout Mountain, eight miles northeast of Fort Payne, and nine miles south of Mentone on CR 89.

From Exit 218 on I-59, follow US 35 south, through Fort Payne to the top of Lookout Mountain. (There are two turns required to fol-

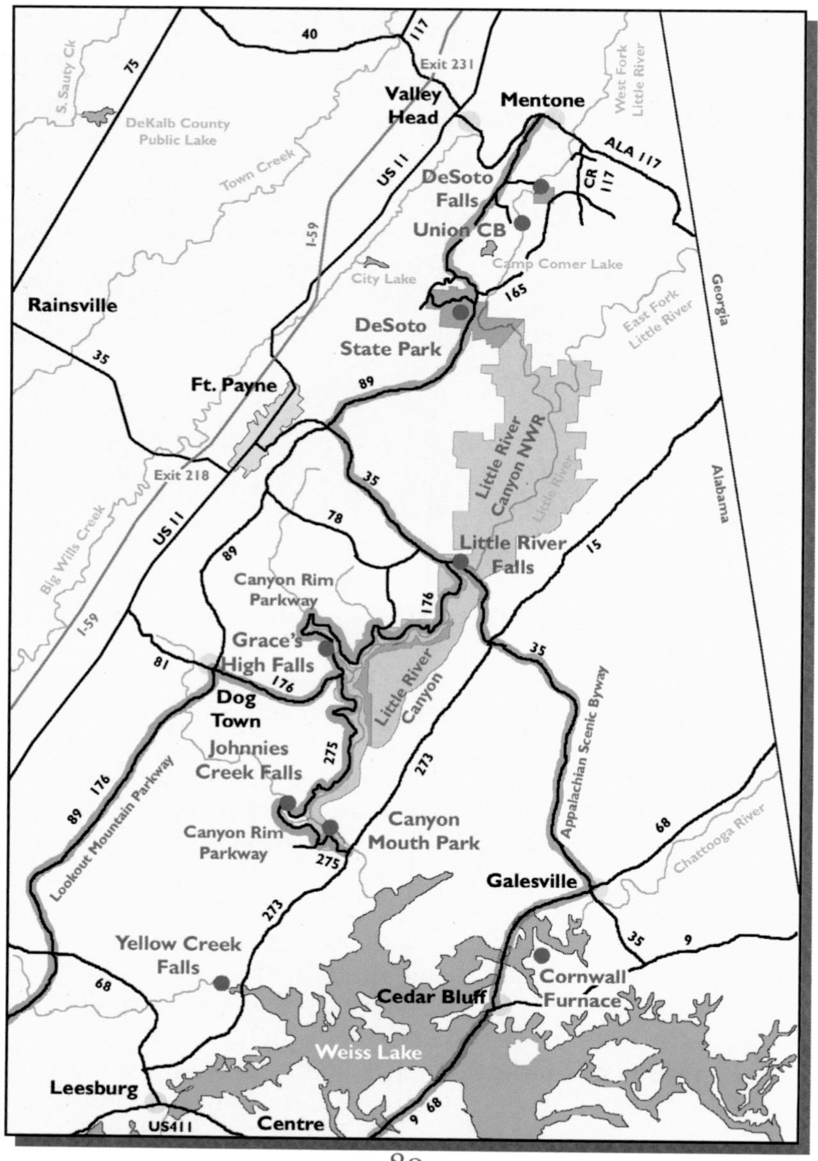

low US 35 through Fort Payne; first, take a left onto US11 north, then turn right at Union Park onto US 35 south). Turn left on CR 89 north at the top of the mountain. The park is five miles ahead.

Lost Falls **in autumn. A double waterfall hidden along Laurel Creek.**

Main Park Area and Trail Map

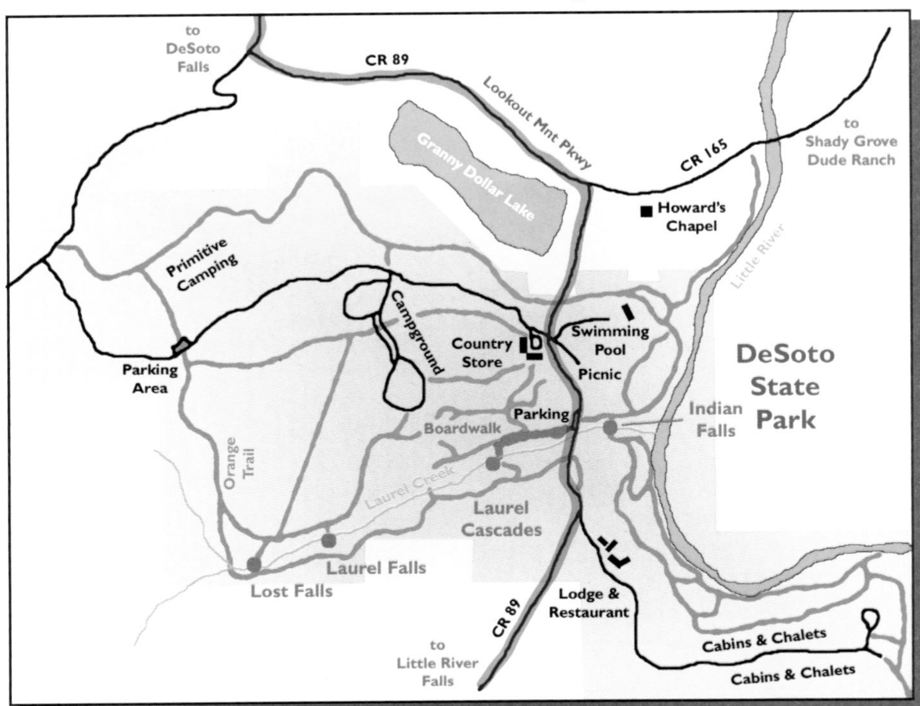

Park Facilities

Lodge and Restaurant:

The lodge is constructed from area stones and features exposed beam ceilings. An extra large fireplace in the restaurant provides a warm, cozy, mountainous atmosphere to meet with family and friends. The restaurant features some of Lookout Mountain's finest, casual dining. There are twenty-five rooms adjacent the lodge. All rooms have telephone and cable TV with a choice of one king, or two double beds. The lodge overlooks Little River below.

Cabins and Chalets:

A total of 22 cabins and chalets are available within the park. Two, four or six-person, newly renovated, rustic cabins constructed of native logs and stones. Modified "A" frame structures, chalets have a double bed in the main bedroom and two twin beds in the sleeping loft, with skylight. All are furnished (including linens, basic cookware and utensils), air conditioned and electrically heated. All cabins and chalets have fireplaces, screened porches, sundecks, and are located in forested areas, away from main roadways to provide additional privacy. Each unit has sufficient parking for several vehicles. Most are situated adjacent Little River.

Campgrounds:

Seventy-eight widely spaced sites with water and electrical connections. Some sites are well shaded, while others are sunlit. A pavilion, two comfort stations and playgrounds are within easy walking distance. Back-in sites for tents or small campers, and pull-through sites available for larger

Scenes

Waterfalls:

There are several waterfalls within the park, ranging in size from small cascades to DeSoto Falls, with its drop of 100 feet. The coke-bottle colored clear waters of Little River forms multitudinous rapids and whitewater as it rushes along Lookout Mountain through the park.

DeSoto Falls has a concrete dam above the falls, built in 1925 for Alabama's historic first hydroelectric power plant. Only a marker, the dam and a few concrete pads remain today. Little River flows over the dam, through the rocks forming several cascades, then plummets 100 feet to the pool below. The small lake above the dam provides a calm area of Little River for picnics, fishing, swimming and canoeing. Steps lead below the dam to overlook the main waterfall. This overlook is not wheelchair accessible.

Indian Falls, Azalea Cascade, Laurel Falls and Lost Falls can be found along Laurel Creek near the boardwalk. The boardwalk follows Laurel Creek upstream 1,080 feet and terminates at Laurel Cascades. Laurel Falls and Lost Falls require a short hike (3/8 and 1/2 mile respectively) beyond the end of the boardwalk. Indian Falls is just a few steps (300 feet) across the road from the boardwalk parking area on CR89. A short downhill hike beyond Indian Falls leads to Little River. **TIP:** Since Laurel Creek is seasonal, check the amount of water as it flows under the roadway at CR89 by the boardwalk or at Indian Falls before hiking to Laurel Falls or Lost Falls. The

vehicles. A dumping station is also available. Gated access enhances your security. A primitive camping area is available.

Country Store & Information Center:

At the heart of the park, this facility includes camper registration, a store for camper and picnic supplies, craft and gift shop, nature center, restrooms and a coin-operated laundry.

Swimming Pool:

DeSoto State Park maintains an Olympic size swimming pool and bathhouse, located near the country store and picnic area. The pool is open Memorial Day through Labor Day.

Picnic Areas:

Picnic areas are located in the DeSoto Falls area and across from the country store. A comfort station is in the DeSoto Falls area. Restrooms and a rustic stone pavilion are in the picnic area near the country store. This area also has a playground, volleyball court, ball field, horseshoe court, tennis court and basketball court. Sports accessories are available for checkout at the country store.

Hiking trails:

The park maintains eight miles of hiking trails. Most trails are located around the lodge, cabins, chalets, and campgrounds. The trails lead along Laurel Creek, Little River and through forested areas. Many natural rock formations, including *Needle Eye Rock* can be seen along the trails. Each trail is marked by colors along the way; pick up a trail map at the country store. For the dedicated hiker, permits are required to hike and camp in Little River Canyon.

Orange trail along Laurel Creek continues westward upstream, then turns north and crosses the campground road by a small parking area. The hike back to Lost Falls from this parking area is about the same distance as from the boardwalk side, but the terrain is much more level.

Little River Falls is visible from the bridge on Ala. 35, approximately 10 miles southeast of the main park area. Across the bridge is a small parking area with a paved trail leading to the falls. Minor restroom facilities are available in the parking area (no running water). Little River Falls drops 45 feet across a gorge width of 250 feet, a very impressive scene during the rainy season. This waterfall begins the 22-mile long Little River Canyon. Follow Ala. 176 south (Canyon Rim Parkway) from the west side of the bridge to tour along the canyon rim (see *Little River Canyon National Preserve*). **TIP:** The southernmost nine miles is rough pavement requiring a slow speed, but along the way you'll find Johnnie's Creek and Grace's High Falls.

Creeks:

Little River flows just below the lodge and cabins, then continues in a southerly direction through Little River Canyon on its journey to Weiss Lake. Little River is classified as an *Alabama Wild and Scenic River*, and was the first river in the state to be awarded the status of *Outstanding National Resource Water*, because of its water quality.

Laurel Creek flows through the center of the main park, originating west of the campground area.

(Continued on page 84)

(Continued from page 83)
The boardwalk follows part of its journey to Little River. Indian Falls, Laurel Cascades, Laurel Falls and Lost Falls are found along this short creek. Laurel Creek is seasonal and may slow to a trickle during summer months.

Foliage:

Mountain laurel and rhododendron are abundant throughout the park. Their blooms peak during May and June, filling the forests with their fragrances. The white and lavender blooms of dogwood and redbud trees are scattered throughout the forests under the taller pines and cedars. Around mid-March, the maple and oak begin blooming with their bright red buds. Rare and endangered plant life can be found along the hiking trails; check with the naturalist at the country store. Shortneedle pines, oak, hickory and elm trees are plentiful throughout the forests. Fern growth is accentuated by the moist, rocky soil.

A small stream hidden under mountain laurel near the picnic area, just above Little River.

Dismals Wonder Garden

Park Description

★★★★

The Dismals is a small canyon located in northwest Alabama just south of Russellville. The canyon features Champion Tree, Dismals Branch, two waterfalls and many unusual rock formations. The scenic 3/4-mile trail through the canyon follows both sides of the stream and takes visitors between narrow crevices in huge moss covered boulders.

Nearby Points of Interest

Russellville is the closest town to the park with Tuscumbia being just 16 miles further north. Rock Bridge Canyon is 16 miles southwest. The Bear Creek Reservoirs are located in this area. Natural Bridge Park is 29 miles southeast. Clarkson Covered Bridge is east of Natural Bridge.

The waters from a natural spring create *Secret Falls* before joining Dismals Branch.

Location and Directions

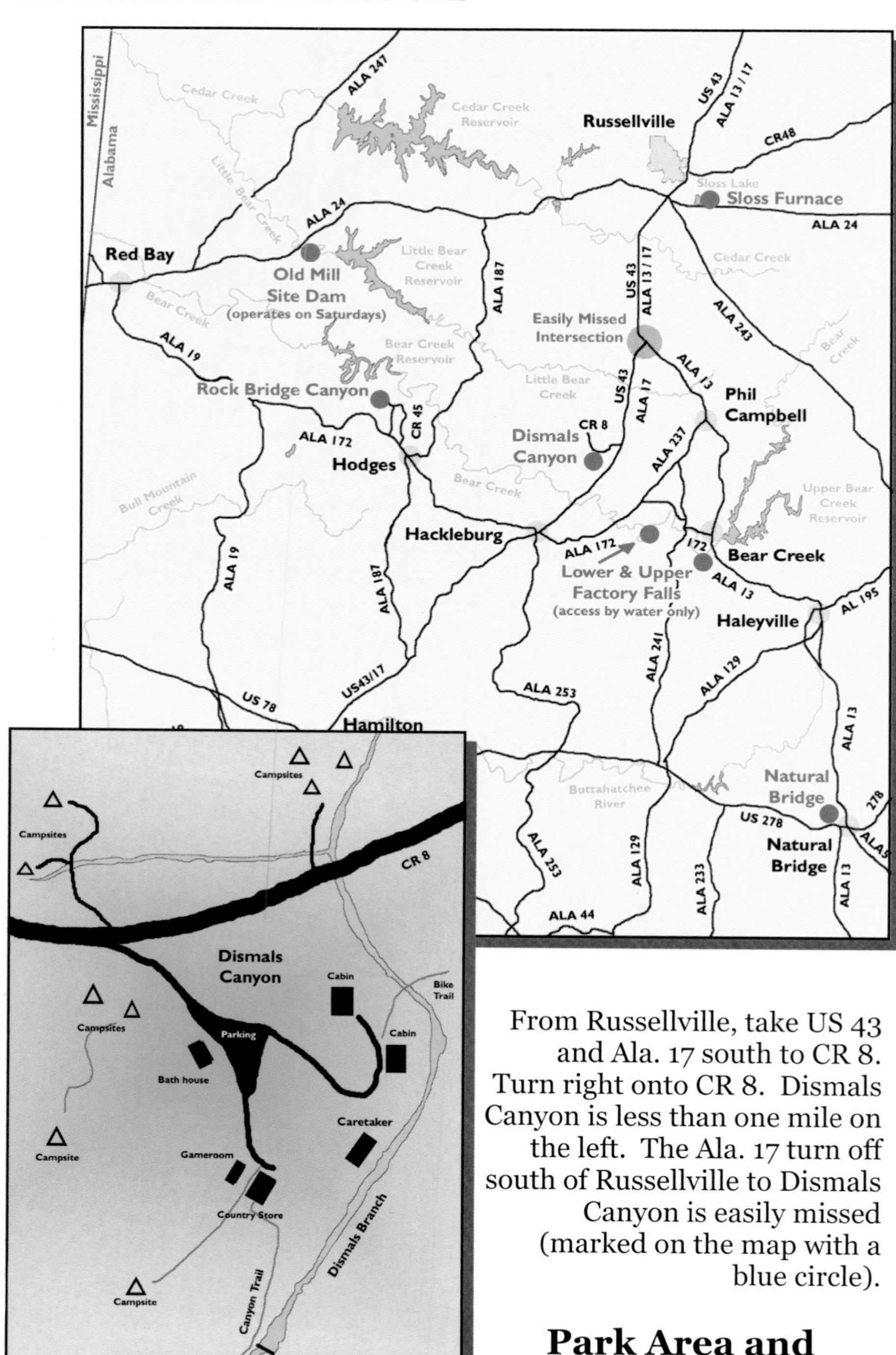

From Russellville, take US 43 and Ala. 17 south to CR 8. Turn right onto CR 8. Dismals Canyon is less than one mile on the left. The Ala. 17 turn off south of Russellville to Dismals Canyon is easily missed (marked on the map with a blue circle).

Park Area and Trail Map

***Rainbow Falls* in Dismals Canyon.**

The swinging bridge over Dismals Branch.

Park Facilities

Lodge and Restaurant:

There are no lodge or restaurant facilities available.

Cabins and Chalets:

The park provides two cabins overlooking Dismals Branch near the country store.

Campgrounds:

Several primitive campsites are available, some along the Dismals Branch. The one bathhouse and a game room are located near the country store.

Country Store & Information Center:

This store includes a gift shop, visitor registration, and camping and picnic supplies.

Swimming Pool:

The park does not have a swimming pool, but did have a swimming area with deck below the country store along Dismals Branch. Due to a recent hole forming in the old mill's dam above Rainbow Falls, the water has drained.

Picnic Areas:

Picnic areas are only located at the campsites.

Hiking trails:

The moderate 3/4-mile trail leads through the canyon along both sides of Dismals Branch. Many unusual rock formations, two waterfalls and Champion Tree, Alabama's largest Eastern Hemlock are seen along the trail. A swinging bridge below Rainbow Falls leads through narrow gaps in huge rocks. A bike trail is available.

Scenes

Waterfalls:

The 18-foot **Rainbow Falls** is the site of an old gristmill. The small dam above the falls provided additional waterpower for the mill and a small pool above. Portions of the dam are still intact, but only the stone cutouts for the mill footing remain today. Rainbow Falls begins the Dismals Branch journey through the canyon.

Upper (6 feet) and **Lower Factory Falls** (18 feet) are popular kayak runs on Bear Creek near Ala. 172 and 241 west of the town of Bear Creek. The flow of Bear Creek is dependent upon TVA (power company) requirements. Access is by water only (no trails).

Canyon:

The canyon contains house-sized boulders lined with bright green mosses. Dismals Branch runs through the canyon, passing under and between the boulders. Rainbow Falls is at the head of the canyon, with the smaller **Secret Falls** along a tributary creek. Many narrow crevices and larger openings in the rocks form cool environments along the trail.

Creeks:

Dismals Branch is a shallow stream that varies in width from 10 to 20 feet.

Double Bridges Falls

Description ★

Scarham and Whippoorwill Creeks join at Double Bridges. Both creeks have waterfalls at this juncture, viewable from a small pull-off along CR 409. An old red mill house remains on Scarham Creek, with its dam just above the falls. These falls are sometimes referred to as Red Mill Falls. About 30 feet wide and dropping 15 feet, it is

***Red Mill Falls* on Scarham Creek. The pull-off is left, above the shrubbery. Whippoorwill Falls is further left. Scarham Creek Cascades is upstream from the right side of the bridge.**

difficult to get a good view. The falls on adjacent Whippoorwill Creek are smaller at 10 feet wide and 10 feet high. Scarham Creek Cascades is on private property 1/4 mile upstream from the Red Mill. This cascade is 35 feet wide and 6 feet tall. There is no trail leading to the cascades. To reach its best viewpoint, hike along the overflow streambed through the underbrush on the southwest side of Scarham Creek (privately owned). Although all these falls are scenic, the surrounding properties are not well maintained and distract from the area's beauty.

Nearby Points of Interest

Private Short Creek Falls is only three miles west on CR414. Lake Guntersville State Park is eight miles north on Ala. 227. High Falls County Park and Buck's Pocket State Park are to the northeast following Ala. 75 and 227.

Location and Directions

From US 431 in Guntersville, take Ala. 227 east three and one-half miles and turn right onto CR 414. Drive 6.4 miles and turn left onto CR 409. It is 1.2 miles to Double Bridges.

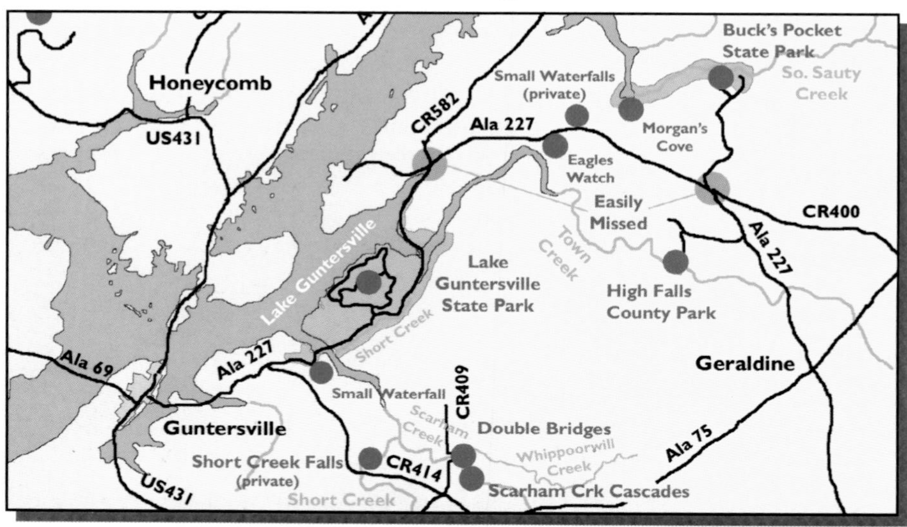

Area Map

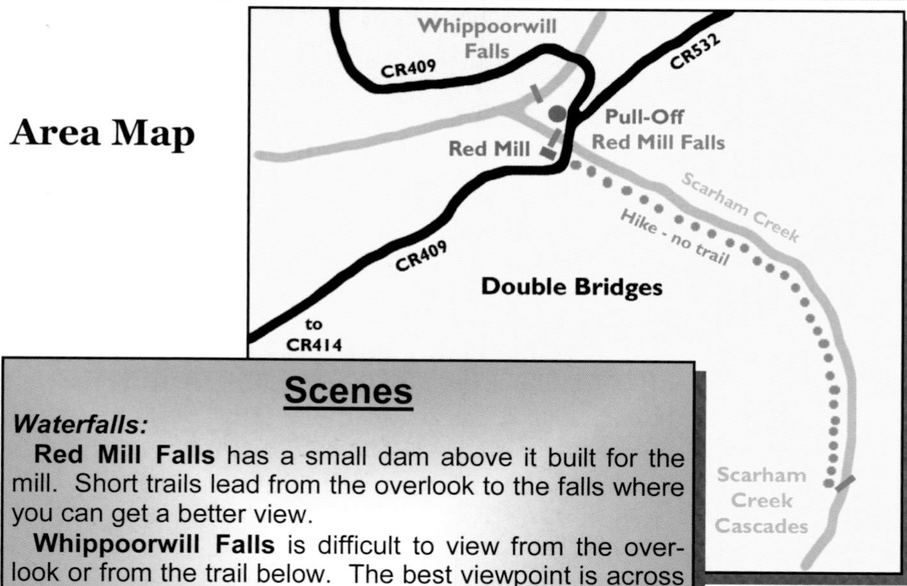

Scenes

Waterfalls:

Red Mill Falls has a small dam above it built for the mill. Short trails lead from the overlook to the falls where you can get a better view.

Whippoorwill Falls is difficult to view from the overlook or from the trail below. The best viewpoint is across the creek, but it is very difficult to get there.

Scarham Creek Cascades is a beautiful waterfall, but again is very difficult to reach. There is no trail leading the 1/4 mile back to the cascades, so you must trek through the underbrush on private property.

Dugger Mountain Scenic Drive

Description ★★

Ala. 9 just south of Piedmont traces the west side of scenic Dugger Mountain in the Talladega National Forest. To continue a scenic drive around the 9,200 acre Dugger Mountain Wilderness Area, turn left (east) onto Rabbittown Road (CR55) in Holley Crossroads (8.7 miles south of Piedmont along Ala. 9). Follow CR55 until reaching Oak Level then turn left (north) onto CR 49. Follow CR 49 to Borden Springs and turn left (west) on CR 70. Follow CR 70 back into Piedmont. This 39-mile route loops around Dugger Mountain through the National Forest. Although not classified as such, Ala. 9 is very scenic all the way to near Montgomery in central Alabama.

Nearby Points of Interest

North is Yellow Creek Falls and Little River Canyon Mouth Park near Leesburg. West in Gadsden, is Noccalula Falls Park and the southern extremity of Lookout Mountain Parkway.
The Choccolocco WMA is just south along Ala. 9. The Forest Roads leading to Coleman Lake Recreation Area from Ala. 9 and Rabbittown Road are all dirt. The best way to reach Coleman Lake is from US 78 on the east side of the forest, where the roads are paved.

Positioned below the Dugger Mountain range, this barn was constructed in the early 1950's. Dugger Mountain's 2,140 foot peak is just left of this image. Dugger Mountain Scenic Drive is to the right, paralleling the mountain range.

Location and Directions

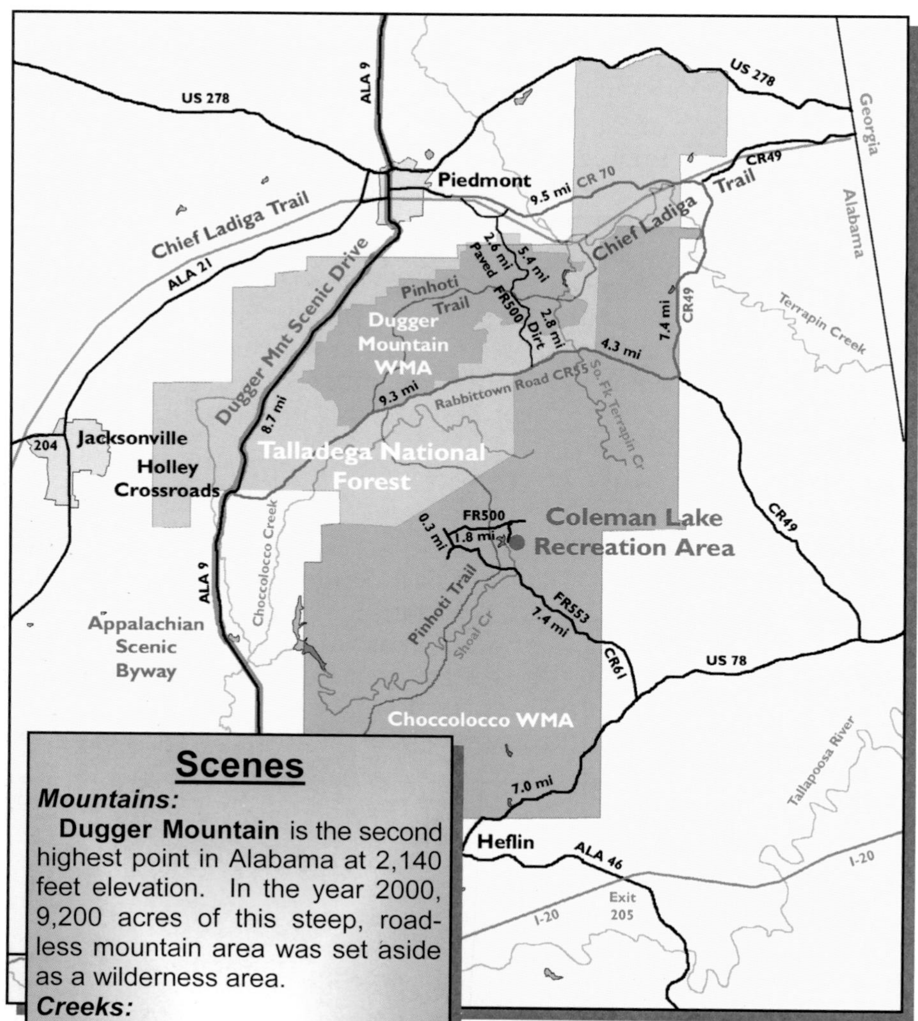

Scenes

Mountains:

Dugger Mountain is the second highest point in Alabama at 2,140 feet elevation. In the year 2000, 9,200 acres of this steep, roadless mountain area was set aside as a wilderness area.

Creeks:

Choccolocco Creek and **Terrapin Creek** flow just east of Dugger Mountain within the National Forest boundaries. Both creeks provide recreational activities such as canoeing and kayaking.

Foliage:

The Talladega National Forest hosts most trees native to North Alabama. The mountains here are too steep for the pines to be harvested, so the forest remains in a natural state.

From Piedmont, follow Ala. 9 south. Dugger Mountain Scenic Drive begins just south of Piedmont and extends six miles southward as Ala. 9 passes Dugger Mountain. Ala. 9 is also part of the newly established Appalachian Scenic Byway.

Ghost Creek Falls and Natural Bridge

Description

★★

This hidden, natural wonder is privately owned and is not open to the public, but one waterfall and the natural bridge are clearly visible from the roadway. The owners have exercised immense effort in clearing and improving the surrounding lands for their residence. The natural bridge spans almost 20 feet, while the traversing cascades descend 50 feet down the rocks behind and beneath the bridge. Three natural springs emerge from the mountainside, creating waterfalls and cascades as the water flows toward an underground stream before reaching Lake Guntersville. The spring water is pure and is often used by the resident.

Nearby Points of Interest

The city of Guntersville is 11 miles south along US 431. US 431 from this point to Guntersville is very scenic as it often intersects Lake Guntersville and crosses the Tennessee River. Lake Guntersville State Park is 21 miles southeast, while Cathedral Caverns State Park is 15 miles northeast. Blowing Wind Cave NWR is 11 miles beyond Cathedral Caverns. Huntsville and Monte Sano State Park are 25 miles north along US431. Buck's Pocket State Park, High Falls County Park and Short Creek Falls are also nearby.

Ghost Creek Falls.

Scenes

Waterfalls, Springs & Natural Bridge:

There are three springs emerging from the mountainside.

Ghost Creek Falls is on the rightmost spring adjacent the residence. The spring emerges from a small cave in the mountainside, then tumbles down the cliff face. This waterfall cannot be seen clearly from the roadway.

Natural Bridge Falls flows under the natural bridge to an underground stream 50 feet below.

The leftmost spring (unnamed) originates from higher on the mountainside and joins the other two springs underground.

The **Natural Bridge** spans 20 feet in front of the waterfall and stands 50 feet above the bottom of the sinkhole. The surrounding land is just below the bridge, providing a close up view.

Foliage:

The owner has invested greatly in improving the surrounding lands by adding stone walls, azaleas and rhododendrons to the hillside.

***Natural Bridge & Falls. Ghost Creek Falls* is just right of this photograph, hidden beside the owners residence. A redbud tree is in bloom above the bridge. I found this natural wonder years ago while driving along the roadway. I could hear this waterfall 150 feet back in the woods.**

Location and Directions

From Guntersville, follow US 431 north toward Huntsville, 11 miles to Cottonville Road. Turn right onto Cottonville Road, go 1/2 mile to the first sharp curve, the falls and natural bridge are on the left in the curve. Cottonville Road is a small paved road 3.2 miles north of CR 5 (the road to Cathedral Caverns) and is across from Honeycomb Campground.

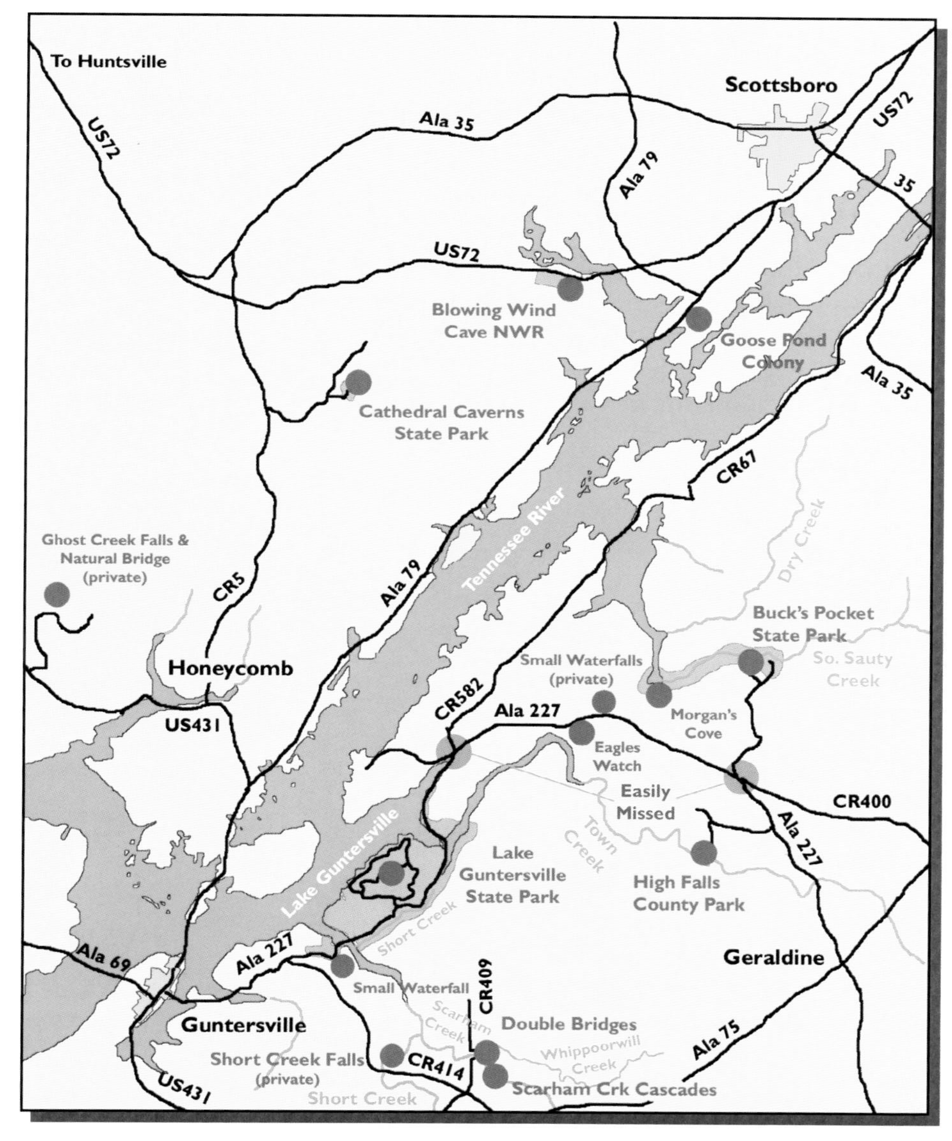

High Falls County Park

Park Description

High Falls is almost an unknown wonder even to Alabamian's. Until recently, the park was not listed on maps, road signs or brochures. After driving through the area many times, I did not know of its existence until traveling in a different direction when I saw a new sign haphazardly placed on a highway marker. This waterfall is large. When first seeing it, I immediately thought of Niagara Falls. The falls are 300 feet wide, with water dropping 55 feet. During heavy rains almost the entire width is falling water. A natural bridge has formed just below the falls and the water gushes through. A restored walking bridge crosses Town Creek above the falls. The bridge is constructed upon the original stone pillars.

Nearby Points of Interest

Buck's Pocket State Park is 8 miles north along Ala. 227. Lake Guntersville State Park is 18 miles west following Ala. 227. Guntersville is 24 miles away, six miles beyond Lake Guntersville State Park. Following Ala. 227 southeast 1.5 miles further you'll find interesting rapids and remnants of an old mill site.

Location and Directions

From US 231 in Guntersville, follow Ala. 227 east 24 miles. Ala.

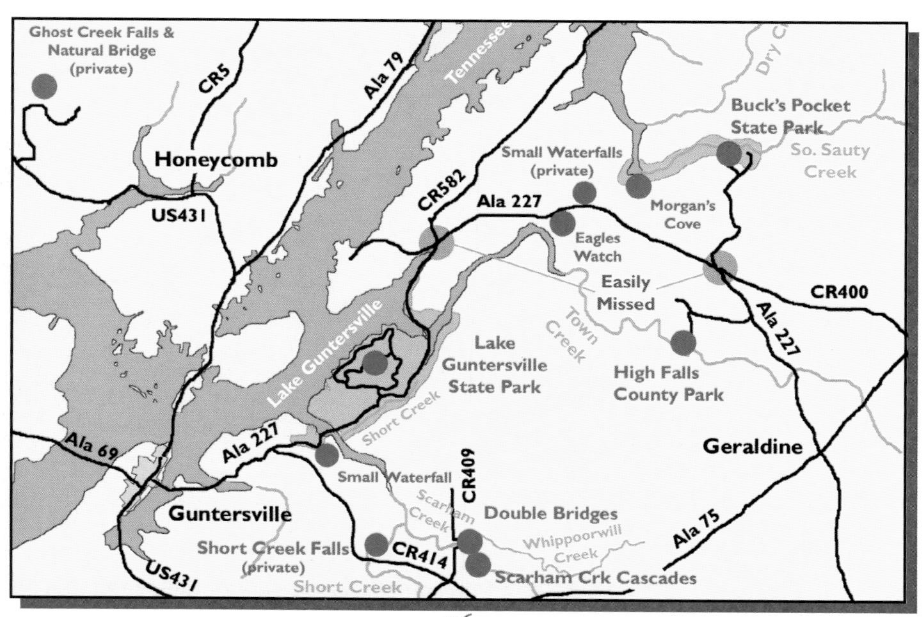

Autumn colors linger over *High Falls* and the *Natural Bridge* in late November. The natural bridge is not visible here, but it is under the rock formation on the left in front of the waterfall.

227 makes an abrupt right turn where you will see the turnoff (left) to Buck's Pocket State Park. Here, continue right on Ala. 227 for an additional 1.5 miles. Turn right on CR 356. Travel west 1.5 miles and turn left onto a paved road. High Falls County Park is one mile ahead.

Park Map

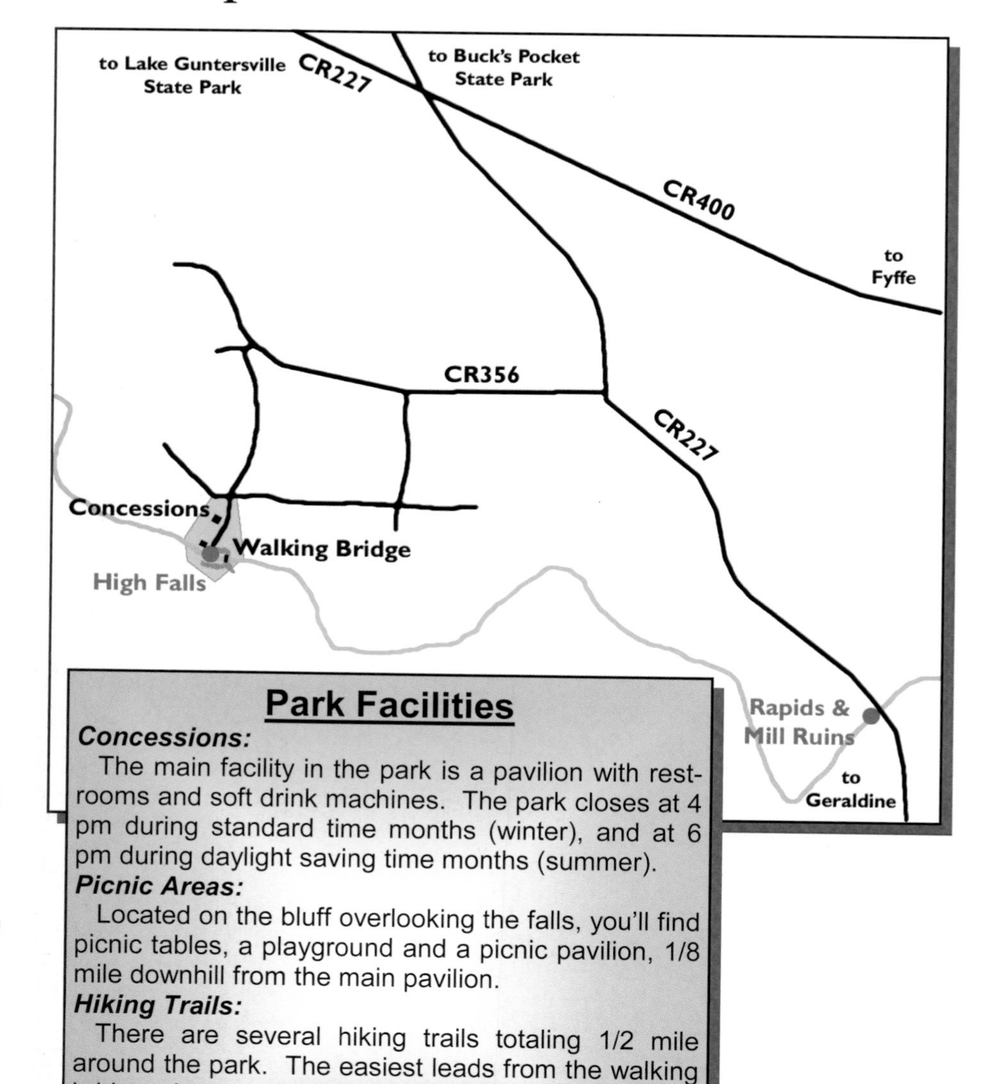

Park Facilities

Concessions:

The main facility in the park is a pavilion with restrooms and soft drink machines. The park closes at 4 pm during standard time months (winter), and at 6 pm during daylight saving time months (summer).

Picnic Areas:

Located on the bluff overlooking the falls, you'll find picnic tables, a playground and a picnic pavilion, 1/8 mile downhill from the main pavilion.

Hiking Trails:

There are several hiking trails totaling 1/2 mile around the park. The easiest leads from the walking bridge along a small side creek back to the picnic pavilion. Across the walking bridge, a moderate trail leads to the south side of the falls. This trail goes to the pool below the falls, but it is a steep and dangerous climb.

Scenes

Waterfalls:

Some water flows over the 55 foot tall and 300 foot wide **High Falls** all year long. During winter months, mist freezes on the foliage growing on the natural bridge below.

Natural Bridge:

The natural bridge, about 20 feet high and 20 feet across, is below the falls just below the picnic pavilion. Water flows through the opening. Its best viewpoint is from the overlook below the picnic pavilion.

Walking Bridge:

This wooden restored walking bridge crosses Town Creek just above the falls. Originally a covered bridge constructed in the 1800's, the stone pillars are still in place and supporting the walking bridge.

Creeks:

Town Creek flows over a shallow rocky streambed above the falls. A small side creek joins Town Creek under the restored walking bridge.

Foliage:

Most trees are long needle pines and hardwoods. Mountain laurel highlight the trails, blooming in May and June.

High Falls **as viewed from the overlook by the picnic pavilion. Part of the natural bridge is visible at the lower left.**

Horseshoe Bend National Military Mon.

Park Description ★★★

Historic Horseshoe Bend formed a natural defensive boundary for the Upper Creek Indians. They established the village Tohopeka along the Tallapoosa River in the deepest part of the bend. Realizing turbulence with the new settlers invading their lands, the Creeks felt confident of their safety on this easily defendable peninsula. Almost 1,000 Upper Creek Indians gathered here under Chief Menawa. However, in 1814 General Andrew Jackson's army of 2,700 men with the assistance of 600 Creek allies overcame the Upper Creeks during the famous Battle of Horseshoe Bend. A 3-mile road leads through the park following the Tallapoosa River. Wild turkey frequently covey around the battlefields.

Nearby Points of Interest

New Site is a small town located nearest the park. Alex City is 18 miles southwest and is large enough to have all major hotels. Wind Creek State Park (not covered in this book) is located south of Alex City on Lake Martin and provides a large campground but no lodging, restaurant or cabin facilities. Talladega National Forest and Cheaha State Park are located 50 miles north of Horseshoe Bend. DeSoto Caverns is 50 miles to the northwest.

A peaceful resting place along the trail beside the creek.

Location and Directions

From Alex City, take Ala. 22 east 12.5 miles. Turn right onto Ala. 49. Go 5 miles south to Horseshoe Bend National Military Park on the left.

Park Facilities

Visitor's Center:

The Visitor's Center includes a Nature Center.

Picnic Areas:

Picnic areas are available throughout the Park.

Hiking trails:

A 2.8-mile trail leads beside the horseshoe along the Tallapoosa River and through the forest. This easy to moderate trail winds by almost all of the park's historic sites and markers. Wide enough for two people to easily walk side-by-side, the trail is covered with small pebbles and is well maintained. There are ample benches along the way strategically placed near hilltops. A small creek meanders beside a portion of the trail.

Scenes

Creeks:

The only creek in the park is near the trail parking area. It follows a portion of the hiking trail as it wanders to the Tallapoosa River.

Foliage:

Long-needle pines and hardwoods are prominent in the park.

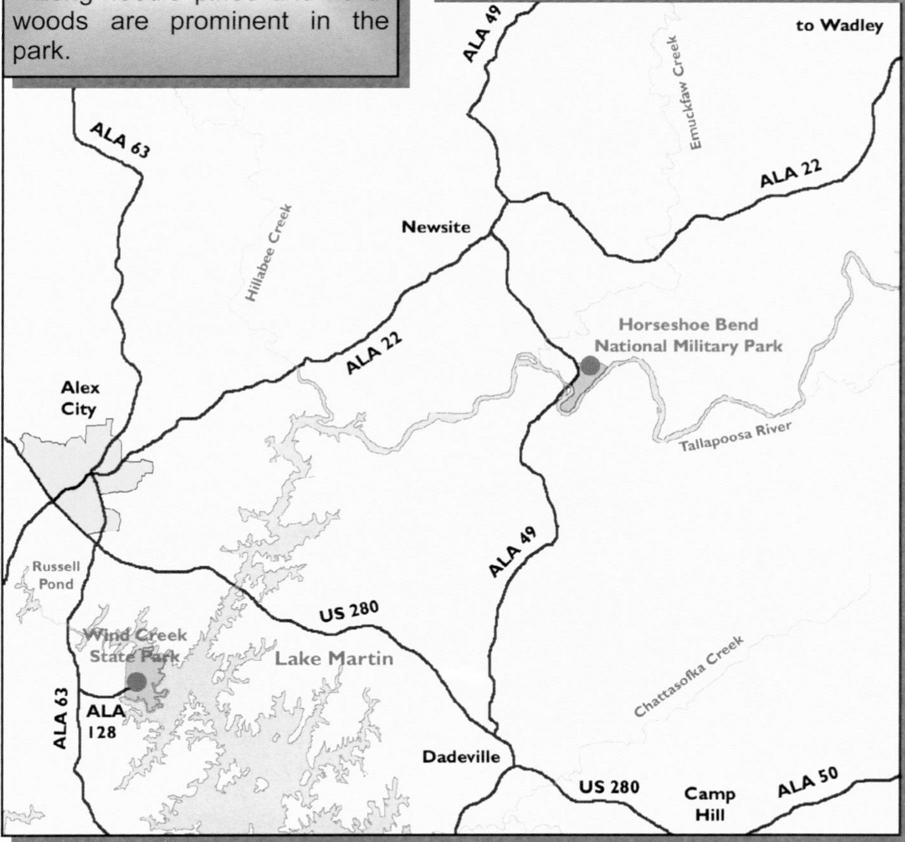

Hurricane Creek Park

Park Description ★★★

Recently donated to the Cullman Parks and Recreation Department, this 60-acre park has trails leading through a small canyon along Hurricane Creek north of Cullman. The park features a natural bridge, several small waterfalls and a picnic area and pavilion beside Hurricane Creek. A scaled down version of The Incline in Chattanooga is available to carry visitors up and down the canyon's slopes. Two miles of trails around the canyon lead visitors by unusual rock formations. The previous owner developed the park's facilities and has maintained the park in outstanding condition.

Nearby Points of Interest

Ave Maria Grotto is on US 278 just east of Cullman. To the north near Decatur is Wheeler NWR. In Huntsville are Monte Sano State Park and Madison County Nature Trail. 30 miles south is Rickwood Caverns State Park. Southwest along US 278 is Clarkson Covered Bridge and Bankhead National Forest. Eastward, the traveler will find Guntersville State Park.

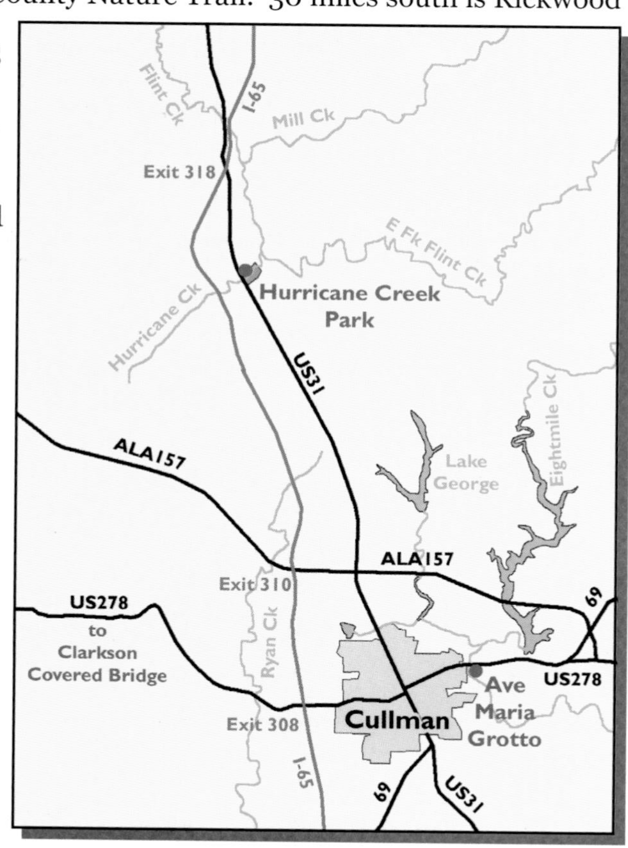

Location and Directions

From Exit 318 on I-65, drive 2.1 miles south on US31 to Hurricane Creek Park on the left. The park is 8.4 miles north of Cullman.

This natural bridge is only 5 feet off the ground, but it spans 18 feet.

The swinging bridge across Hurricane Creek by the picnic area and pavilion.

One of the many small rapids along Hurricane Creek.

Park Map

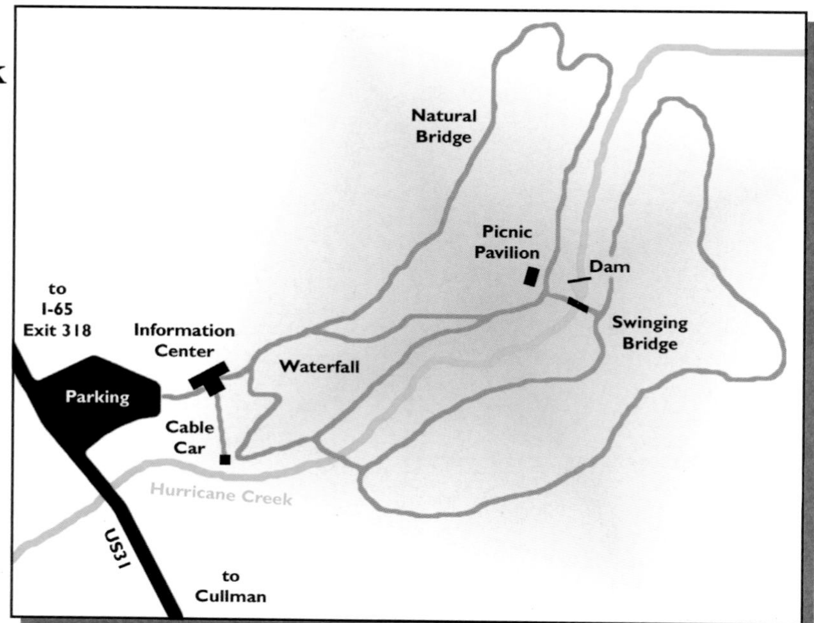

Park Facilities

Information Center:

This facility includes the upper landing for the cable car. The car carries visitors 100 feet below to near the bottom of the canyon and picnic area.

Picnic Areas:

The picnic area adjacent Hurricane Creek includes a small pavilion. The previous owner constructed a dam in front of the pavilion providing a peaceful location to relax. A swinging bridge above the dam adds to the area's aesthetics.

Hiking trails:

2 miles of easy to moderate, well-maintained hiking trails lead around and through the canyon. The trails guide hikers by the natural bridge, Hurricane Creek, waterfalls and unusual rock formations.

Scenes

Waterfalls:

Several unnamed waterfalls along the trails exist after rains. Small creeks flow over the canyon walls to Hurricane Creek below.

Natural Bridge:

The natural bridge spans 18 feet and is only 5 feet above the ground. A small trail leads to the top of the bridge.

Creeks:

Hurricane Creek is the only major creek in the park. It's waters flow over small boulders at the bottom of the canyon.

Foliage:

Mostly pines, cedar and hardwoods are in the park boundaries. Markers along the trails describe many of them. Poison ivy is found near the canyon floor.

Joe Wheeler State Park

Park Description

Joe Wheeler State Park is located on Wheeler Lake 27 miles east of Florence following US 72. The park includes outstanding extras such as a championship par-72 golf course, waterfront lodge, restaurant, convention center and a modern 134-slip marina. The State Park, NWR, dam and lake are named after General Joe Wheeler, who served 18 years in Congress for Alabama and survived 3 wars. His estate encompasses 1,500 acres south of the Tennessee River near Courtland.

Nearby Points of Interest

27 miles west in Florence and Tuscumbia are Pope's Tavern Museum, Shiloh Battlefield, the W. C. Handy Home & Museum, Helen Keller's Birthplace, the Alabama Music Hall of Fame, Tuscumbia Falls (a man-made work of art!) and the Tennessee Valley Arts Center and Museum. Further westward is the Natchez Trace Parkway. The Space & Rocket Center, Monte Sano State Park, Gilbert and Cambron Covered Bridges and Madison County Nature Trail are located to the east near Athens and Huntsville. Joe Wheeler NWR is south of the Tennessee River east of Decatur. The Dismals Wonder Gardens and Rock Bridge Canyon are south of the park. The Trail of Tears Corridor follows US 72 just north of the park.

Sailboats at the marina. The restaurant and lodge are behind.

Location and Directions

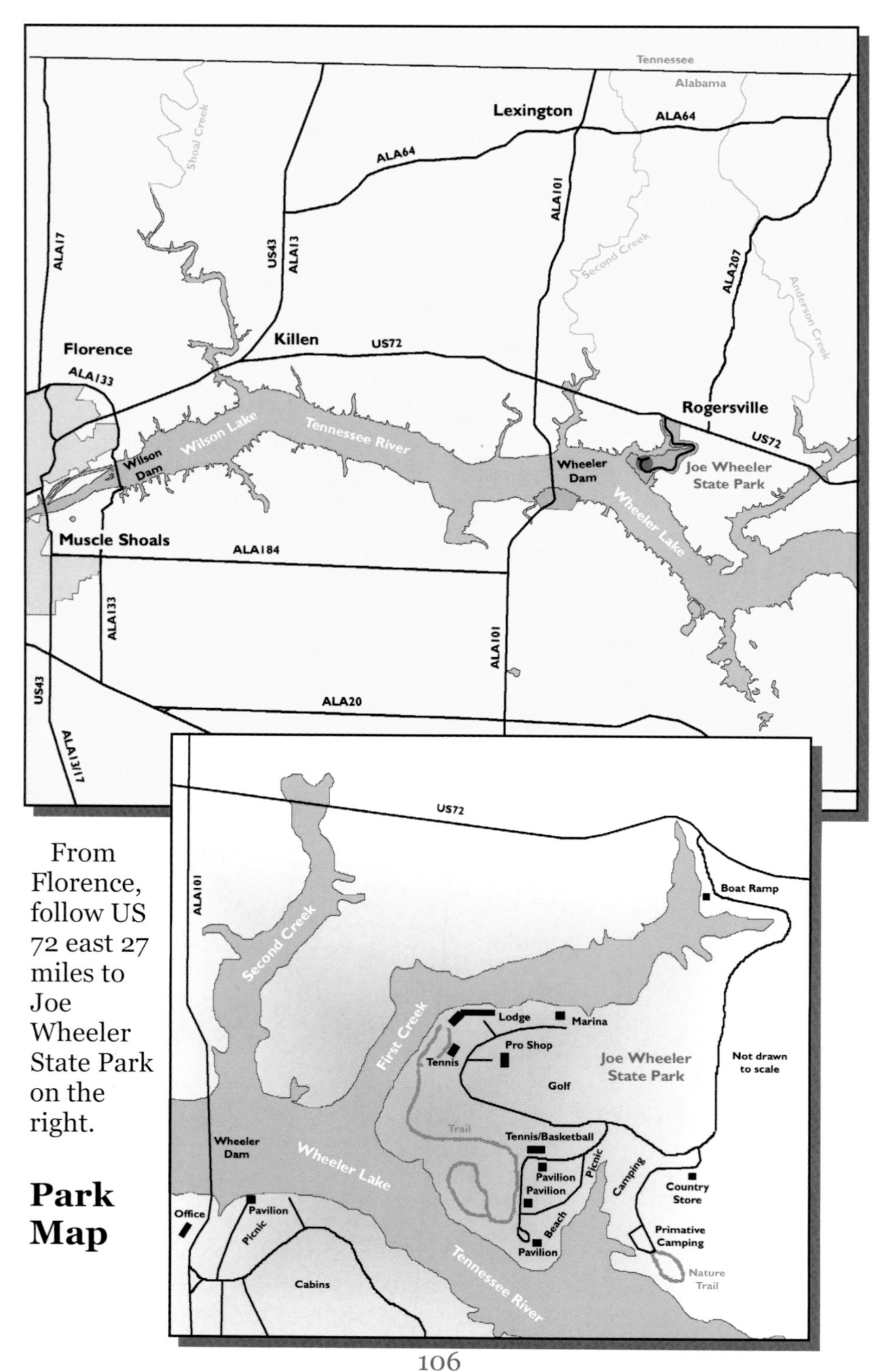

From Florence, follow US 72 east 27 miles to Joe Wheeler State Park on the right.

Park Map

Park Facilities

Lodge:

The waterfront 75-room lodge and restaurant complex overlook First Creek adjacent the marina.

Cabins and Chalets:

The park maintains 30 brick and wooden cabins across the river near Wheeler Dam. All cabins are furnished for light housekeeping.

Campgrounds:

The park's 116 campsites are spacious and wooded along the shores of the Tennessee River. Three comfort stations and one pavilion are centrally located. Almost all sites have water, electric and sewer connections for tents or RV's.

Country Store & Information Center:

A well-stocked country store and camper registration office is located at the campground entrance.

Marina:

The 134-slip marina is on First Creek adjacent the lodge. The marina's store provides gasoline and boating supplies.

Swimming Pool:

The Olympic size swimming pool area is situated on the waterfront between the lodge and restaurant.

Picnic Areas:

The 2 picnic areas include 4 pavilions. Three pavilions are located in the main park area, while the fourth is near the cabins.

Hiking trails:

The park maintains 5 miles of easy hiking trails, some along the riverbanks.

Scenes

Waterfalls:

The terrain in this area is nearly flat, so few waterfalls exist here. In nearby Tuscumbia, the city has developed a man-made waterfall in their downtown park. With several cascades and falls, it looks very natural.

Creeks:

First Creek encircles the main park area, with the lodge, restaurant and marina on its southern shores.

Foliage:

Pine, cedar and various hardwoods abound in the park area.

Near the picnic grounds, a small creek joins the Tennessee River.

Kymulga Covered Bridge & Gristmill

Park Description ★★★★

A 57-acre park owned and operated by the Alabama Historical Commission with the assistance of Talladega County, this park has Alabama's only operating gristmill, churning out corn meal daily. A uniquely designed water turbine powers the mill. An historic covered bridge crosses Talladega Creek adjacent the mill. Both the bridge and mill, remaining at their original locations, were constructed during Civil War years in the early 1860's. The covered bridge is a single span bridge 105 feet long and 10 feet wide, built on two piers of native stone. The park is listed on the National Register of Historical Places and includes 2 miles of hiking trails, picnic areas and campgrounds.

Nearby Points of Interest

DeSoto Caverns Park is just 3.5 miles southeast on Ala. 76. Waldo Covered Bridge and Old Mill Restaurant are 19 miles east following Ala. 76, 21 and 77 through Talladega. The Talladega Speedway and Museum is located just north of Talladega. Horseshoe Bend National Military Monument is southeast following US 280. Childersburg is 5 miles west along Ala. 76. Oak Mountain State Park is 42 miles west.

Kymulga Covered Bridge, constructed in 1860.

Kymulga Gristmill reflects in the calm waters above the dam.

Kymulga Gristmill (right), Covered Bridge (center) and dam with its unique turbine are shown here. Notice how the camera captures the effect of the turbine on the falling water. Ducks enjoy the calmer waters behind the rock barrier.

Location and Directions

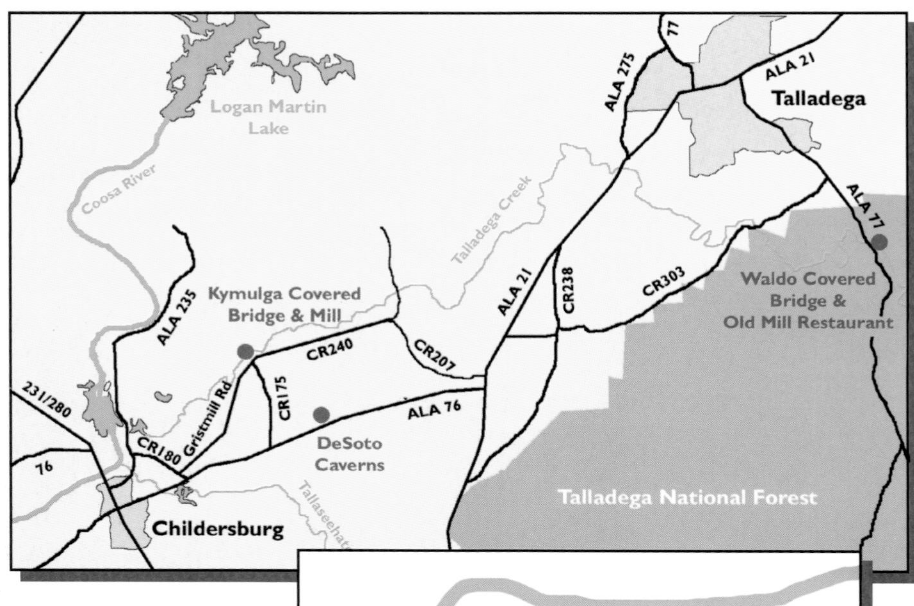

From US 231 in Childersburg, take Ala. 76 east 1.8 miles to CR 180 (Forest Hill Drive). Go 0.2 miles north and turn right onto CR 240 (Grist Mill Road). Follow CR 240 east 3.2 miles to Kymulga Park on the left.

Park Map

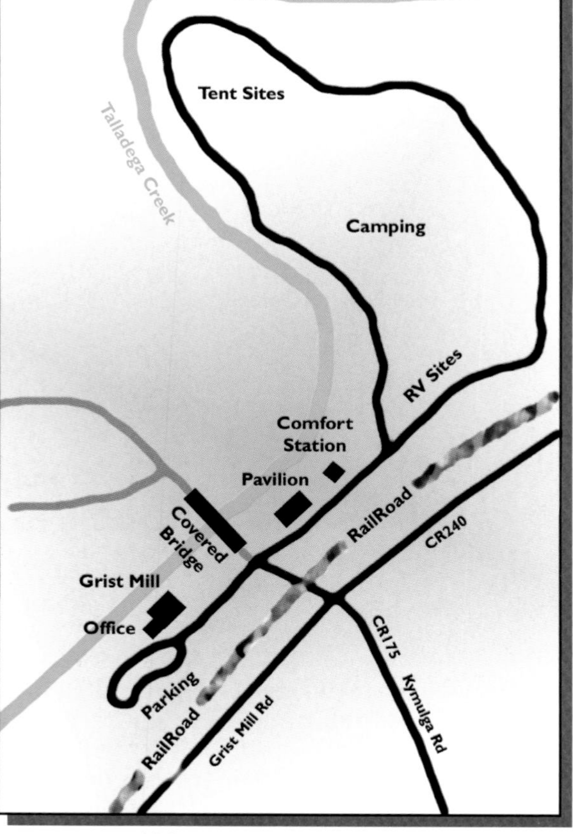

Park Facilities

Mill Office:

Adjacent the old mill, the office has minimal camping and picnic supplies and gifts. Tours through the gristmill begin here.

Campgrounds:

The campground includes sites for tents or RV's. The RV sites have water and electrical connections. One comfort station is conveniently located between the campground and picnic area.

Picnic Areas:

The picnic area and pavilion are adjacent the covered bridge along the banks of Talladega Creek.

Hiking trails:

Two miles of trails lead through forests of large white oaks. The trails are open for horseback riding or hiking.

Scenes

Covered Bridge:

Constructed in 1860, **Kymulga Covered Bridge** is a single span town-truss bridge 105 feet long and 10 feet wide. Still in use until 1958, it is now open to pedestrians only.

Gristmill:

Constructed in 1864, this working gristmill still grinds cornmeal. It uses a uniquely designed water turbine to power the mill's grinding stones.

Creeks:

Talladega Creek flows around the campgrounds, under the covered bridge then to a small dam by the gristmill where the turbines capture it's power.

Foliage:

The park hosts the largest grove of white oak trees in the southeast, along with the State Champion sugarberry tree.

Kymulga Covered Bridge spanning Talladega Creek.

Lake Guntersville State Park

Park Description ★★★★

Six miles northeast of Guntersville on Ala. 227, Lake Guntersville State Park encompasses 5,909 acres of mountainous regions as high as 1,140 feet above sea level. The Lodge and Convention Center Complex is perched atop Taylor Mountain on a 500 foot bluff overlooking the Tennessee River and 66,470 acre Lake Guntersville. Facing northwest, the numerous decks and patios overlook this fantastic scene for gorgeous sunsets. The park has everything needed for a relaxing stay, including restaurants, gift shop, swimming pool, beaches, scenic drives, hiking trails and a scenic, par 72 mountaintop golf course. The lodge has 94 rooms available adjacent the main complex with chalets and cabins just a short drive away. Deer are often seen around the facility, in the parking area and all through the park at dawn and dusk. Campgrounds are located next to the beach area on the lakefront. The Town Creek area provides additional camping, fishing and canoeing. Bald Eagle viewing is an annual winter event at Lake Guntersville State Park in the Town Creek area.

Rainbow over Lake Guntersville State Park from Guntersville Harbor (The SP is on the mountain at the rainbow's base).

Nearby Points of Interest

Lake Guntersville and the breathtaking overlooks are the major attractions for this park. Take the short drive to Buck's Pocket State Park and High Falls County Park located just 18 miles east on Ala. 227 near one another. Cathedral Caverns State Park and Blowing Wind

Cave are across the river near Grant and Scottsboro. Ghost Creek Falls and Natural Bridge is also in this direction. Goose Pond Colony, located south of Scottsboro on Ala. 79/279, offers a par 72 lake front golf course and public access to Lake Guntersville for boating, fishing and swimming. Several other waterfalls and two natural bridges are nearby as denoted on the map (one bridge at High Falls).

Location and Directions

From US 431 in Guntersville, take Ala. 227 east 6 miles to the Lake Guntersville State Park entrance on the left.

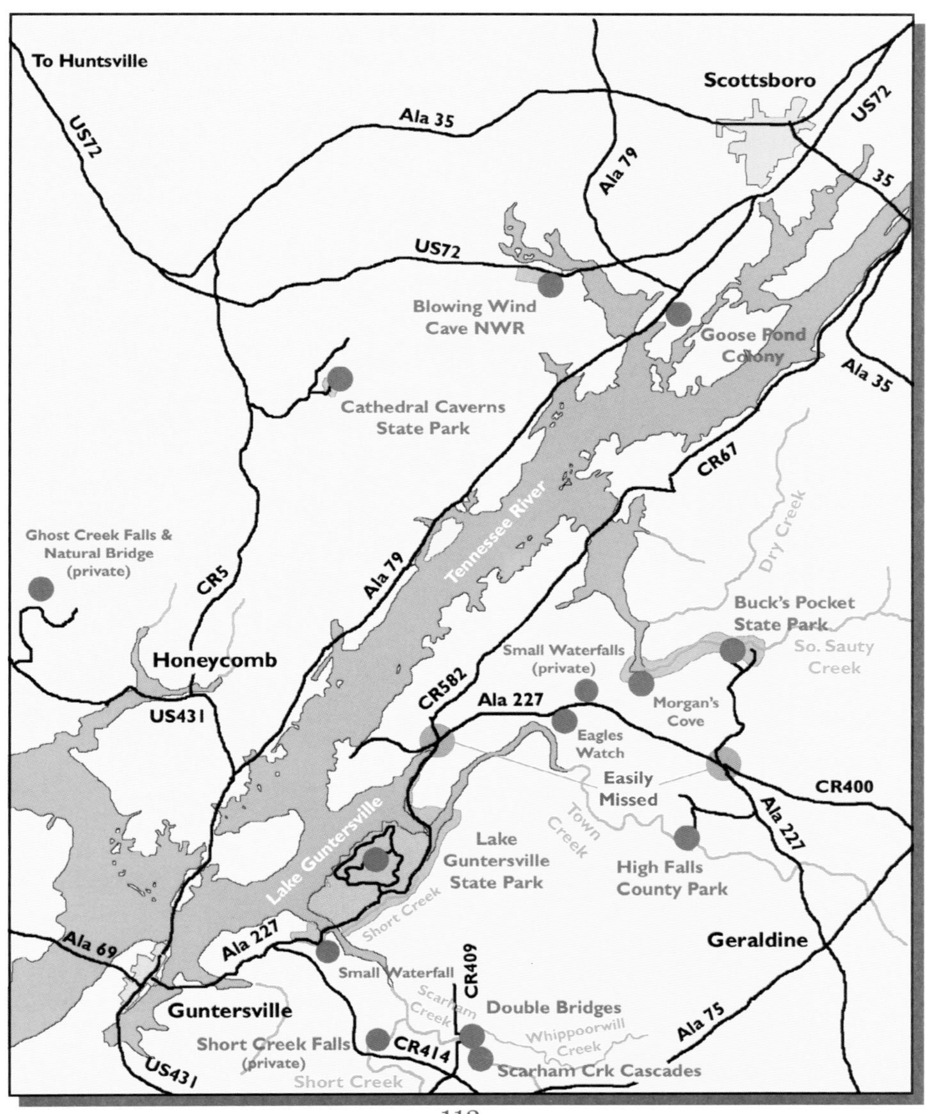

Park Facilities

Lodge and Restaurant:

Opened in 1974, Lake Guntersville State Park Lodge and Convention Center is constructed of native stone and stained pine with exposed beams and 7 large fireplaces. The lodge houses the registration and information office, meeting rooms, gift shop, restaurant, coffee shop and swimming pool overlooking the bluff. On either side of the lodge are 94 rooms and 6 suites, some with a bluff view. Rooms have 2 double beds, color television and telephone. Suites have a living room with wet bar, refrigerator and icemaker, 1 king bed and 2 TVs.

(Continued on page 116)

Scenes

Waterfalls:

There are no continuous waterfalls within park boundaries, however there are several in the area. Along Ala. 227 toward Guntersville, you may see a small waterfall adjacent the roadway in a sharp curve as you ascend the mountain leaving the park. **High Falls County Park**, located just 18 miles to the east along Ala. 227 is well worth visiting. A large waterfall, it also has a natural bridge that formed just below the falls. Another small waterfall can be viewed from Ala. 227 on the north side just before reaching the top of the mountain near Morgan's Cove.

(Continued on page 116)

A small six foot waterfall along Ala. 227 near the park's western border.

A post-rainstorm sunset over Lake Guntersville.

Park Map

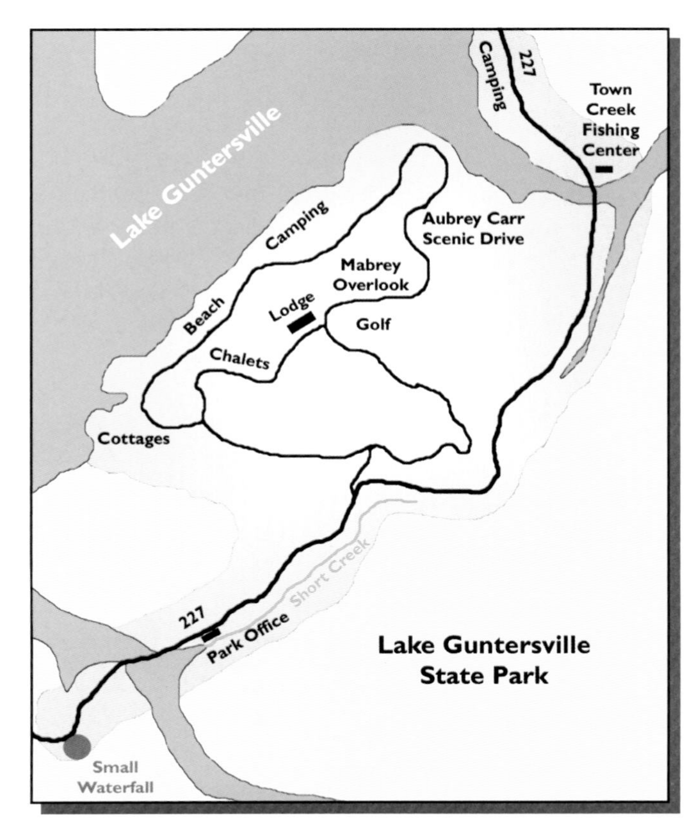

(Continued from page 114)

Cabins and Chalets:

Twenty chalets positioned near the lodge accommodate 1-6 people each. All have a living room with fireplace, 1 king or 2 double beds. 15 cottages are located on the lakefront near the beach area accommodating 1-8 people each. Cottages have a sitting room with color television, 2 baths and 2 bedrooms with 1 king and 2 double beds.

Campgrounds:

A total of 364 sites bordering the beach area. The nature center, 7 comfort stations, 2 laundries and public telephones are conveniently located throughout the camp area. The activity center, playground and recreation area is centrally located. A pavilion is situated on the waterfront, along with 2 fishing piers. The dump station is located near the campground exit. Gated access enhances security.

Country Store & Information Center:

The country store and registration office provides camping and picnic supplies.

Swimming Pool:

On the bluff overlooking Lake Guntersville, a large swimming pool is conveniently located alongside the lodge and rooms.

Picnic Areas:

Several picnic areas are located around the park. The most scenic is on the bluff near the golf pro shop at Mabrey's Overlook.

Hiking trails:

There are 20 trails totaling 36 miles. Most are rated easy to moderate. The country store and lodge office has trail maps available.

(Continued from page 114)

Overlooking Town Creek Valley, this rise is excellent for Bald Eagle viewing during winter months. Located just 8 miles south of Lake Guntersville State Park, the top of **Short Creek Falls** can be seen from the bridge on CR414, four miles south of Ala. 227. The surrounding land is privately owned. This is a large waterfall that I wish were open to the public. Short Creek flows into Lake Guntersville near the Park Office located on Ala. 227. Northwest of Guntersville on US 431 toward Huntsville in the Honeycomb area, **Ghost Creek Falls** and **Natural Bridge** exist together. This feature can be seen from the roadway but is on private property. On US 431 near the Honeycomb Campground, turn north on CR 466 (Cottonville Road) and drive 1/2 mile. Look on the left in the first sharp curve.

Creeks:

The only creek in the park, **Short Creek**, follows Cutchenmine Trail and Ala. 227 as you enter the park from the city of Guntersville. This Short Creek is not the same creek as mentioned above under Waterfalls.

Foliage:

The abundant dogwood and redbud begin blooming in mid-March. Abounding fern grows under the dense cover of pine and cedar.

Lake Lurleen State Park

Park Description ★★

Named after Alabama's only woman governor, Lurleen B. Wallace, this 1,625-acre park includes 250-acre Lake Lurleen. Located only 15 miles northeast of Tuscaloosa, the park originally opened in 1954 around the man-made lake. In 1972, the state purchased the land and developed it into a state park. There are no lodging or cabin facilities available, but the park does maintain 91 developed campsites beside the lake. The lake is open to power boats; water or jet skiing is not allowed. Canoes and paddle-boats are available for renting. Five miles of hiking trails lead over the hills around the lake.

Nearby Points of Interest

Just 15 miles southeast in Tuscaloosa the Paul W. Bryant Museum, by the University of Alabama campus, honors Alabama players and relives Crimson Tide history under the "Bear". Moundville Archaeological Park is 12 miles south of Tuscaloosa. Oakmulgee NWA in the southwest portion of Talladega National Forest begins east of Moundville. Following the paved roads CR 50, CR 49 and Ala. 25

The north extremity of Lake Lurleen near the picnic area.

eastward to Centreville is a scenic drive through the National Forest.

Location and Directions

From Exit 71A/B on I-20/59, take I-359 north through Northport to US 82 west. Turn right onto CR 21, then turn right onto CR 49. The park is just ahead on the left.

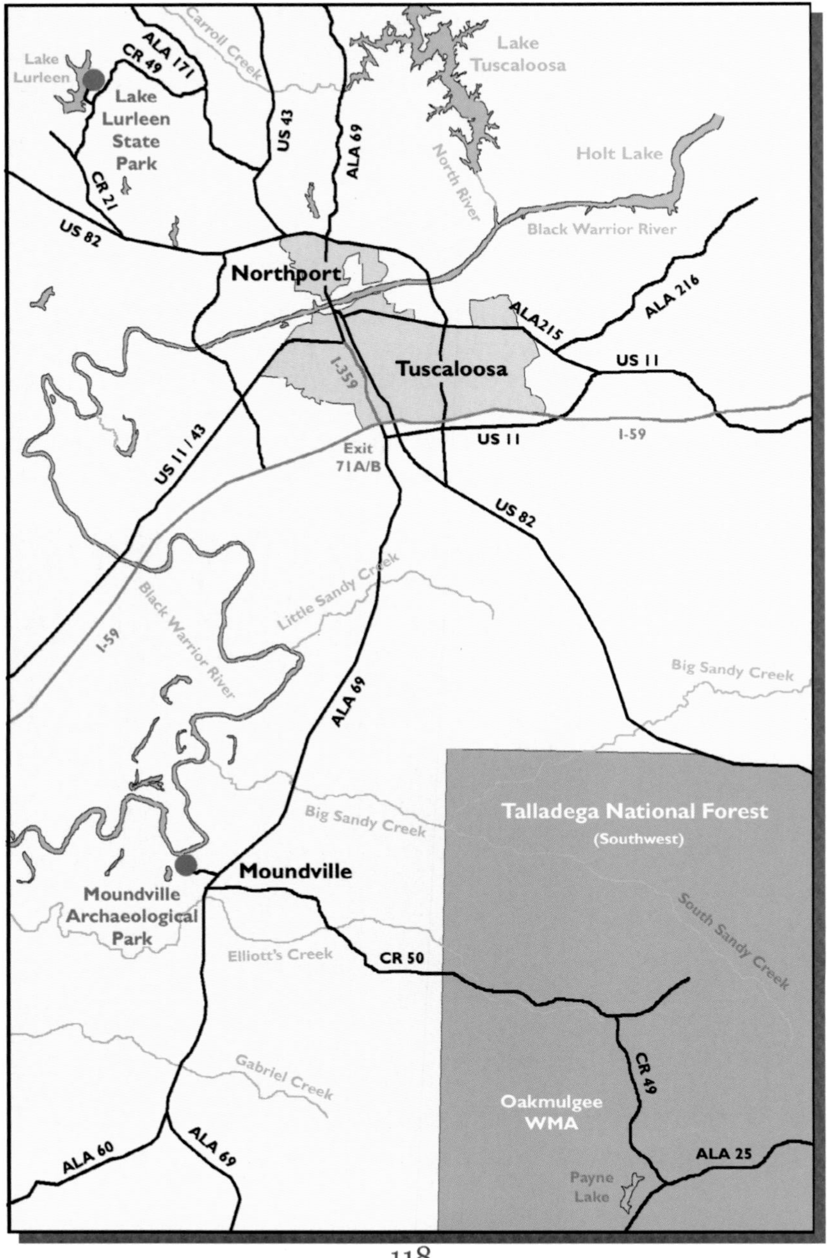

Park Map

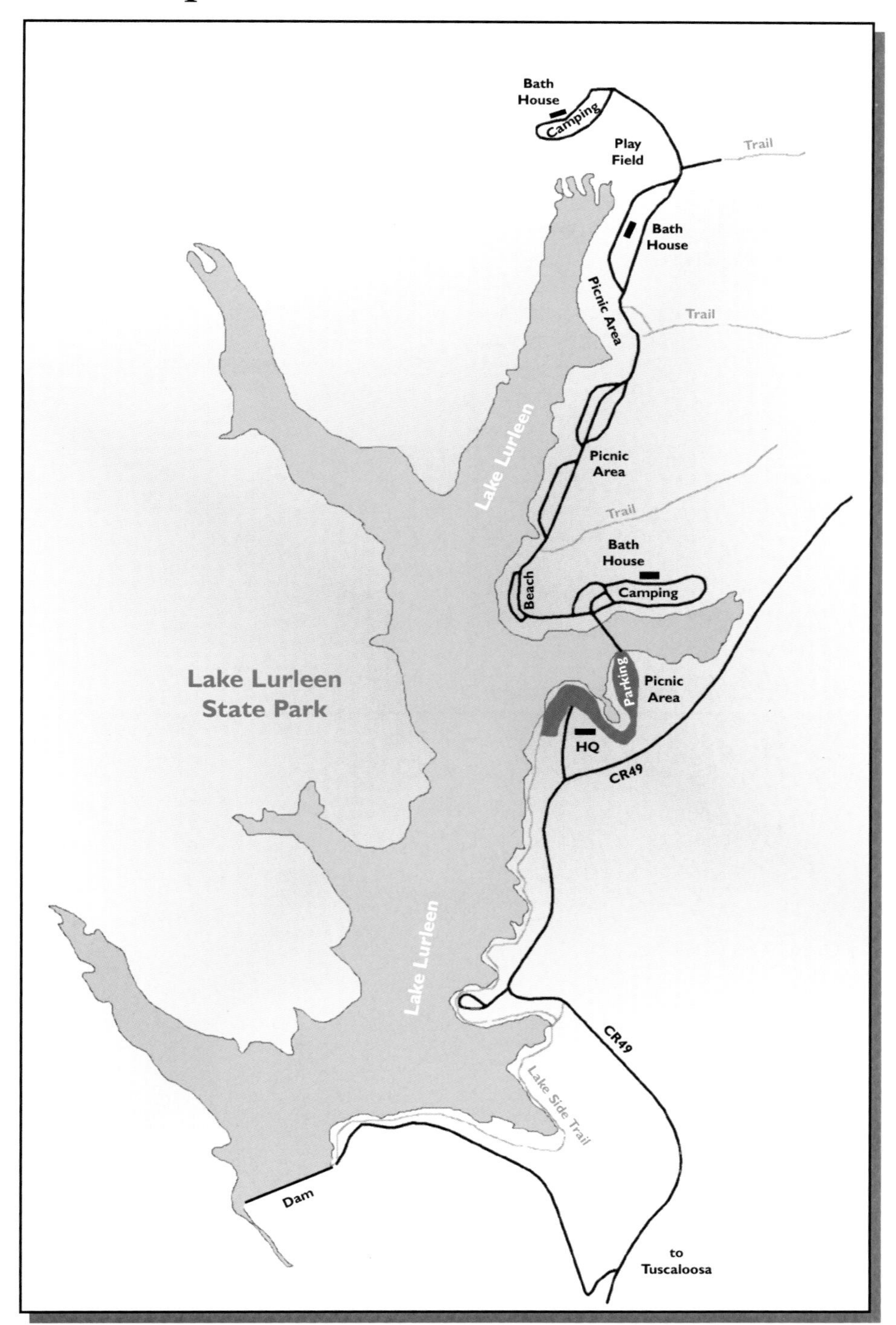
Bath House
Camping
Play Field
Trail
Bath House
Picnic Area
Trail
Lake Lurleen
Picnic Area
Trail
Bath House
Camping
Beach
Parking
Picnic Area
Lake Lurleen State Park
HQ
CR49
Lake Lurleen
CR49
Lake Side Trail
Dam
to Tuscaloosa

Park Facilities

Country Store:

Located near the park entrance, the country store maintains camping and picnicking supplies.

Campgrounds:

Lake Lurleen State Park has 91 total camp sites around the lake. All sites have water and electrical connections, and some sites have sewer connections. All sites are located on or near the lake. The sites will accommodate tents, pop-ups, and large RV's. A dump station is also available.

Picnic Areas:

Several picnic areas are around the lake, with tables and grills.

Hiking trails:

5 miles of trails extend through the park.

Lake Side Trail follows the lake edge from the main parking area to the dam.

Scenes

Lake:

This 250-acre lake is man-made. Opened to the public as a county park in 1952, the state developed it into a state park in 1972. Being up to 48 feet deep, it measures 1.5 miles in length by 1/2 mile width in places.

Foliage:

Pines are predominant, with various hardwoods in the surrounding forests.

Looking across the lake toward the park entrance, the fishing pier juts into Lake Lurleen.

Little River Canyon National Preserve

Park Description ★★★★★

Added to the National Park System in 1992, Little River Canyon is one of America's deepest and most extensive canyon systems east of the Mississippi River. Within the Preserve's 14,000 acres exists one of Alabama's highest waterfalls; the seasonal Grace's High Falls. The canyon features breathtaking overlooks where the turquoise waters of Little River flow 700 feet below. Rocky sandstone outcrops add to the splendor. During the colder months when rainfall is abundant, numerous smaller creeks and small waterfalls can be seen along the 22 mile Canyon Rim Parkway. Little River Canyon Mouth Park is positioned alongside Little River where it exits Lookout Mountain. Little River is classified as an *Alabama Wild and Scenic River*, and was the first river in the state to be awarded the status of *Outstanding National Resource Water*, because of its quality. With a remarkable number of waterfalls, awesome canyon overlooks, forested trails and the close proximity of facilities at DeSoto State Park, this area should be top on your list of places to visit.

Little River Canyon National Preserve encompasses some of Alabama's most scenic natural beauty. Be extremely careful in this area. Dangerous overlooks and rushing waters exist throughout the Preserve. Refer to the cautions posted in the front of this book.

Nearby Points of Interest

Partnering DeSoto State Park provides complete camping and lodging facilities for the Preserve. DeSoto Falls with its 100-foot drop and several smaller waterfalls are located in the State Park. If there were not enough waterfalls in the Preserve and State Park, Yellow Creek Falls is on Weiss Lake near Leesburg just 5 miles south of Little River Canyon Mouth Park on Ala. 273. High Falls County Park is 48 miles west of Canyon Mouth Park, reached by following Ala. 273 south, 68 west and 227 north. High Falls is an impressive waterfall 55 feet high and 300 feet wide, comparable to Little River Falls. Fort Payne, the *Official Sock Capitol of the World*, is within 10 miles of Little River Falls and DeSoto State Park at the north end of the canyon. Privately owned Cloudmont Ski and Golf Resort with the historic Union Covered Bridge is also near the north end. Sequoyah Caverns is just 13 miles north of DeSoto State Park.

Location and Directions

Little River Canyon National Preserve is located in DeKalb County on Lookout Mountain, seven miles east of Fort Payne on Ala. 35. From Exit 218 on Interstate 59, follow Ala. 35 south, through

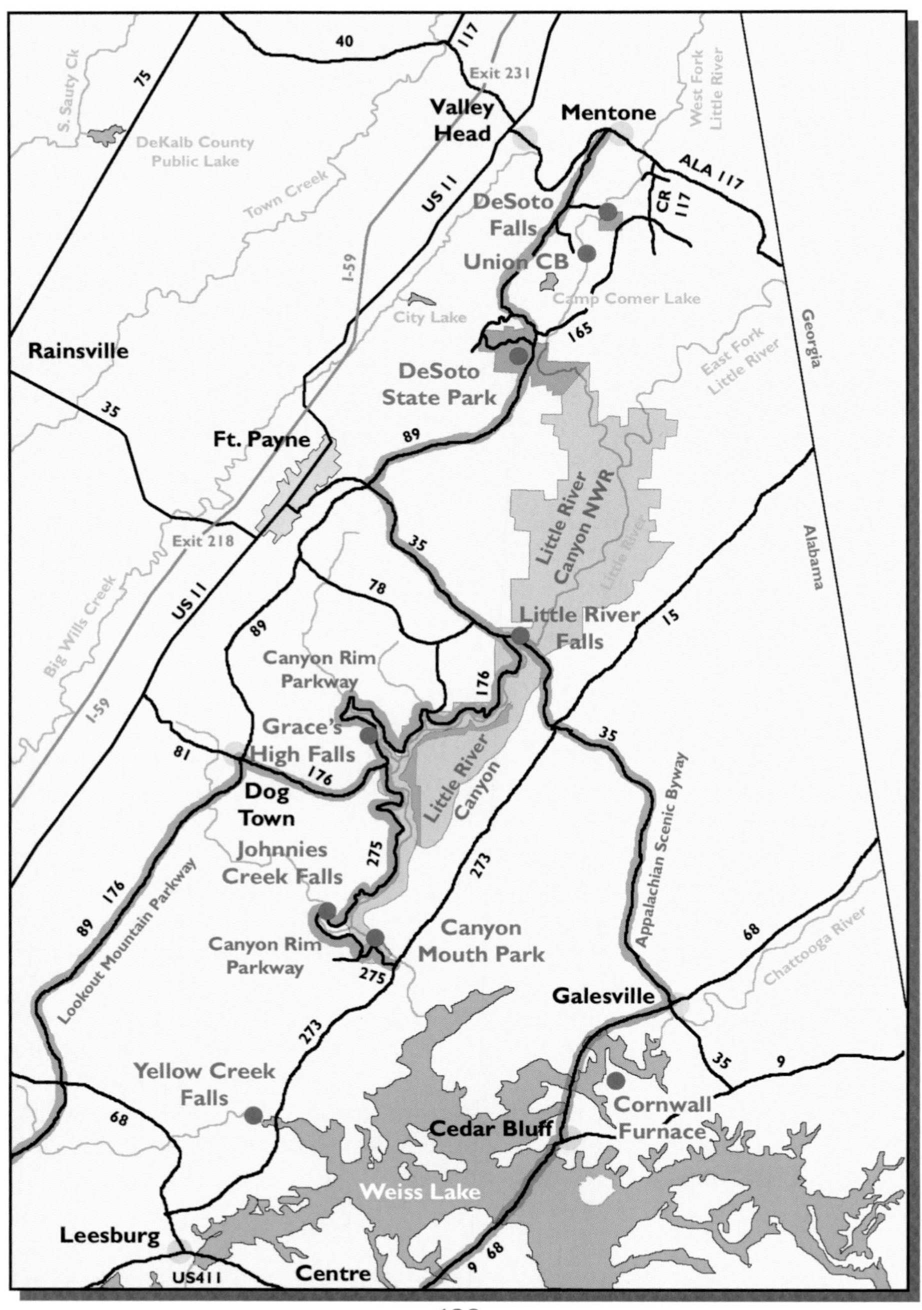

Fort Payne to the top of Lookout Mountain. (There are two turns required to follow Ala. 35 through Fort Payne; first, take a left onto US 11 north, then turn right at Union Park onto Ala. 35 south). Continue 5 miles eastward on Ala. 35 beyond CR 89 (the turnoff to DeSoto State Park). Turn right onto Ala. 176, Lookout Mountain Parkway and Canyon Rim Parkway. Little River Falls is just beyond this intersection on Ala. 35.

Park Map

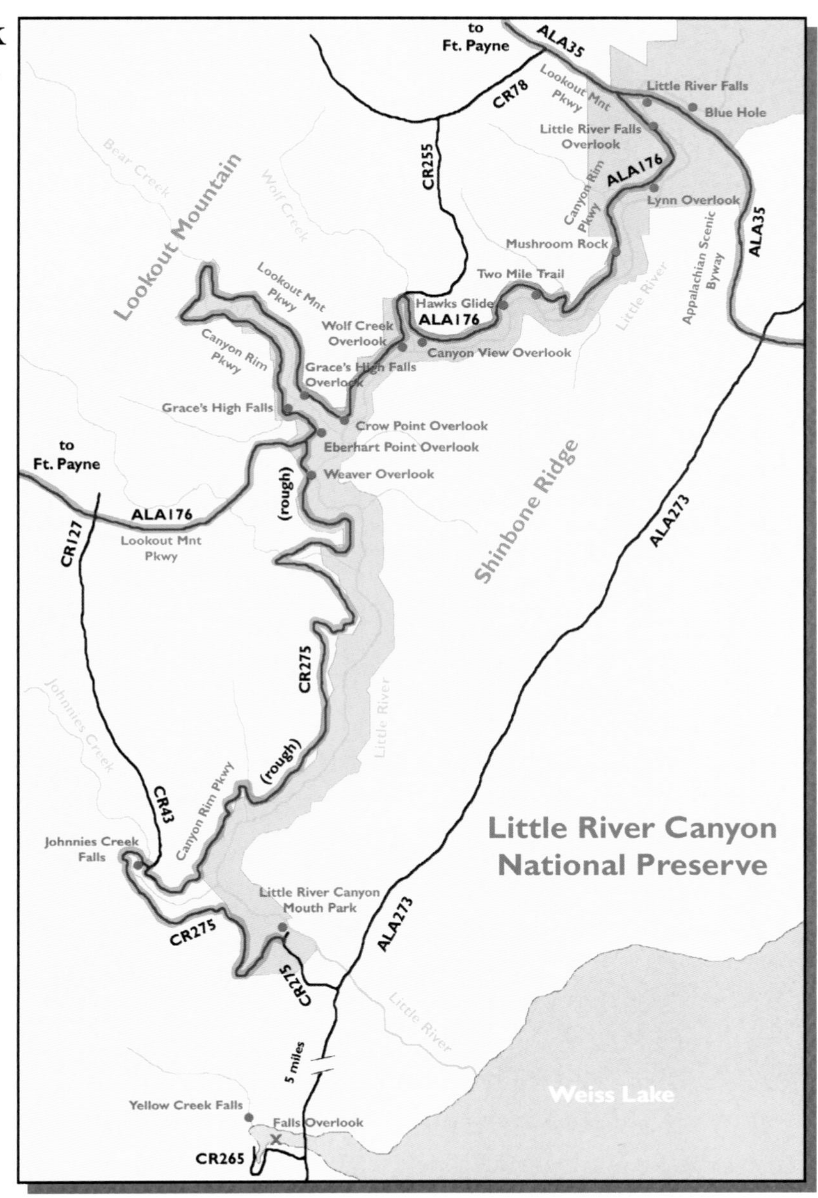

Little River Falls **from the overlook deck.**

Park Facilities

Facilities:

DeSoto State Park provides restaurant, lodging and camping facilities for the National Preserve. Camping by permit is also available at Little River Canyon Mouth Park adjacent Little River at the southern Preserve boundary. Three other primitive camping sites next to Little River are Slant Rock, Billy's Ford and Hartline Ford. In the canyon area, restrooms are located at Little River Falls and Canyon Mouth Park at the north and south canyon extremities. Little River Canyon Mouth Park is a day use area only, except to registered visitors.

Canyon Rim Parkway (Ala. 176 & CR 275):

Canyon Rim Parkway follows the west rim of Little River Canyon 22 miles from Little River Falls to Little River Canyon Mouth Park. Along this drive, you'll find unusual rock formations such as Mushroom Rock situated in the middle of the roadway, many canyon overlooks and several large waterfalls including Alabama's highest, Grace's High Falls. Deer and other wildlife are often seen along this excursion. The parkway leads around the tributary Wolf Creek and Bear Creek Canyons. During warmer months, kayakers descend the canyon to challenge Little River's turquoise whitewaters below. The northern portion of Canyon Rim Parkway (north of Eberhart Point) is part of the scenic Lookout Mountain Parkway. **TIP**: Canyon Rim Parkway (CR 275) south of Eberhart Point is outside Preserve boundaries and is ill maintained. A better option when traveling south

Scenes

Waterfalls:

Little River Falls embarks Little River Canyon at the north end. 250 feet wide and 45 feet high, this waterfall is one of Alabama's most scenic. An adjacent parking area and paved trail make it easily accessible.

Seasonal **Grace's High Falls** is one of Alabama's highest waterfalls. Its best viewpoint is from Grace's High Falls Overlook along the Canyon Rim Parkway.

Johnnie's Creek Falls is a popular swimming area during warmer months. Just 4 miles north of Little River Canyon Mouth Park along Canyon Rim Parkway, this waterfall is adjacent the roadway by an undeveloped pull-off. This waterfall is not within Preserve boundaries. **Tip**: If traveling north through the canyon, when leaving Johnnie's Creek Falls, cross the bridge, drive up the hill then turn left at the intersection onto CR 43. Follow this road to the stop sign at Ala. 176 and turn right to reach Eberhart Point. Although turning right at Johnnie's Creek Falls follows The Canyon Rim Parkway, this portion is under poor repair with minimal overlooks.

Overlooks:

Little River Falls Overlook has a short boardwalk leading from the parking area to the canyon rim providing an excellent up river view of Little River Falls.

Lynn Overlook is the first view of Little River Canyon on your southerly journey along Canyon Rim Parkway. Rocky sandstone outcrops line the distant canyon wall.

At **Hawks Glide Overlook** you

is to take Ala. 176 west to CR 127, turn left (south) and continue to Johnnie's Creek Falls. Turn right onto CR 275, drive down the steep hill, cross the bridge and pull into the turnoff on the left. Johnnies Creek Fall is below the turnoff.

Swimming:

Blue Hole is a favorite swimming and fishing area. From the Little River Falls parking area, go east on Ala. 35 to the first dirt road on the left.

Picnic Areas:

Picnic areas are located at Little River Falls and at some of the nine overlooks along Canyon Rim Parkway and in the Little River Canyon Mouth Park area.

Hiking trails:

Little River Falls Trail is an easy to moderate paved trail leading 1/8 mile from the parking area to Little River Falls. Although it is wheelchair accessible, the incline is rather steep.

Lower Two Mile Trail is located on Canyon Rim Parkway between Mushroom Rock and Hawks Glide Overlook. This is a difficult trail that leads from the canyon rim to Little River below. The trail is used primarily by kayakers to access Little River.

Eberhart Point Trail is another difficult trail that leads to Little River below, used mainly by kayakers for river access.

Little River Canyon Mouth Park Trail leads 3/4 mile up stream beside Little River to Johnnie's Creek. Along this easy to moderate trail, experience close-up the enormity of the boulders you've seen from above while touring Canyon Rim Parkway. The beautiful turquoise color of Little River's clear water is evident around rapids and whitewaters.

may see hawks and crows gliding on the air currents.

Canyon View Overlook affords one of the canyon's most magnificent views overlooking Little River where Wolf Creek joins. Across Wolf Creek Canyon, people and vehicles at the Wolf Creek Overlook give perspective to the proportions of the canyon.

Wolf Creek Overlook, another magnificent viewpoint. Often you'll spot rock climbers ascending the canyon walls. An excellent location to view the rapids of Little River.

At **Crow Point Overlook, v**iew Bear Creek as it unites with Little River. You may see kayakers navigating the rapids.

Grace's High Falls Overlook has a viewing platform along the roadside. In fall, winter and spring, Grace's High Falls, one of Alabama's highest waterfalls is seen free-falling over 100 feet into Bear Creek Canyon.

Eberhart Point Overlook has a 3/4-mile trail leading down to Little River where kayakers often descend. A picnic area and a short 1/8-mile concrete pathway leads to two overlooks and the trailhead. Adjacent the overlook is the site of the old Canyonland Park which years ago, maintained a chair lift to the canyon floor.

Weaver Overlook is just south of Eberhart Point Overlook along the less maintained portion of the Rim Parkway. Experienced rock climbers like this highest climbing point in the canyon.

Creeks:

Little River is one of the few rivers in America flowing almost its entire length on top of a mountain. Little River is classified as an *Ala-*

(Continued on page 128)

Little River Canyon from Wolf Creek Overlook.

(Continued from page 126)
bama Wild and Scenic River, and was the first river in the state to be awarded the status of *Outstanding National Resource Water*, because of its water quality.

Johnnie's Creek has formed a tributary canyon to Little River Canyon. Johnnie's Creek Falls, located just 4 miles north of Little River Canyon Mouth Park on Canyon Rim Parkway, is a popular destination for swimmers during summer months.

Bear Creek composes Little River's largest tributary canyon. Water from a privately owned mountain top lake plunges over the canyon wall into Bear Creek below, forming Grace's High Falls.

Wolf Creek forms a smaller tributary canyon of Little River. It's two overlooks along Canyon Rim Parkway, Canyon View and Wolf Creek, provide magnificent views of Little River and overhanging rock outcrops.

Foliage:

As in DeSoto State Park, mountain laurel and rhododendron are abundant throughout the Preserve, with blooms at peak during May and June. The white and lavender blooms of dogwood and redbud trees are scattered in the forests under the taller pines and cedars. Rare and endangered plant life can be found along the hiking trails, such as the carnivorous green pitcher plant. Short-needle pines, oak, hickory and elm trees are plentiful throughout the forests. Fern growth is accentuated by the moist, rocky soil.

The turquoise waters of Little River at Canyon Mouth Park.

Locust Fork Falls

Description

★★★

Located on private property, Locust Fork of the Black Warrior River is about 130 feet wide at the falls. An elevated rocky area in the middle splits the creek into twin waterfalls about 75 feet apart, on either side of the streambed. Dropping 6 feet in a distance of 10 feet, the falls are really more like cascades. Locust Fork usually has a significant amount of water flowing, making the falls superb for kayak runs.

Nearby Points of Interest

Swann Covered Bridge is located at the trailhead to the falls. Easley and Horton Mill Covered Bridges are located not far away near Rosa and Oneonta. Nectar Falls is also nearby on Ala. 160. Rickwood Caverns State Park is to the west near I-65. The *Falls at Grave's Creek* is a popular input point for kayaks and canoes.

Location and Directions

From I-65 Exit 284, take Ala. 160 east to Cleveland. Turn left on Ala. 79 north and drive one mile to Swann Bridge Road then turn left. Drive one mile across Swann Bridge and park on the side of the road. Hike 1.2 miles downstream to the falls.

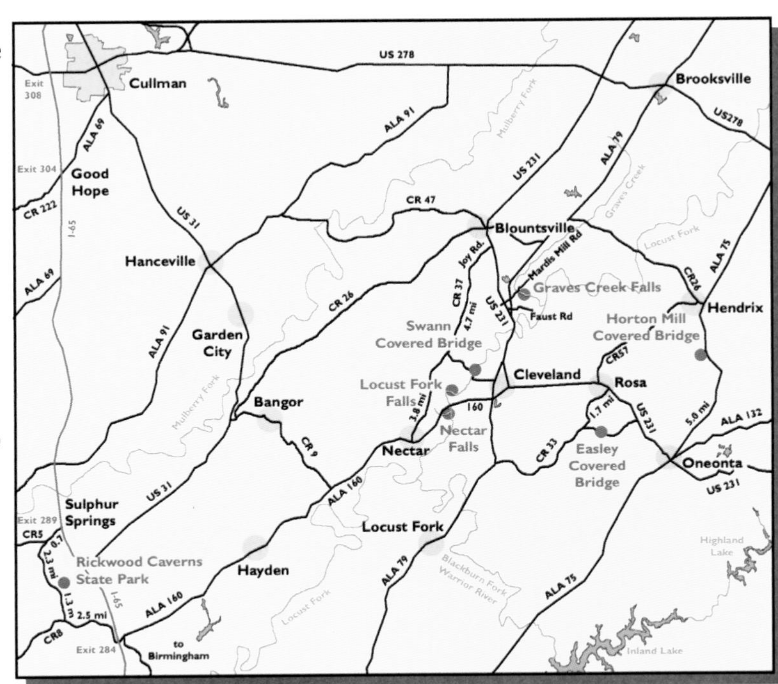

Area Map

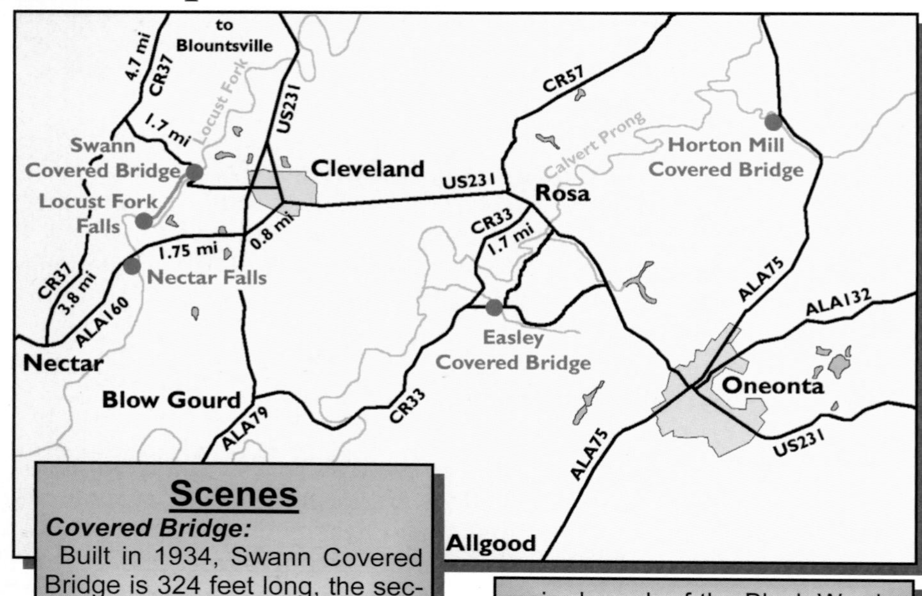

Scenes

Covered Bridge:

Built in 1934, Swann Covered Bridge is 324 feet long, the second longest in Alabama. It spans a small canyon on Locust Fork and is open to local traffic. It is only wide enough for a single vehicle, so look cautiously for oncoming traffic.

Waterfalls:

The twin falls at **Locust Fork** are a beautiful sight. If you're lucky, you may see kayakers challenging the falls.

Graves Creek Falls drops 16 feet and is 35 feet wide. It is on private property, but is frequently visited by swimmers.

Creeks:

Locust Fork is about 130 feet wide at the falls. Water is usually flowing here since this is a major branch of the Black Warrior River. Kayaks and canoes often launch under the covered bridge.

Facilities

Hiking trails:

Along the northwest side of the creek, a 1.2-mile hard, but mostly level trail leads from Swann Covered Bridge to Locust Fork Falls. Most of the trail is frequently traveled, although it does become difficult to follow at times. Before the covered bridge is out of sight, the trail leads across boulders adjacent the streambed for about 200 feet. This is the hardest part to traverse.

Locust Fork is a twin waterfall.

***Locust Fork Falls*,**
left side.

***Locust Fork Falls*,**
right side.

Swann Covered Bridge is a three span bridge.
The canyon wall can be seen in the distance below the bridge.

Lookout Mountain Parkway

Description ★★★★

Lookout Mountain Parkway extends from Gadsden to Mentone following CR 89 and Ala. 176. A portion of its journey follows Little River Canyon Rim Parkway (Ala. 176), overlooking one of the most extensive canyon systems east of the Mississippi River. Along this route are many old barns remaining from the early 1900's. Noccalula Falls Park in Gadsden is at the Parkway's southern extremity. *Griffin Falls* is 2.9 miles west of I-59 on Ala. 68 on dirt road CR 221. Two of Alabama's largest waterfalls are near the north end of the Parkway; DeSoto Falls and Little River Falls.

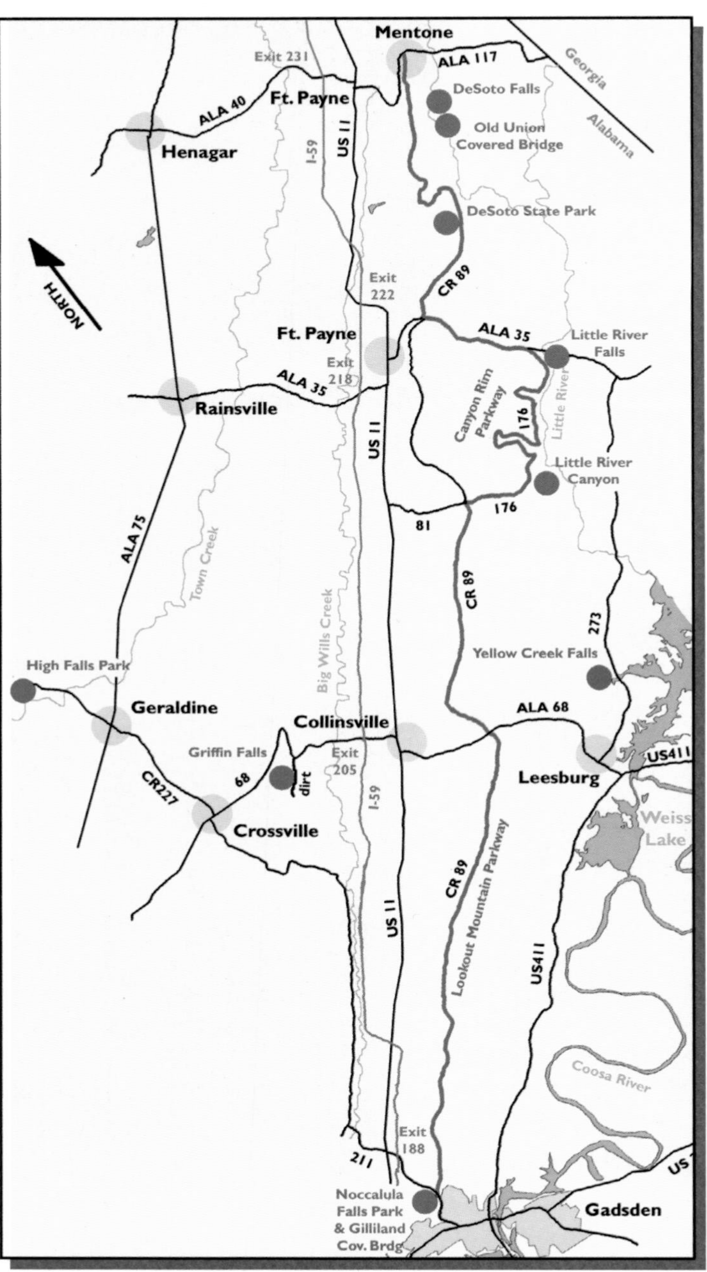

Madison County Nature Trail

Park Description ★★★★

Atop Green Mountain in Huntsville, this park features Cambron Covered Bridge, 17-acre Skye Lake, a pioneer homestead, an outdoor chapel and two miles of hiking trails around the lake. Opened in 1975, this 72-acre park is a day use area.

Nearby Points of Interest

In nearby Huntsville, there are many museums, the Botanical Gardens, Monte Sano State Park and the Space & Rocket Center. Wheeler National Wildlife Refuge surrounds the Tennessee River and extends west to Decatur. The Trail of Tears follows US 72. Ghost Creek Falls and Natural Bridge is southeast following US 431.

Location and Directions

From Memorial Pkwy (US 231) in Huntsville, drive east on Airport Road 6 miles. Airport Road changes to Carl T. Jones Dr., then to Bailey Cove Road southbound. Turn left on Green Mountain Road (at the flashing yellow traffic signal). Drive 1.7 miles up Green Mtn. and turn right at the top onto South Shawdee Drive. The Nature Trail is 1.5 miles on the right.

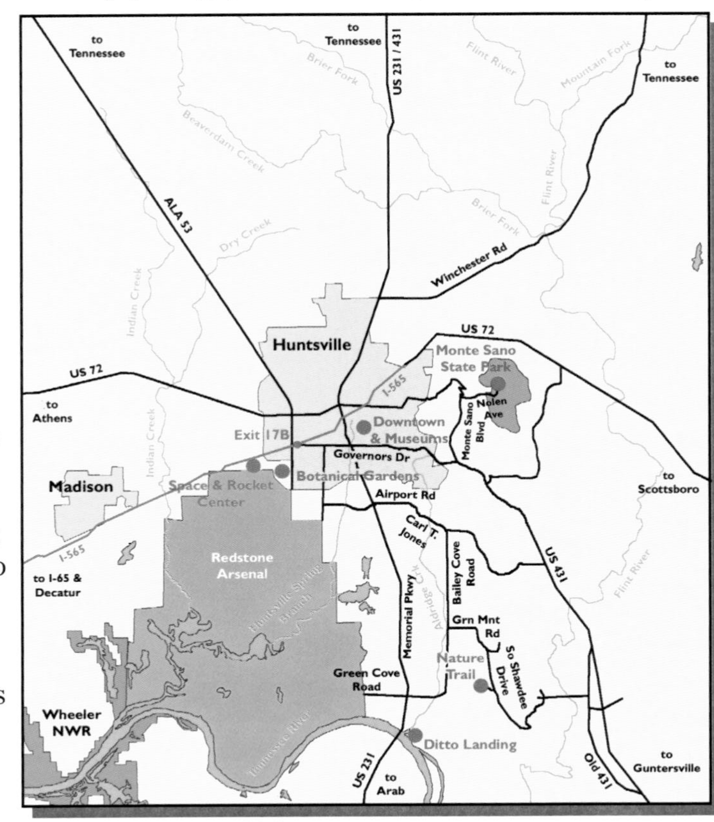

Park Facilities

Pavilion:

The picnic pavilion with restroom facilities is located near the parking area.

Picnic Areas:

The picnic area is beside the lake and near the parking area and pavilion for convenience.

Hiking trails:

The main trail leads two miles around the perimeter of Skye Lake. Along this trail you will cross Cambron Covered Bridge and pass the pioneer homestead and chapel.

Scenes

Waterfalls:

The park's only waterfall is at the beginning of the lake trail below the parking area.

Covered Bridge:

Cambron Covered Bridge is a replica, but very scenic. About 10 feet wide and 50 feet long, it crosses a marsh along the lake's edge.

Chapel:

The open front chapel is located several hundred yards north of the picnic area.

Creeks:

Several small, unnamed creeks flow into the lake, crossed on the main trail.

Foliage:

Spring or fall is the best time to visit. The gardens near the waterfall are in full bloom in springtime. Fall spreads shades of color throughout the park.

Cambron Covered Bridge.

Monte Sano State Park

Park Description ★★★

Monte Sano State Park, established in 1933, is perched atop Monte Sano Mountain, on the east border of Huntsville city limits. It is a short, six-mile drive to downtown Huntsville. The Park has 2,340 acres, with 730 acres on the plateau, 1,650 feet above sea level. "Monte Sano" in Spanish means "Mountain of health". The area was originally settled in the 1820's around a town named "Viduta" (from

Monte Sano Tavern Ruins. Constructed in 1937, destroyed by fire in 1947. Now under reconstruction.

"vida", the Spanish word for "life"). In 1887, the nationally acclaimed Hotel Monte Sano opened, but soon closed in 1900 due to the economy. In the 1930's, stones were removed from the old hotel and used by the CCC to construct the facilities present today.

Highlights of the park include overlooks, ruins of the historic Monte Sano Tavern (now under reconstruction), an amphitheater overlooking the bluff, a Japanese Pagoda and Gardens, hiking and biking trails and an adjacent planetarium operated by the Von Braun Astronomical Society. The Park doesn't have a lodge any longer but does maintain 14 rustic cabins along the bluff overlooking Mills Hollow to the east. The cabins, campground and picnic area provides a peaceful resting point for the weary traveler. The park closes at sunset to all non-registered visitors.

Nearby Points of Interest

With highly populated Huntsville close by, there are many diverse restaurants and businesses convenient for visitors. Major attractions include the Space & Rocket Center and NASA tour, the Early Works Museum (a hands-on museum for children) and Constitution Village (celebrating Huntsville life of the 19th century). Also nearby is the Huntsville Museum of Art, the Huntsville Botanical Gardens, the Madison County Nature Trail with its covered bridge replica, and the old Huntsville Depot & Museum, one of America's oldest remaining railroad structures. The nearby Hampton Cove Golf Course is on Alabama's famous Robert Trent Jones Golf Trail. Not far away in Decatur, Point Mallard Water Park provides many activities including a wave pool and par 72 golf course. On Memorial Day, the park is host to the annual Hot Air Balloon Festival. Wheeler Wildlife Refuge surrounds the Tennessee River southeast of Decatur and extends eastward to Huntsville.

Apollo/Saturn V
Space & Rocket Center
30th Anniversary Celebration.

Location and Directions

From I-65, take Exit 340 and follow I-565 east toward Huntsville. Take Exit 17B to Governors Drive, then continue east seven miles to the top of Monte Sano Mountain. Turn left at the traffic signal at the mountain peak onto Monte Sano Blvd. Continue north for 2.5 miles, then turn right on Nolen Ave. Monte Sano State Park is one mile ahead.

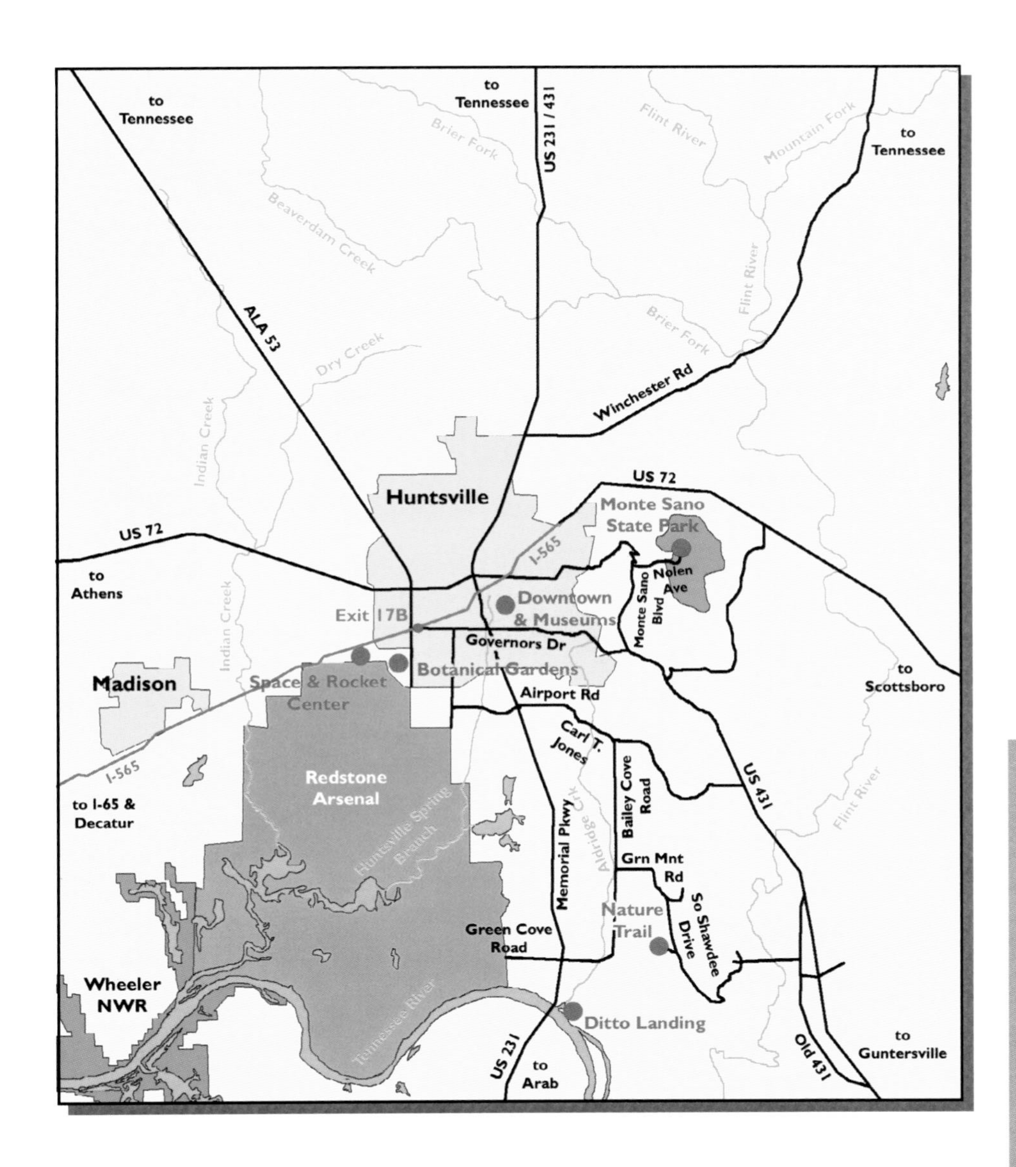

Park and Trail Map

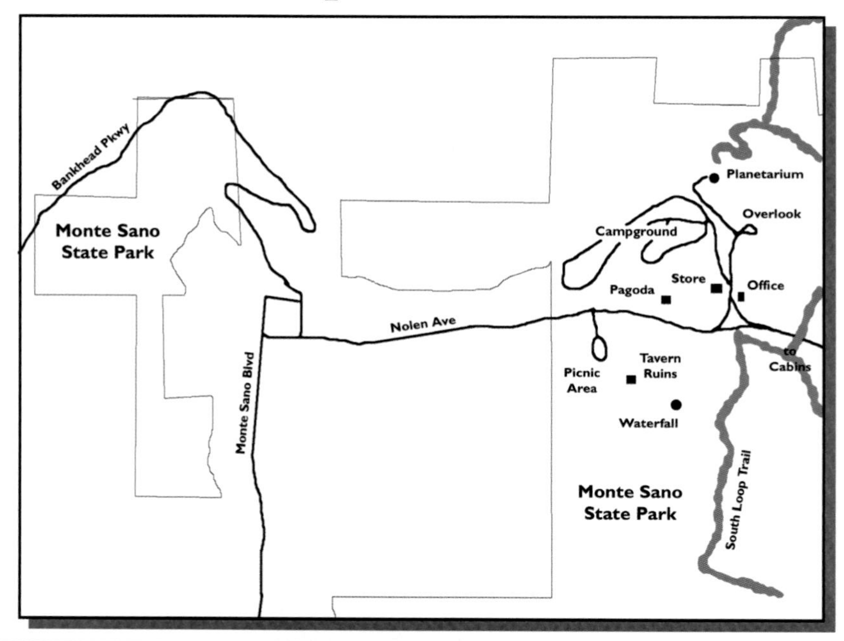

Park Facilities

Lodge and Restaurant:

No lodge or restaurant facilities are available.

Cabins and Chalets:

The park maintains 14 rustic cabins constructed by the CCC using native logs and stones. All cabins are located along the bluff overlooking Mills Hollow. Through traffic is prohibited, except to bikers and hikers, adding to privacy and security.

Campgrounds:

There are 89 sites total, several being pull-through sites for larger campers, plus 20 more sites in the primitive area nearby. Nineteen sites have full hook-ups. The two comfort stations and pavilion are conveniently located near all sites, as is the country store.

Country Store & Information Center:

Stop by the country store for camper and cabin registration and check-in. The store maintains minimal supplies, but with the close proximity to Huntsville, anything you may need can be found.

Swimming Pool:

No swimming facilities are available within the park.

Picnic Areas:

The large picnic area provides a playground and an open field for children. Located nearby you'll find the amphitheater, a native stone pavilion and the old Monte Sano Tavern ruins. Across the road from the picnic area you'll find the Japanese Pagoda and Gardens. Another short trail

Scenes

Waterfalls & Creeks:

There are no perpetual waterfalls in the park, however after rainstorms the creeks can still produce beautiful falls. The waterfall in this photograph is just such an instance. The creek which flows beside the Japanese Pagoda crosses Nolan Avenue, joins with another creek, then cascades down the gorge forming this waterfall before reaching McKay Hollow below.

Foliage:

Most of the park acreage is undeveloped. Along the trails, you will find all sorts of hardwoods indigenous to this climate, such as cedar, pine, oak and hickory.

leads from the country store to the Pagoda.

Hiking trails:

There are a total of 14 miles of hiking trails within the park, ranging from easy to very difficult. A few of the easy and moderate trails are open for bicycling and mountain biking. Pick up a detailed trail map at the country store.

Seasonal waterfall below the Tavern Ruins.

Montevallo-Ashville Stagecoach Route

Description

This two-lane scenic drive extends from Montevallo at the southern end to Ashville at the northern end, following an old stagecoach route between the two cities. Today, much of the route is developed, but mostly residential with light traffic. It is a scenic method to bypass Birmingham's congestion. This drive borders Oak Mountain State Park southeast of Birmingham. Another nearby scenic drive follows Ala. 25 from Leeds. Rambling to the southeast across scenic Coosa Mountain, this drive leads to US 231 at Childersburg near DeSoto Caverns Park and Kymulga Gristmill and Covered Bridge.

Nearby Points of Interest

Kymulga and DeSoto Caverns Parks are east near Childersburg. The peaceful Twin Pines Resort is located just off Ala. 25 southeast of the scenic drive. The *Saunders Family Covered Bridge* is located at the resort on the edge of Lake Lauralee. Oak Mountain State Park is parallel to the scenic drive southeast of Birmingham. Tannehill Historical State Park and Tannehill Valley Covered Bridge are west of Birmingham near I-20/59. Brierfield Ironworks Historical State Park is near Montevallo. Rickwood Caverns State Park is north of Birmingham on I-65.

Near Ashville, horses graze in front of an old home site.

Location

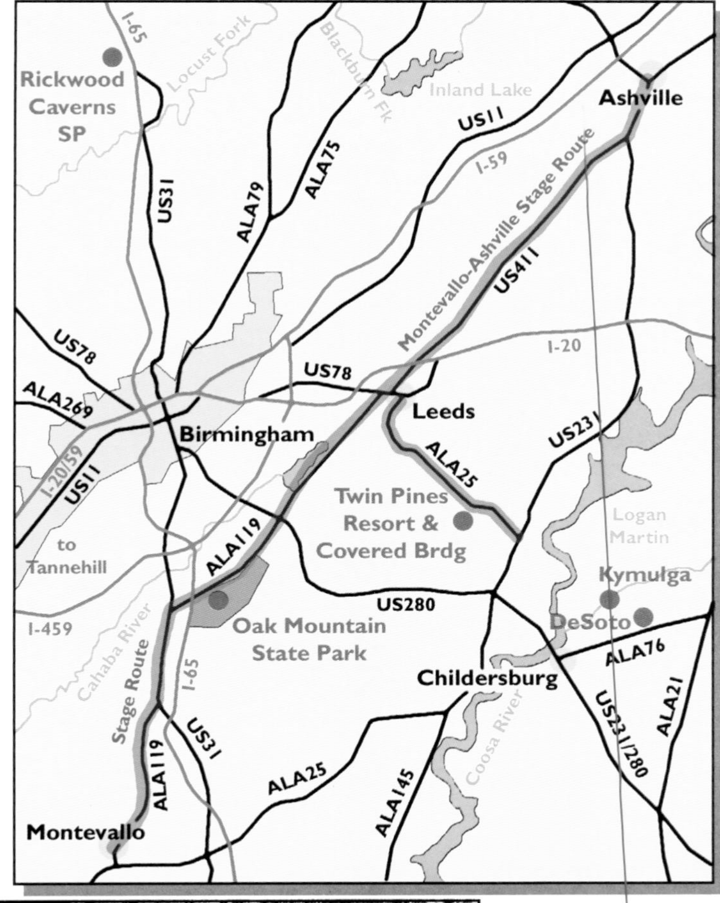

This old structure stands on the edge of the Stagecoach Route.

A lone fisherman on the waters of Lake Purdy.

Moundville Archaeological Park

Park Description ★★★★

With 320 acres adjacent the Black Warrior River, Moundville is one of Alabama's richest sites of ancient native American Indian culture. Archaeological digs date civilization here as far back as 12,000 years. Twenty-six flattop pyramid mounds are celestially aligned, with the highest peaking at 60 feet. The one and a half-mile tour through the park can be driven or hiked. An Indian Village and museum are along the tour.

Nearby Points of Interest

Just 15 miles north in Tuscaloosa the Paul W. Bryant Museum, by the University of Alabama campus, honors Alabama players and relives Crimson Tide history under the "Bear". Lake Lurleen State Park is 12 miles northwest of Tuscaloosa. Oakmulgee NWA in the southwest portion of Talladega National Forest begins east of Moundville. Following the paved roads CR 50, CR 49 and Ala. 25 eastward is a scenic drive through the forest.

One of the lakes where Indians removed soil to construct the mounds seen across the lake and in the distance against the tree line.

Location and Directions

From I-20/59 Exit 71A/B in Tuscaloosa, follow Ala. 69 south 12.7 miles to Mound Parkway. Turn right to Moundville Archaeological Park.

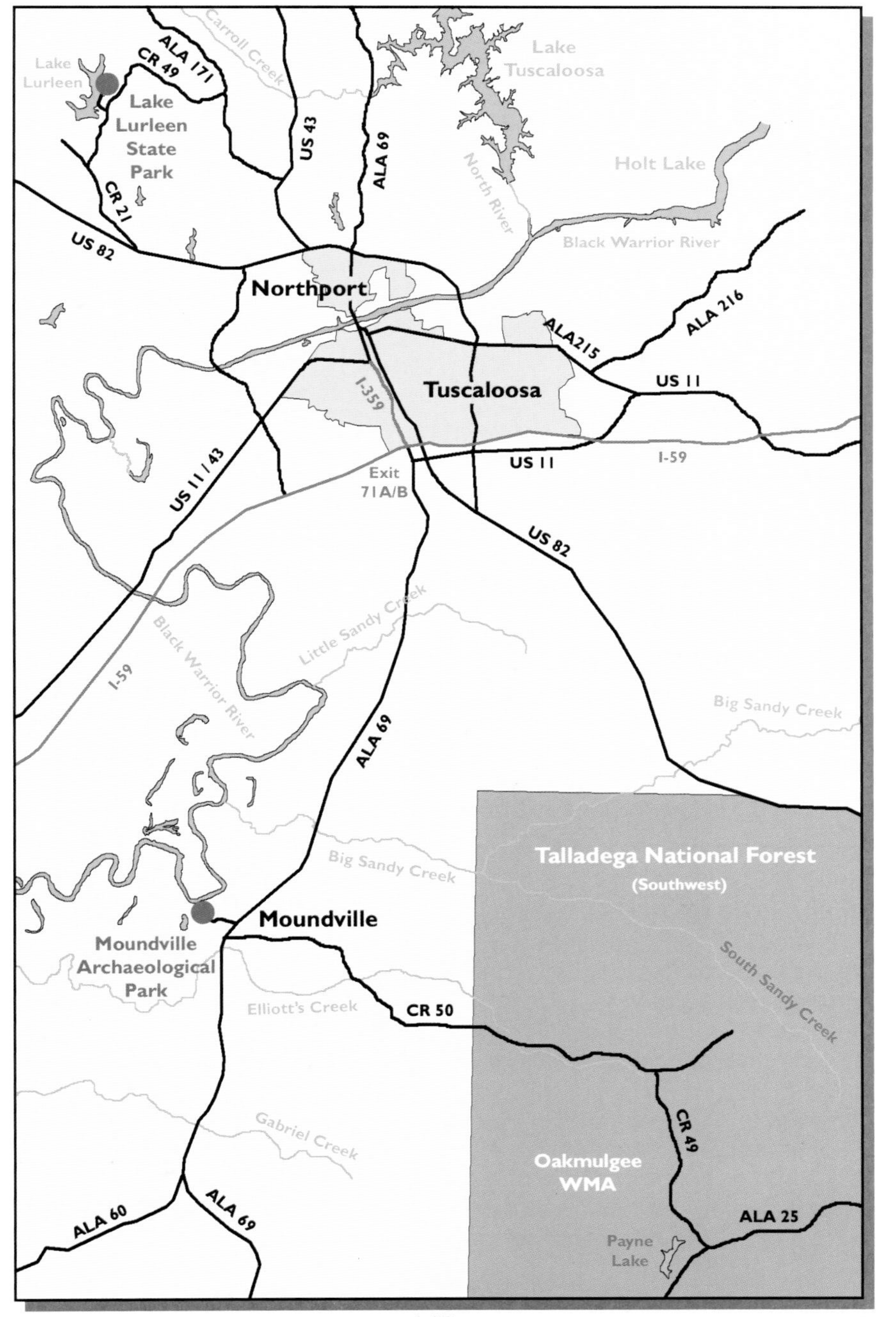

Park Map

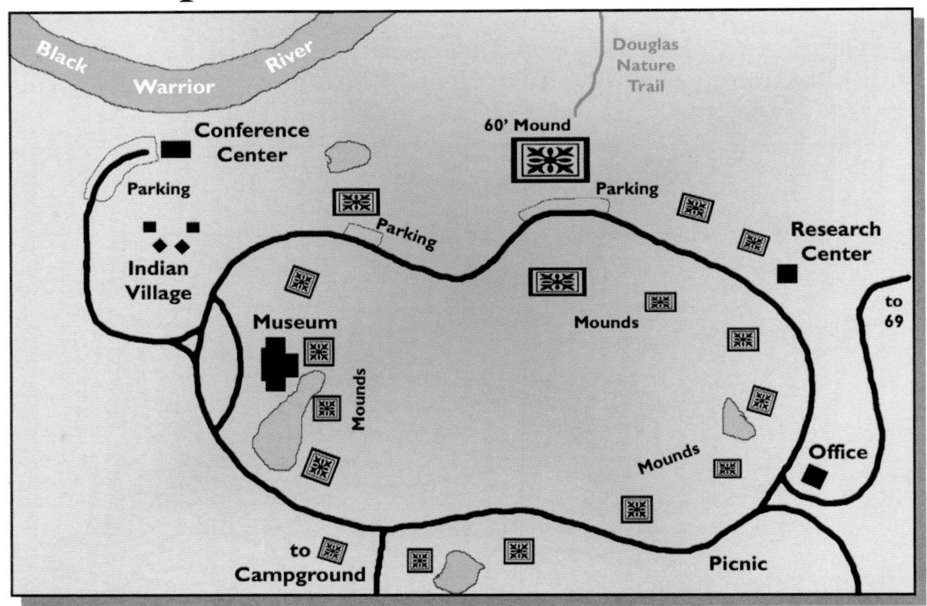

The largest, 60-foot mound with reconstructed hut.

Park Facilities

Visitor's Center:

Located at the park entrance, the theater provides a short movie on the area's history. Camper registration, visitor check-in and park information is available in the lobby.

Museum:

Constructed of concrete by the CCC, the museum displays many artifacts found at this historical site. A gift shop is located in the museum.

Scenes

Mounds:

Twenty-six mounds cover the area, ranging in height from 20 feet to 60 feet. It is believed the chieftain's house or temple was built upon the largest. Four small lakes remain where the Indians removed earth to construct the mounds.

Foliage:

The huge oaks provide cover for the smaller dogwoods beneath.

Picnic Areas:

The picnic area is situated under a grove of trees near the Visitor's Center.

Camping:

The 30 campsites are positioned away from the main tour loop to provide privacy. All sites provide water and electrical connections, with several sites also having sewer connections for RV's. The comfort station is centrally located.

With a perspective from the 60-foot mound, the mid-day sun casts an unusual shadow under this large oak tree.

Natchez Trace Parkway

Park Description 

The National Park Service established Natchez Trace in 1938. The Trace extends 33 miles through the northwest corner of Alabama. Following an historic Indian trail 445 miles from Natchez, Mississippi to Nashville, Tennessee, the Trace later became a well-traveled path for settlers and traders. The parkway closely follows the original Trace (just to the northwest of the parkway) for most of its journey through Alabama. As part of the National Scenic Byways Program, the National Park Service preserves historic sites along this excursion. Designated an "All American Road" in 1995 to recognize its beauty, landscape features and historic qualities, this two-lane parkway is open to non-commercial vehicles, has limited access and no commercial businesses.

Nearby Points of Interest

The quad cities of Florence, Tuscumbia, Sheffield and Muscle Shoals are closest to the Trace. In Florence you'll find Pope's Tavern Museum, Shiloh Battlefield (nearby in Tennessee) and the W. C. Handy Home & Museum. Tuscumbia has Helen Keller's Birthplace, the Alabama Music Hall of Fame and the Tennessee Valley Arts Center and Museum. Don't bypass *Tuscumbia Falls*, a man-made waterfall in Tuscumbia's downtown Spring Park. This waterfall consists of several cascades and falls on a small hillside at the edge of the park. Appearing very natural, it is truly a work of art. The Trace crosses the Tennessee River near Lake Pickwick. Further south are Dismals Wonder Gardens and Rock Bridge Canyon. Joe Wheeler State Park is 27 miles east of Florence following US 72. The *Trail of Tears Corridor* follows Ala. 20 then US 72 east.

Location and Directions

From Florence, follow Ala. 157 north to CR 10 and turn left. Natchez Trace is 0.4 miles ahead. Turn left onto the Trace.

If approaching the Trace from the Russellville or Red Bay area, take Ala. 24 to Ala. 247 and turn north. Turn left onto CR 23. CR 23 is a short four-mile road along Little Bear Creek that is very scenic, however the road is bumpy. Turn left at the end onto CR 90 west. Drive two miles and turn right onto CR 190. Follow CR 190 to the end and turn right onto CR 290. (CR 290 is also Sally Burns Road).

CR 290 ends at CR 1, where you'll turn left. Follow CR 1 through Maud to the Trace access road. CR 190 and CR 290 are also bumpy, but very scenic. Wild turkey are often seen along this forested route. **TIP:** Be sure to have sufficient fuel; there are no stations along the Trace or this backcountry route.

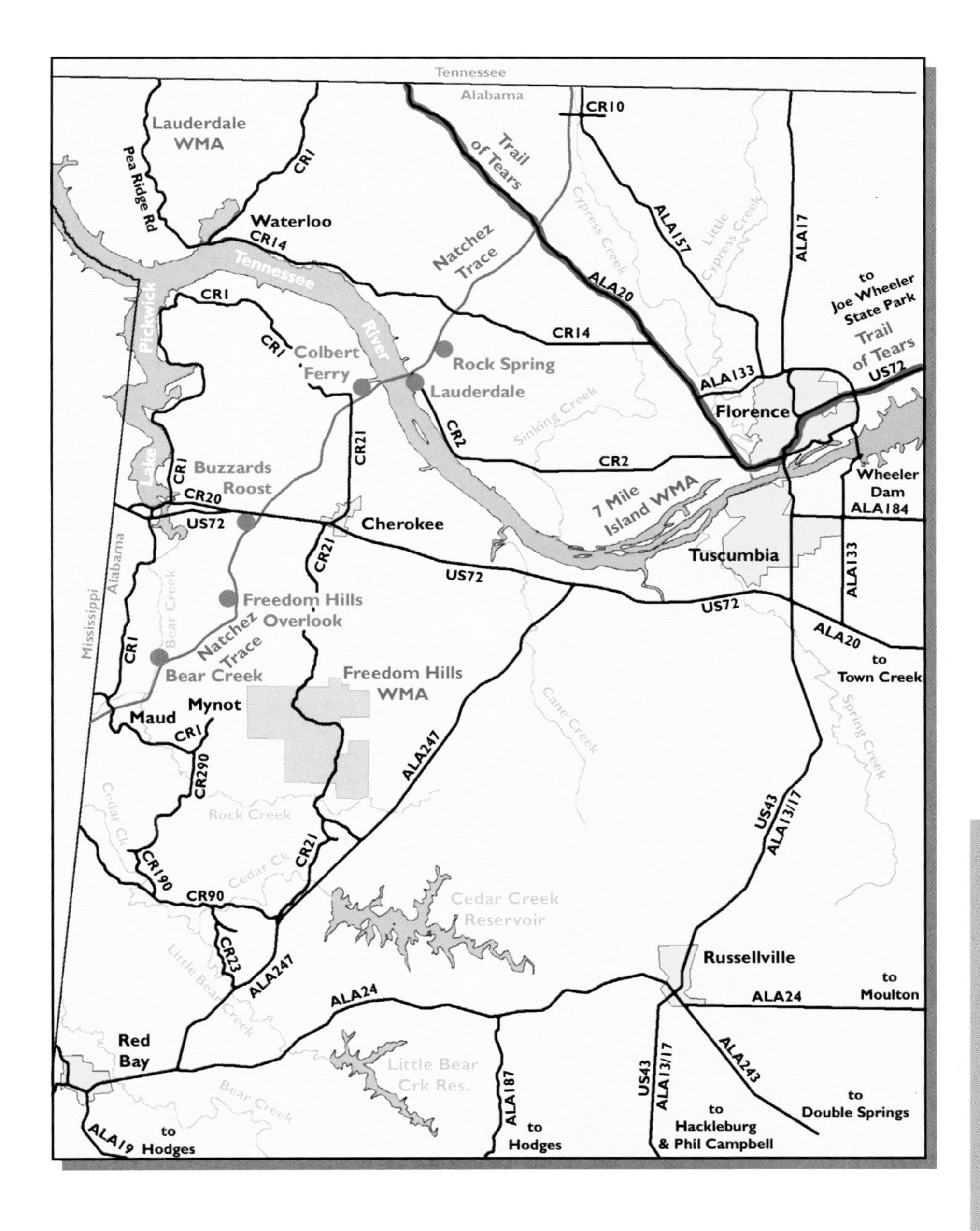

Park Facilities

Facilities:

There are no lodging facilities along the parkway. No commercial business is allowed on the Trace. Colbert Ferry is Alabama's most developed area along the Trace, with an Information Center, picnic areas, bike trails and boat ramps.

Campgrounds:

The parkway's three campgrounds are located in Mississippi and Tennessee; none in Alabama.

Picnic Areas:

Picnic areas are located all along the Trace at Bear Creek, Buzzard's Roost Spring, Colbert Ferry, Lauderdale and Rock Spring.

Hiking trails:

The **Freedom Hills Overlook Trail** is paved from the parking area 300 yards uphill to the overlook. The first half of the trail is moderately uphill. The upper portion levels out and becomes easy. The overlook faces eastward overlooking the Freedom Hills WMA.

Buzzard's Roost Spring has a short moderate trail leading just a few yards downhill from the parking area to the natural spring.

Colbert Ferry has a short easy trail leading 50 yards to the site of Colbert's Stand, the Inn he established near the banks of the Tennessee River where he maintained a ferry crossing.

Rock Spring Nature Trail leads an easy 50 yards to the spring where you'll find stepping stones crossing the stream. Beyond the stream, the trail leads moderately uphill through the forest several hundred yards to open fields.

Scenes

Overlooks:

Freedom Hills Overlook provides an easterly view of the forests in the Freedom Hills WMA.

Creeks:

Buzzard's Roost Spring emerges from a small cave under the parking area.

The **Tennessee River** flows under the Trace between the 328 and 329 mile markers.

Rock Spring flows into Colbert Creek before reaching the Tennessee River.

Bear Creek follows Alabama's southern portion of the Trace about two miles. Bear Creek flows northward into Pickwick Lake at the Tennessee River.

Foliage:

Near this scenic drive are plentiful oak and hickory, along with pine and cedar. Many of the roadside fields are covered with wildflowers during spring and summer.

Stepping stones across Rock Spring.

Natural Bridge Park

Park Description

★★★★

Privately owned and operated, Natural Bridge Park is a peaceful place to visit with shady, creek side picnic areas and trails leading through the forest to the natural bridge. One of America's longest, this sandstone bridge has a span of 148 feet and is 60 feet high. It is so large, it is difficult to photograph all of it in one picture.

Nearby Points of Interest

Dismals Wonder Garden and Rock Bridge Canyon are northwest near Hackleburg. William B. Bankhead National Forest is northeast. Many waterfalls and trails are in the forest boundaries. Kinlock Falls is easily accessible beside dirt road FS 210. Most other waterfalls in the forest require longer hikes. Clarkson Covered Bridge is east following US 278.

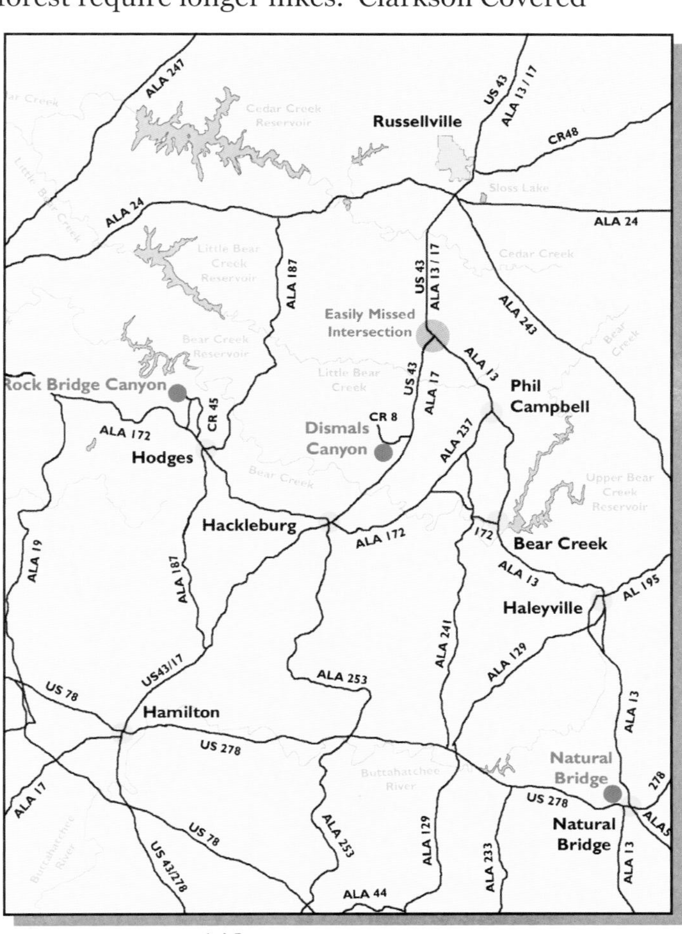

Location and Directions

From Russellville, follow Ala. 13 south to US 278 in Natural Bridge. Turn right onto US 278. The park entrance is less than a mile on the right.

Park Map

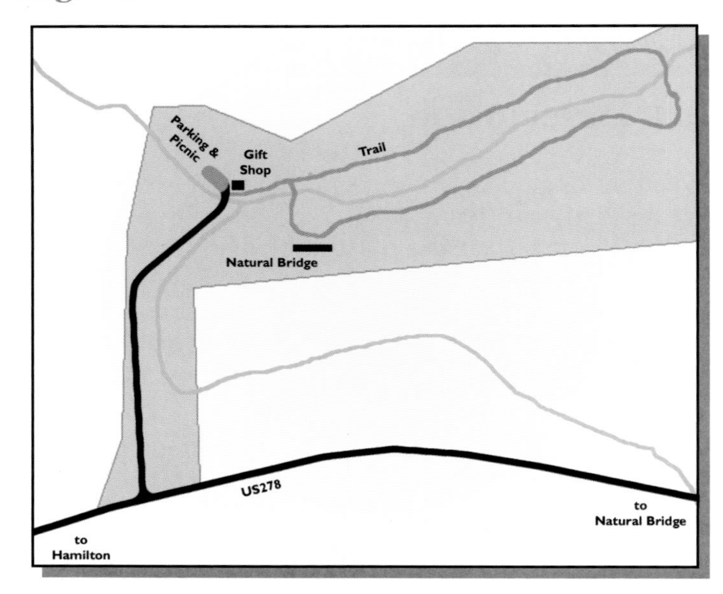

Natural Bridge is actually two bridges.

Park Facilities

Gift Shop:

In addition to gift items, the store has minimal picnic supplies.

Picnic Areas:

The picnic area is conveniently located by the parking area and gift shop. A small stream flows beside the area under the trees.

Hiking trails:

Almost 1/2 miles of easy hiking leads along the creek through the forest. The natural bridge is found along the trail.

Scenes

Natural Bridge:

The natural sandstone bridge spans 148 feet, 60 feet above the ground. It is one of America's longest natural bridges.

Creeks:

Small creeks flow through the park by the picnic area and along the hiking trails.

Foliage:

All of the indigenous hardwoods are found in the park, along with pine and cedar.

Noccalula Falls Park

Park Description ★★★★

Noccalula Falls, just 2.5 miles from Exit 188 on I-59 in Gadsden, is at the southern end of Lookout Mountain Parkway. The waterfall is named after a Creek Indian princess who hurdled herself into the canyon when her chieftain father exiled her lover. Noccalula's 13-foot statue, poised to leap, was erected on the canyon rim in 1958.

Black Creek free-falls 90 feet to the large pool at the canyon floor. At times, a rainbow will appear in the mist of the falls. Several trails lead around the canyon rim and along Black Creek at the bottom of the ravine, where Indian carvings and other artifacts remain from the 1800's. Originally built in 1899, *Gilliland Covered Bridge* was moved to the park from nearby Reece City in 1966. The park also includes campgrounds, a miniature train ride, playground, botanical gardens, deer park, pioneer homestead, souvenir shop, picnic pavilions, carpet golf and sand volleyball courts. Don't miss the lights of *Christmas on the Rocks* in season.

Nearby Points of Interest

Lookout Mountain Parkway begins at the park and goes northeast to Mentone following Tabor Road (CR 89). This scenic drive tours Little River Canyon National Preserve and DeSoto State Park. Cornwall Furnace, Griffin Falls and Yellow Creek Falls are located northeasterly near Leesburg. Silver Lakes just south of Gadsden is part of the Robert Trent Jones Golf Trail.

Location and Directions

From I-59, Exit 188, take US 211 south 2.5 miles to Noccalula Falls Park on the right.

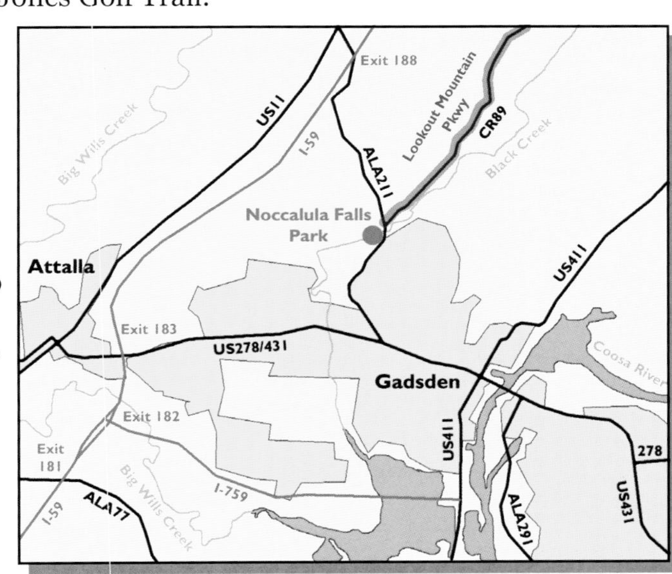

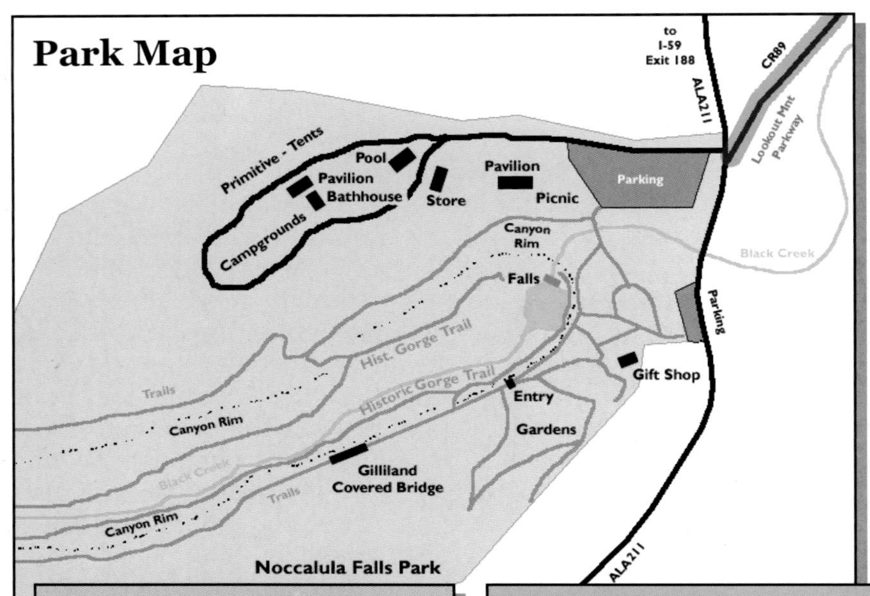

Park Facilities

Main Park:

The botanical gardens, deer park, Gilliland Covered Bridge and the pioneer village are all on the south side of the ravine in the main park area.

Country Store:

The country store serves for camper registration. It maintains minimal picnic and camping supplies, but many shops are located in nearby Gadsden, providing any item you might need.

Campgrounds:

Located on the north side of the canyon, there are 130 sites in the campground for tents, pop-ups or RV's. Twenty-nine sites have full hookups with water, electric and sewer connections. Fifty-four additional sites have water and electricity. There are 34 tent sites in the primitive area nearby, but away from the ravine. There are also 5 pull-though sites for large RV's. Most sites with water and electrical connections overlook the ravine. A large screened pic-

Scenes

Waterfalls:

Noccalula Falls free-falls 90 feet to the canyon floor. Under normal rain conditions, the falls are 20 feet wide with a smaller fall just to the right. After heavy rains, the two merge into one and become much wider.

Creeks:

Black Creek flows through the ravine after plunging over Noccalula Falls. Black Creek parallels Lookout Mountain Parkway, enters the park area and continues through Gadsden to join the Coosa River. On the north side of the ravine, another small creek enters the canyon and sometimes creates a small waterfall along the gorge trail.

Foliage:

Mountain laurel and wild hydrangea bloom in May and June along the gorge trail. In the botanical gardens, thousands of azaleas and flowers bloom in May. Tall pines surround the ravine.

Noccalula Falls **from the ravine.**

nic pavilion and comfort station is located centrally to all sites.

Swimming Pool:

A large swimming pool near the country store is available for registered campers.

Picnic Area:

The picnic area sits on the north bluff adjacent the parking area. It is a peaceful shady area with a large pavilion overlooking the falls.

Hiking trails:

Historic Gorge Trail is a hard trail that leads hikers 1.5 miles around the canyon floor along Black Creek. One end of this trail leads under and behind the waterfall. Many large moss-covered boulders and unusual rock formations are seen along this trail, along with several historic sites.

TIP: The gorge trail can be reached from the north or south bluff. The southern entry point has a steep stairway descending halfway into the canyon, just inside the park entrance. On the north side, an easily accessible steep trail at the back of the campground area leads into the ravine.

Wild roses and vines mark the entrance to Gilliland Covered Bridge.

Noccalula Falls from the southern rim.

Oak Mountain State Park

Park Description ★★

Peavine Falls.

This is Alabama's largest State Park with 9,940 acres on Double Oak and Little Oak Mountains 15 miles south of Birmingham. The park has a Demonstration Farm, horse boarding, riding facilities and trails, scenic overlooks, four large lakes, a waterfall and 50 miles of trails. A 150 site campground is located adjacent Beaver Lake. Ten rustic cabins are secluded around Tranquility Lake. An 18-hole championship golf course, marina and beach area are also available. The park includes the Wildlife Rehabilitation Center that houses injured raptors.

Nearby Points of Interest

The scenic Montevallo-Ashville Stagecoach Route extends along the northwest border of the park. DeSoto Caverns Park and Kymulga Park with its historic covered bridge and operating gristmill are 35 miles west following Ala. 119 and US 280 to Childersburg. Rickwood Caverns State Park is 40 miles north along I-65. Ala. 25, northeast of the park, is a scenic drive over Coosa Mountain in a suburban area of Birmingham. The route passes several horse ranches and is near Twin Pines Resort with its Saunders Family Covered Bridge replica. Tannehill Historical State Park and Tannehill Valley Covered Bridge are 27 miles west. Brierfield Ironworks Historical State Park, located to the southwest, is similar to Tannehill Historical State Park. Oxmoor Valley golf course is listed on Alabama's famous Robert Trent Jones Golf Trail.

Location and Directions

From I-65, Exit 246, take Ala. 119 south (west) 0.1 miles to the first traffic signal and turn left (south) onto State Park Road CR 33. Go 1.8 miles to the stop sign, then turn left to the park entrance.

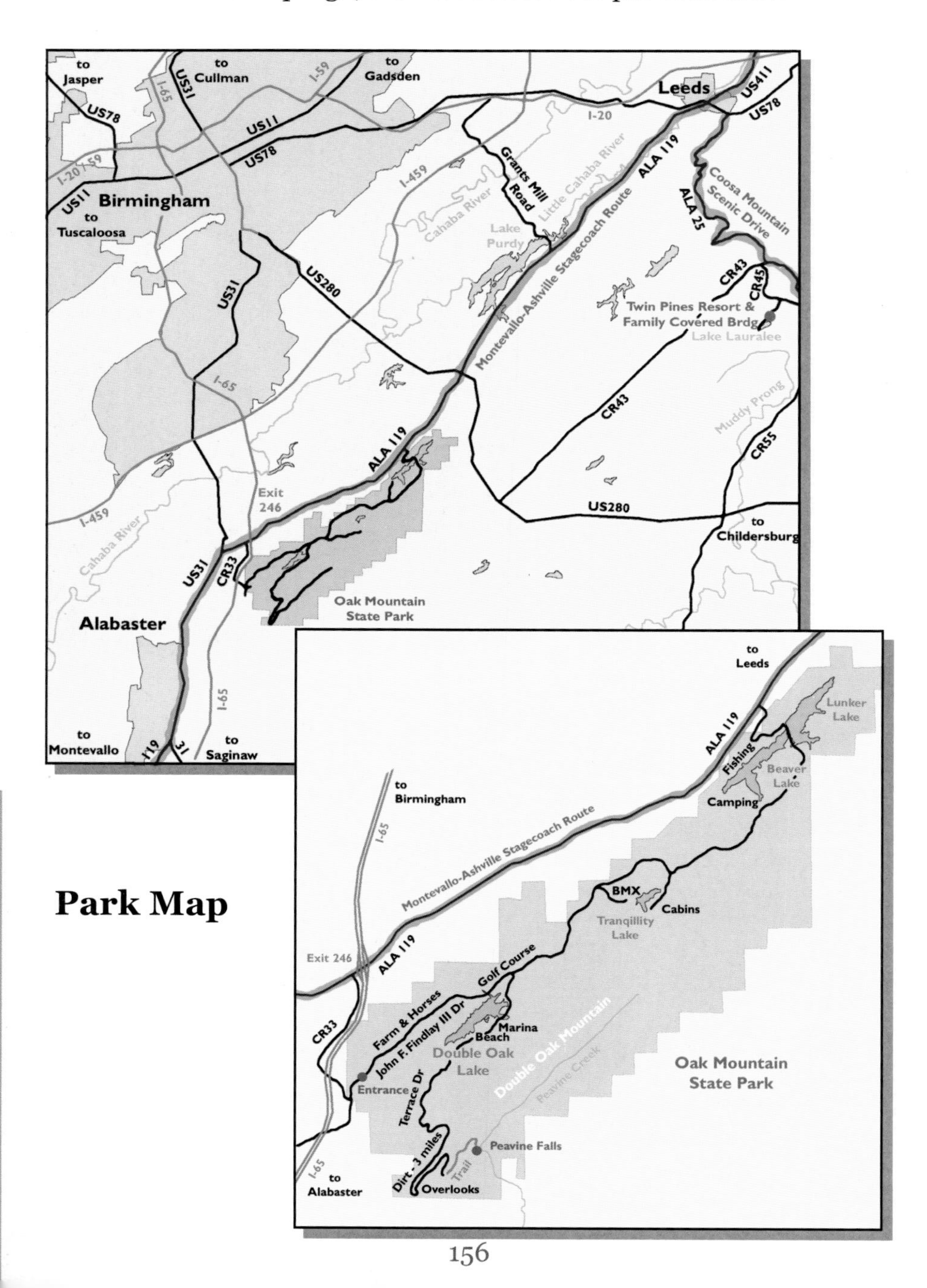

Park Map

Park Facilities

Lodge:

The park has no lodge or restaurant, but does maintain a Conference Center. A snack shop is located adjacent the pro shop at the golf course. The Demonstration Farm is located near the horse boarding facilities. A Wildlife Rescue Center is located on the mountain. The fishing store maintains minimal supplies.

Cabins and Chalets:

Ten secluded cabins, furnished for light housekeeping, surround the 45-acre Tranquility Lake near the center of the park. Small boats with life vests are provided. Open year round, they include two bedrooms, one bath, kitchenette, heat and air conditioning and porch.

Campgrounds:

One hundred-fifty total campsites along the shores of Beaver Lake. Fifty-eight sites have full connections for water, electricity and sewer. Thirty-three sites have water and electricity. Sixty tent sites include six with water and electrical connections. Seven comfort stations, two with laundries, are conveniently situated near sites. **Tip:** Area A, mainly for tents and pop-ups, has spacious wooded campsites near the beach on Beaver Lake. Area B's layout is designed more compact for RV's.

Country Store:

Located at the campground entrance, the store provides minimal picnic and camping supplies. The close proximity of Birmingham allows quick access to unique supplies not stocked by the country store.

Scenes

Waterfalls:

The park's only waterfall, Peavine Falls, is located at the southern extremity of the park near the top of Double Oak Mountain. Driving to the end of a 3-mile long dirt road, a well-maintained 3/8-mile hard trail leads downhill to the top of the falls. From here, a tough downhill trail winds 0.1 miles to the bottom of the falls. Peavine is a beautiful 20-foot high waterfall nestled in a small canyon.

Lakes:

74-acre **Beaver Lake** has a beach area on the south side by the campground area and a small fishing store on its north side.

Lunker Lake provides fishing activities.

Double Oak Lake includes a marina, providing canoeing, paddleboat and flat-bottom boat activities. Tennis courts and parking areas are adjacent the lake's south shore.

Tranquility Lake is a small 45-acre peaceful lake set aside for the enjoyment of cabin guests.

Foliage:

The park abounds with long-needle pines at higher elevations, with many hardwoods being lower on the mountain.

Demonstration Farm.

Swimming Pool:
An Olympic size swimming pool is available. A beach and bathhouse are also available on Beaver Lake near the campgrounds and another on Double Oak Lake. Two tennis courts are near Double Oak Lake.

Picnic Areas:
Twenty-one picnic pavilions are located throughout the park around Double Oak Lake, Beaver Lake, the campgrounds and in surrounding wooded areas. All are available by reservation.

BMX Track (Bike Moto-Cross):
A recently constructed BMX track is situated just off John F. Findlay III Drive near the cabins. Paved bike trails also lead along both sides of John F. Findlay III Drive for its full length. There are miles of mountain biking trails available.

Hiking trails:
Fifty miles of trails reach all across the park. Four miles are available for horseback riding. Mountain bike trails total 17 miles. Thirty miles are available for backpacking. A trail map is available at the Country Store.

Pisgah Gorge

Description ★★★

This small gorge is tucked in Sand Mountain at Pisgah. Through the canyon, Little Bryant Creek drops a total of 600 feet from the mountaintop to the Tennessee River in a distance of only 1.5 miles. Along its journey are two large waterfalls, each near 100 feet tall. A moderate trail leads along the bluff overlooking the creek and falls. The lower waterfall has a point overlook downstream providing a majestic view of the 100-foot waterfall and cascade below the overlook. The upper waterfall is difficult to view from its overlook due to overgrown foliage, but the trail leads to the top of the falls where you get a good view of water falling into the canyon. From here, the trail continues upstream along Little Bryant Creek. There are few barriers at the overlooks making this a very hazardous area.

Nearby Points of Interest

The Trail of Tears follows US 72 just northwest of the gorge. Both Mud Creek and Raccoon Creek WMAs offer very scenic drives. Gorham's Bluff, a mountaintop residential community, is just north of Pisgah. With a Bed-and-Breakfast and outstanding views overlooking the Tennessee River valley, Gorham's Bluff is a popular host to wedding parties. Russell Cave National Monument is north along US72. Sequoyah Caverns Park, DeSoto State Park and Little River Canyon National Preserve are east near Ft. Payne. To the south are Buck's Pocket State Park and High Falls County Park. Westward, you'll find Blowing Wind Cave NWR and Cathedral Caverns State Park. The Pinnacle is a very large rock outcrop on a point of Sand Mountain. It may be seen as you ascend or descend Sand Mountain on Ala. 40. Its better view point is from below along the Tennessee River. Near the intersection of Ala. 35 and Ala. 40, take CR 24 toward Camp Jackson. A trail leads from the end of CR 24 into Pisgah Gorge along Jones Creek. This trail follows the foot of The Pinnacle.

Pisgah Gorge Lower Falls.

Location and Directions

From US 72 in Scottsboro, follow Ala. 35 south 3.2 miles across the Tennessee River and turn left onto Ala. 40. Follow Ala. 40 east 6.9 miles and turn left onto Ala. 71 north. It is 2.4 miles to CR 58 where you turn left toward Pisgah and Gorham's Bluff. Follow CR 58 northwest 2.1 miles and turn left onto CR 374 (just before the Pisgah Cemetery). Pisgah Civitan Park is 0.6 miles ahead on the left. The gate is usually closed due to vandalism. Please don't block the gate. Pisgah Town Park is just beyond, providing a good place to park your vehicle.

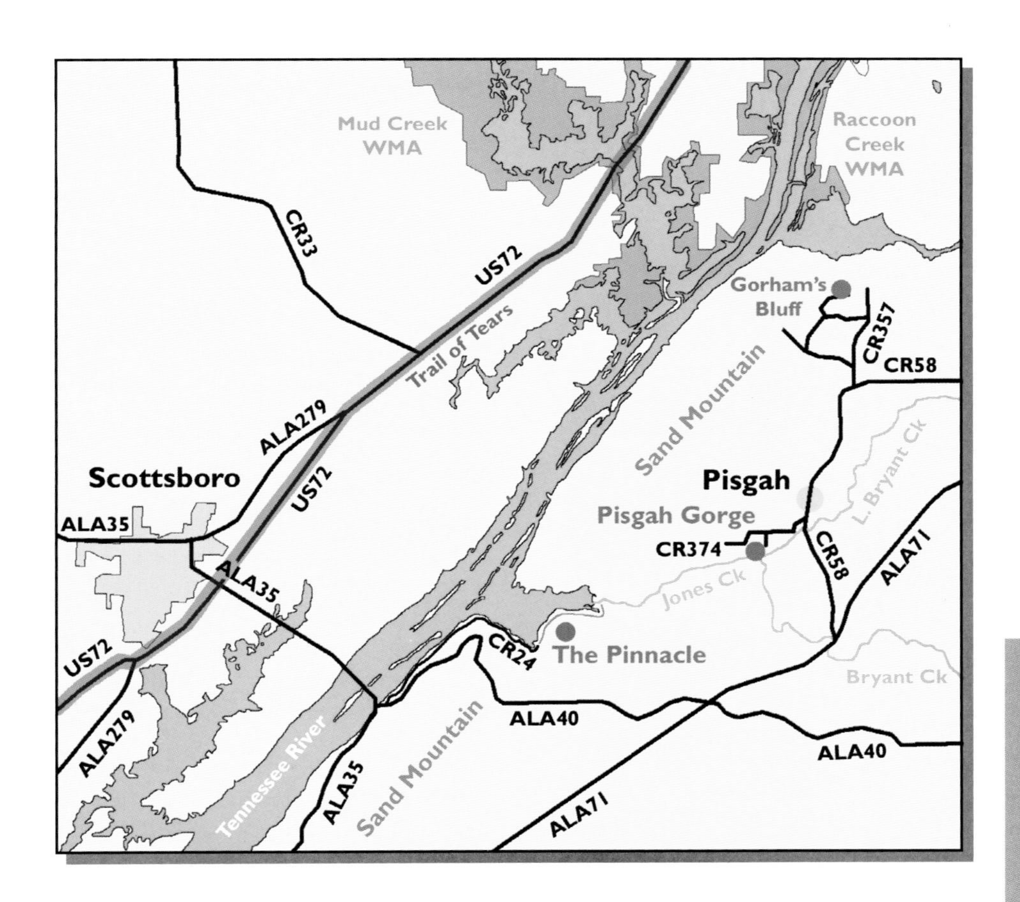

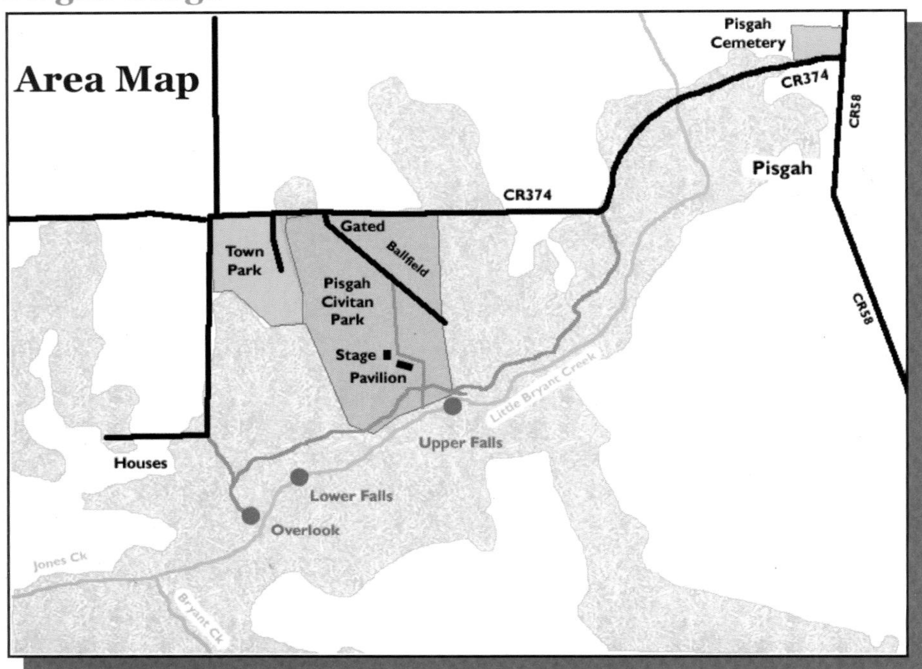

Facilities

Facilities:

There are no facilities in the gorge.

Hiking trails:

A well-traveled 1/4-mile moderate trail leads through the forest along the ridge between the two large waterfalls. The trail continues upstream following Little Bryant Creek. To reach the trailhead, stop at the entrance of Pisgah Civitan Park, then walk 1/4 mile to the back of the park near the picnic pavilion and stage. The trail begins near the pavilion, where you will hear water falling over the upper falls.

Scenes

Waterfalls:

Lower Pisgah Falls is a combination waterfall. As Little Bryant Creek plummets over the top, it free-falls 25 feet, then cascades down the rocks for another 75 feet before reaching the pool below. The point overlook is on a ledge 150 feet above the canyon floor with no safety barriers. Be extremely careful here.

Upper Pisgah Falls drops about 100 feet. It is difficult to view from the overlook because of thick overgrown foliage at the ridge. A fence prevents getting to close to the edge. The trail leads to the top of the falls providing a magnificent view over the falls into the canyon below.

Foliage:

Mountain laurel and rhododendron bloom along the trail in May and June. Hardwoods fill the surrounding forest.

The turbulent waters above the *Upper Falls* before cascading into the gorge. A small dam is just below this image.

A view from the *Lower Falls* overlook.

Rickwood Caverns State Park

Park Description ★★

Located between the Locust Fork and Mulberry Fork of the Black Warrior River, this State Park is a popular destination for kayakers and canoeists. Both rivers provide great rapids and calm waters. The park features the water carved cavern's "miracle-mile" underground tour with active living formations of stalactites and stalagmites. The caverns were formed 260 million years ago when this area was at the ocean's floor, as testified by the shells and fossils lining the cavern walls and ceilings. Blind cave fish inhabit the cavern's crystal clear pools. A miniature train ride winds through portions of the park.

Nearby Points of Interest

Locust Fork and Mulberry Fork have many input points near the park for canoes and kayaks. Oak Mountain State Park is 15 miles southeast of Birmingham. Nectar Falls, Locust Fork Falls and three historic covered bridges are 22 miles east following Ala. 160 to Cleveland. Clarkson Covered Bridge is north, seven miles west of I-65, Exit 308 near Cullman.

A large stalactite drapes from the ceiling in the first room of Rickwood Caverns, as a red glow highlights a small alcove beside the main trail.

Location and Directions

From I-65, Exit 284, take Ala. 160 west 0.2 miles. Turn right onto CR 8 and travel 2.5 miles to the Rickwood Cutoff Road (unmarked, follow State Park signs). Turn right and go 1.3 miles to the park entrance on the right.

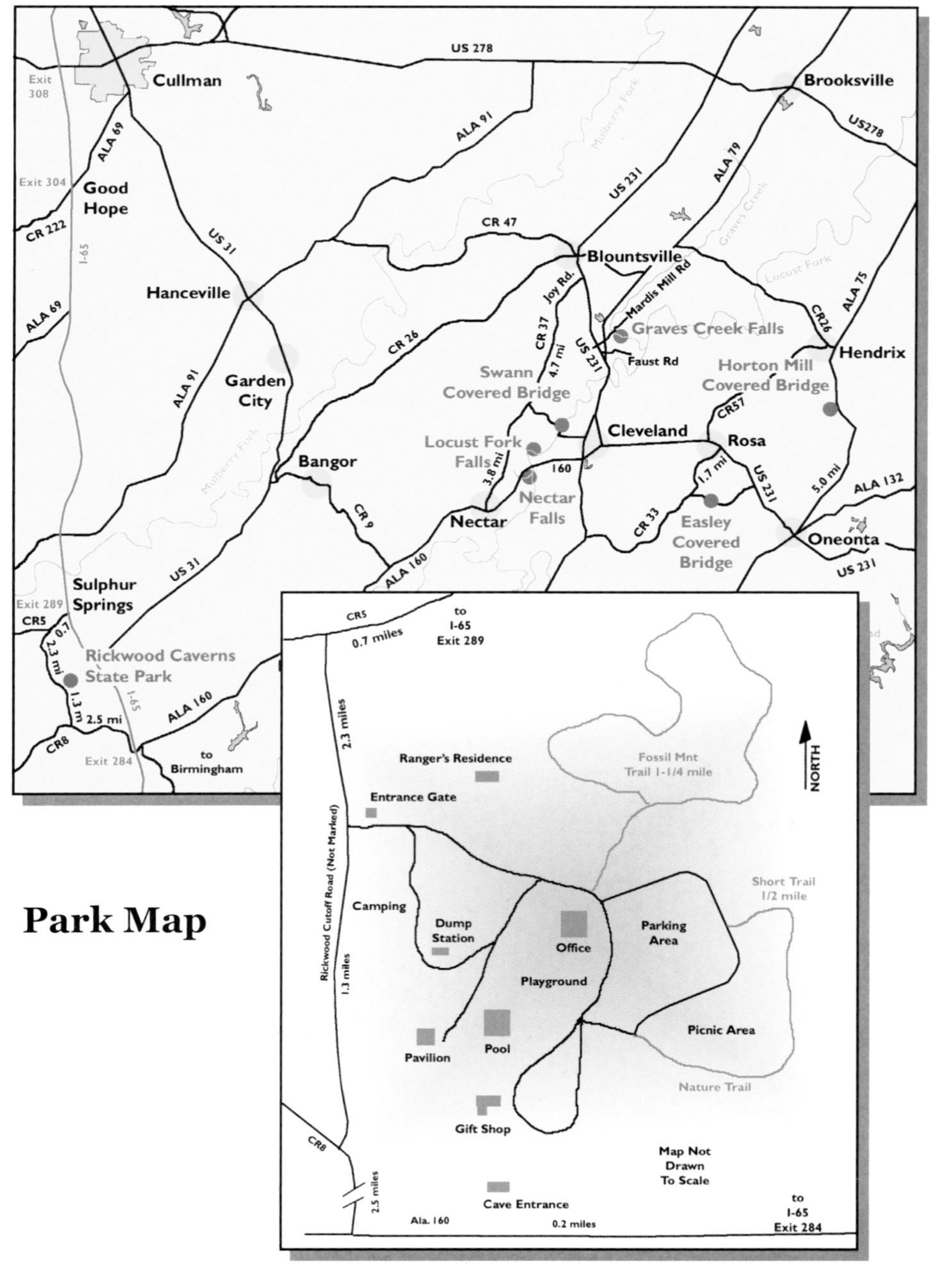

Park Map

Park Facilities

Lodge:

The park does not include a lodge or restaurant.

Cabins and Chalets:

There are no cabins or chalets available.

Campgrounds:

The park maintains 18 total campsites for tents and RV's. There is one site available for group tents. Four other individual tent sites have water connections. Four additional sites have water and electrical connections available for tents or pop-up campers. Nine sites have full connections for pop-ups or RV's. A dump station is available.

Country Store & Gift Shop:

The store maintains gifts, camping and picnic supplies.

Swimming Pool:

An Olympic sized swimming pool is open during season.

Picnic Areas:

The park maintains a picnic area, playground and several large pavilions.

Hiking trails:

There are a total of three miles of hiking trails around the park. The **Nature Trail** continues onto **Short Trail** for 1/2 mile. The **Fossil Mountain Trail** loops 1-1/4 miles through forested areas.

Scenes

Waterfalls:

There are no waterfalls within the park. Locust Fork Falls and Nectar Falls are 22 miles east near Cleveland following Ala. 160 east.

Foliage:

Long and short needle pines and a variety of hardwoods fill the park.

The mini-train railway tracks through the campgrounds.

Rock Bridge Canyon

Park Description ★★★★

This outstanding small canyon is not found on most roadmaps. It appears the property owners intended to open the canyon as a park, but circumstances hindered its full development, with the steps, railings and small bridges now badly deteriorating. This does not at all distract from the canyon's natural beauty. In fact with fewer visitors, the canyon remains in its beautiful natural state. The canyon contains a huge 50-foot span, 50-foot high natural bridge, with a smaller 20-foot span, 5-foot high natural bridge above it (both cannot be seen at the same time due to trees and positioning). To the right of the main bridge is a gigantic concave cliff face that curves overhead. A small 50-foot waterfall trickles over the rocks on the main bridge. Two other impressive waterfalls are found along the creek running through the canyon. This creek forms a small, interesting cascade between the waterfalls as it meanders through and under the huge moss covered boulders. A small lake is positioned in the middle of the canyon's many features.

***Upper Falls*, at the head of Rock Bridge Canyon.**

Nearby Points of Interest

The Dismals Wonder Gardens is only 16 miles northeast of Rock Bridge Canyon. Natural Bridge, one of America's longest spans, is just to the southeast. Bankhead National Forest with Kinlock Falls and South Caney Creek Falls is just east of Natural Bridge along US 278. Follow US 278 12 miles east to Double Springs, turn left (north) onto Ala. 33. At CR 2 turn left (west). (See William B. Bankhead National Forest). Clarkson Covered Bridge is 41 miles east of Natural Bridge following US 278. The Bear Creek Reservoirs are also in this area.

Location and Directions

From Russellville, take US 43 and Ala. 17 south to Hackleburg. Turn right onto Ala. 172 toward Hodges. 0.7 miles past Ala. 187 in Hodges, turn right onto Canyon Road, CR 45. Drive 1.9 miles to a sharp left curve in the road, but continue going straight. An honor pay box is immediately on your right. Continue to the parking area at the end of the road. The Ala. 17 turn off south of Russellville to Dismals Canyon is easily missed (marked on map below).

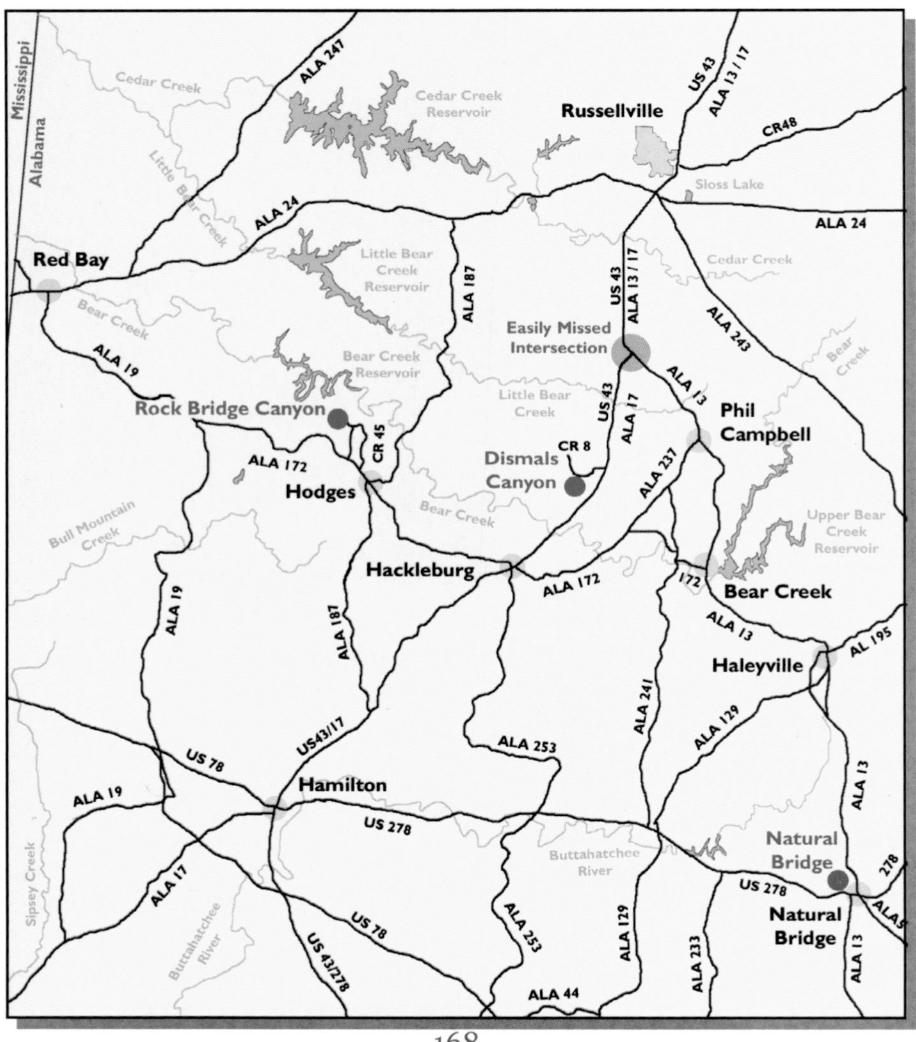

Moss covered boulders surround *Upper Rock Bridge Falls.*

Hodges/Rock Bridge Canyon Directions

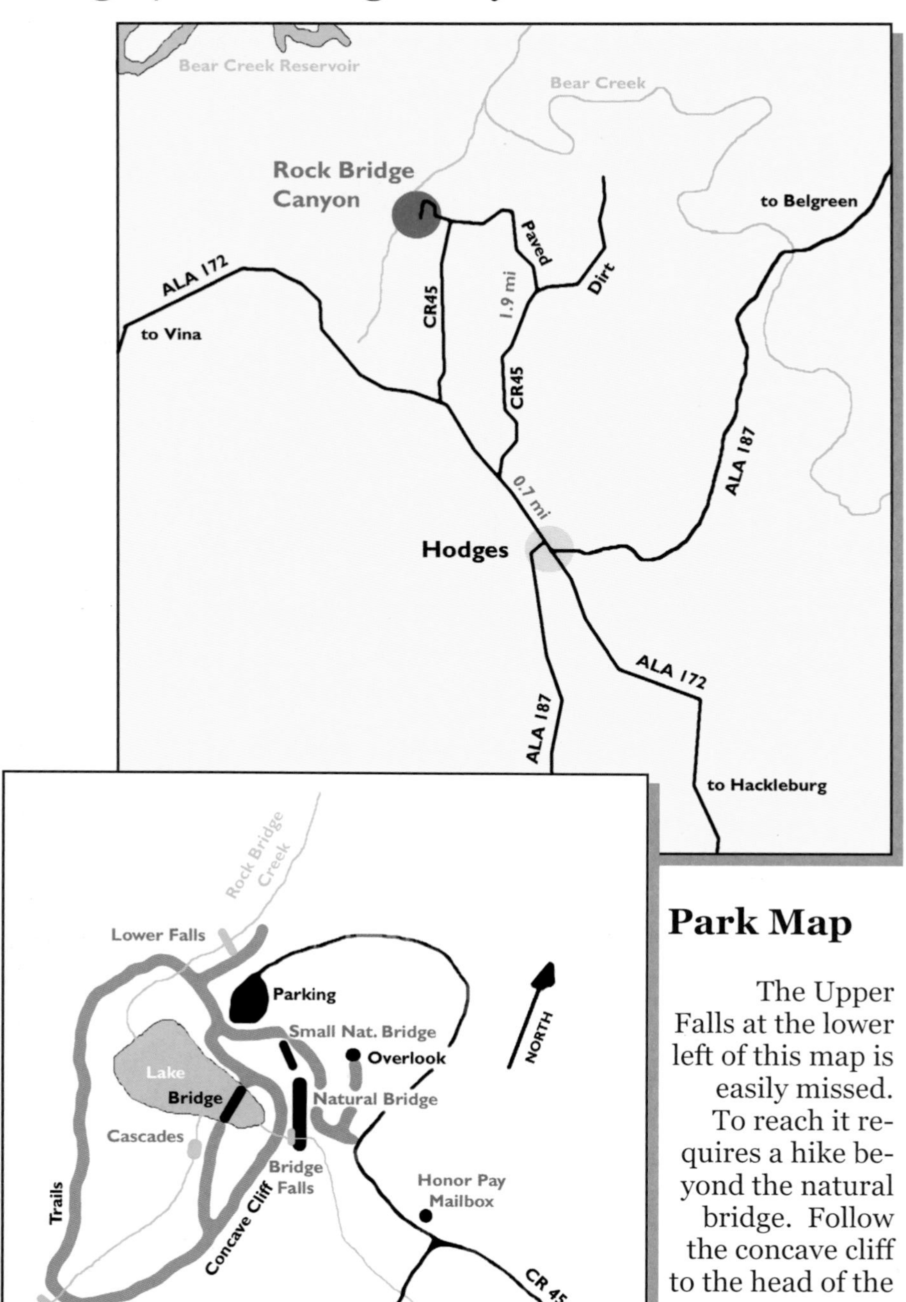

Park Map

The Upper Falls at the lower left of this map is easily missed. To reach it requires a hike beyond the natural bridge. Follow the concave cliff to the head of the canyon.

Two views of the *Lower Falls*, just below the parking area. In the image below, the deteriorating steps descend the left side of the falls. The Upper and Lower Falls in Rock Bridge Canyon are two of the most peaceful, beautiful waterfalls I've found in northern Alabama, possibly because of their secluded natural environment.

Park Facilities

Facilities:

There are no facilities in the park. Check out the pink and blue seats in the outhouses above the main natural bridge.

Picnic Areas:

There are no developed picnic areas. Several picnic tables are found along the trails and provide a convenient place to rest, but their access for picnics is limited, except under the main bridge.

Hiking trails:

About 3/4 miles of tough, undeveloped trails (marked in gray on the park map) wind by all major features. Most wooden steps and small bridges are badly deteriorating and may require bypassing. At some places, stairs missing planks require high steps over boulders. The bridge spanning the lake is in good shape.

Scenes

Waterfalls:

The park's three waterfalls are well worth risking the tough trails to view.

Bridge Falls, the easiest accessible waterfall is just right of the main natural bridge and plummets 50 feet from the rock above the bridge.

Upper Rock Bridge Falls, hidden at the head of the canyon, free-falls 35 feet over the rock face. Moss covered rocks surround the falls. To reach this waterfall, hike under the main natural bridge. Follow along the concave cliff to the right of the natural bridge and continue along the trail until reaching Upper Falls.

Lower Rock Bridge Falls is adjacent the parking area and lake. This waterfall is rather easy to access if the steps are bypassed. A beautiful waterfall with cascades above and falls below, its height totals 20 feet. You'll hear this waterfall from the parking area.

The **Cascades** are found between the upper and lower falls across the bridge spanning the lake. As the creek emerges from the boulders, the water cascades over a slightly sloping streambed of small rocks.

Creeks:

Rock Bridge Creek flows through the canyon forming two waterfalls and several cascades.

Foliage:

The canyon is filled with all types of trees indigenous to this area. The abundance of trees inhibits viewing canyon features until getting close up.

The concave cliff is on the right, with picnic tables below and at center left beside the natural bridge, behind the trees.

The natural bridge is directly overhead, with the small waterfall trickling off its far right side. The rust colored rock wall at center right is the concave cliff. Follow the path by this cliff to reach *Upper Falls*.

Ripples in the crystal clear blue waters of this natural spring reveal its speed as it rushes into the dark opening of Russell Cave. The spring emerges beneath this rock as a small side stream joins it from the left.

Russell Cave National Monument

Park Description ★★★

Secluded in the countryside of the Appalachian foothills, this 310-acre park provides a relaxing, serene atmosphere for a leisurely picnic or stroll. This area holds one of the longest and most complete archaeological records in the eastern United States. Archaeological digs at Russell Cave and the adjacent Cave Shelter have recovered artifacts revealing human habitation for over 8,000 years. The cave itself is closed to the public due to frequent flooding. A 700-foot ADA accessible boardwalk leads visitors to a point overlooking a natural spring flowing into the mouth of the cave. The boardwalk continues on a tour through the Cave Shelter. A 40-foot deep sinkhole is found along the park's nature trail.

Nearby Points of Interest

The *Trail of Tears Corridor* follows US 72 west all the way to Waterloo near the western state line. Sequoyah Caverns Park is southeast following Ala. 117 from Stevenson to US 11 in Hammondville. Just south of Sequoyah is DeSoto State Park and Little River Canyon. Also to the south across the Tennessee River from Scottsboro is Pisgah Gorge. All three of these locations have several large waterfalls. CR 91 is a small paved but rough scenic farm road leading along the east bank of the Tennessee River in the shadows of Sand Mountain. Here you will have great views of Widow's Creek coal power plant on the west riverbank. The plant's enormous smoke stacks can be seen from all over the area. At CR 91's northern end, scenic CR 93 ascends Sand Mountain and terminates at Ala. 73. CR 93 is also a rough and winding roadway.

Indian pink or pink root.

Location and Directions

From Stevenson, follow US 72 north 5.5 miles to CR 75. Turn left (west) onto CR 75. Drive one mile and turn right (north) onto CR 98 west. The park entrance is 3.7 miles ahead on the left.

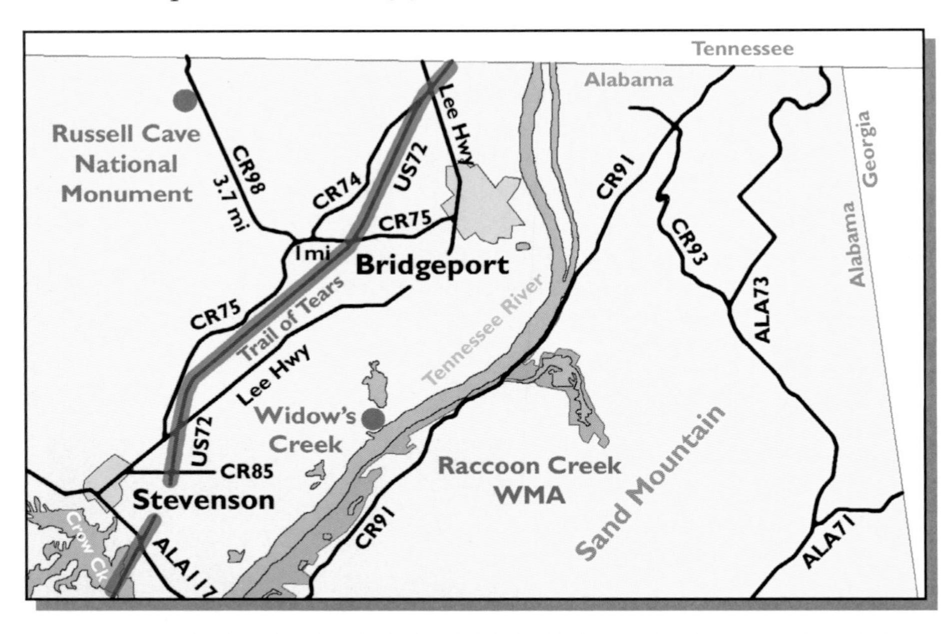

Park Map

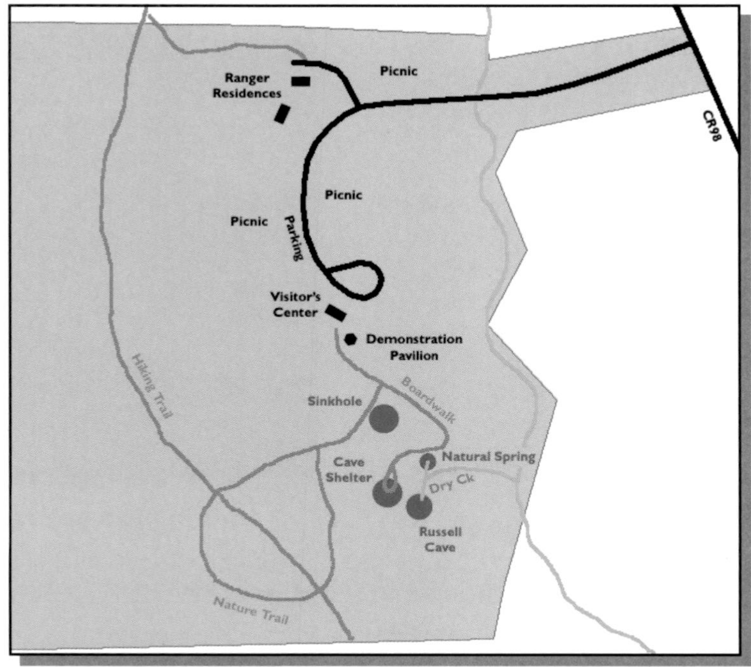

Park Facilities

Visitor's Center, Museum & Information Center:

The Visitor's Center is staffed daily 10 am to 5 pm except holidays. The museum includes artifacts recovered from lands surrounding the caverns and a 20-minute video on the cavern's 8,000-year history. An interesting park feature is a performance by rangers demonstrating primitive tool use such as fire starting, spearhead tooling and atlatl usage, a wooden device enhancing spear throwing.

Picnic Areas:

3 picnic areas are available in the park.

Hiking trails:

Trails include a 0.6-mile nature trail looping up the mountain beside the caverns. This moderate asphalt trail leads by a small sinkhole with a creek flowing through its depths. Another moderate 1.2-mile hiking trail intersects the nature trail and follows an old roadbed along the mountainside.

Scenes

Cave Shelter:

The Cave Shelter adjacent Russell Cave is the location of primitive Indian habitation. Most archaeological digs were near this shelter. The shelter itself is large; about 60 feet across and 50 feet back into the mountainside.

Creeks:

Dry Creek (actually a natural spring) gushes from under the hillside and flows into the mouth of Russell Cave 100 yards away. The flow varies significantly with rainfall. Usually dry, during heavy rains the spring may cover almost half of the cave's entrance.

Foliage:

The surrounding forest is abundant with hardwoods and cedar. Indian pink, sometimes called pink root, blooms along the trails during May. This flowering plant grows up to 2-feet tall with opposing dark green oval leaves up a central stalk, topped with one inch bright red flowers, terminating with bright yellow-green flaring petals.

Dry Creek gushing into the clearly delineated opening of Russell Cave. The boardwalk leads into the Cave Shelter.

Sequoyah Caverns Park

Park Description ★★★★★

Secluded in Sand Valley, this 74-acre park is located between Lookout Mountain and Sand Mountain. The caverns extend under Sand Mountain. Sequoyah Caverns contain many formations and fossils, along with the "Looking Glass Lakes". With all the water surfaces reflecting the cavern's natural formations, this is one of the more beautiful caves in Alabama. The park also includes pastures where White Fallow Deer and American Bison graze. There are also goats, peacocks and rainbow trout.

Sequoyah was a Cherokee Indian who fought with General Andrew Jackson against the Creeks at Horseshoe Bend in the early 1800's. He is the only man known to have developed an entire alphabet, which helped his tribe understand the new settlers. In 1838, he walked with his people along the Trail of Tears when the Cherokee were removed to Oklahoma. The giant Sequoia trees and Sequoia National Park in California were named in his honor.

Nearby Points of Interest

DeSoto State Park and Little River Canyon are just south of the caverns near Ft. Payne. Lookout Mountain Parkway begins in Mentone and goes south to Gadsden. The Alabama Fan Club Museum is in nearby Ft. Payne, the *Official Sock Capitol of the World.* Buck's Pocket State Park and High Falls County Park are to the southwest. Pisgah Gorge is also west. Russell Cave National Monument is northwest.

A family of Canada Geese enjoy the pond below the entrance to Sequoyah Caverns.

Location and Directions

From I-59, Exit 231 north of Ft. Payne, take Ala. 117 south 1.2 miles to US 11. Turn left and follow US 11 north six miles to CR 731 in Rogers. Turn left and drive 1.4 miles to the park entrance on the left.

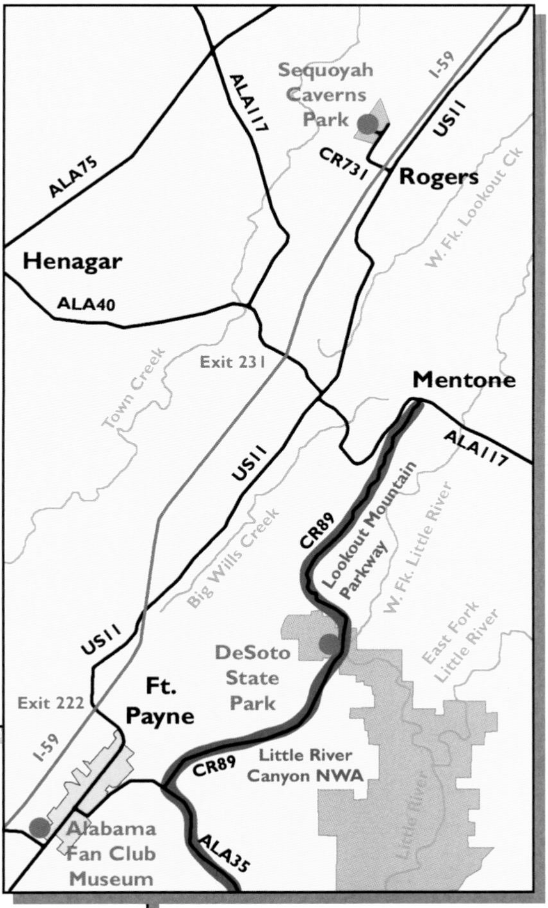

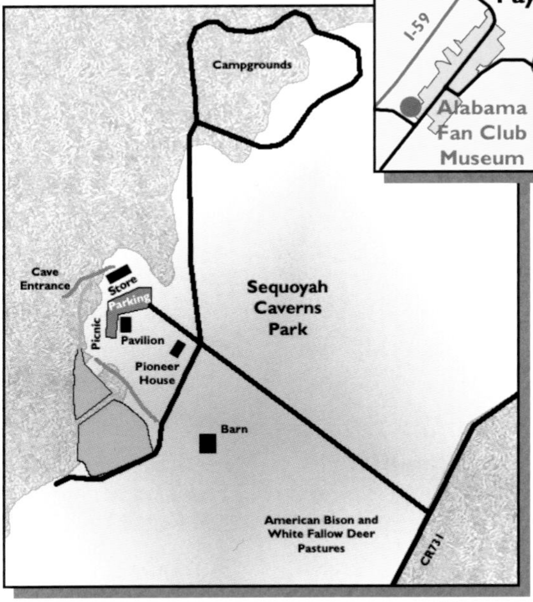

Park Map

Park Facilities

Campgrounds:

The park maintains 85 sites for tents or RV's with water and electrical connections. Fifteen sites also have sewer connections for RV's. A dump station is available.

Country Store & Information Center:

A small convenience store is adjacent the campground. The store includes a gift shop, camper registration and tours for the caverns.

Swimming Pool:

A large pool is available for registered campers.

Picnic Areas:

A picnic pavilion is available near the convenience store. The picnic area extends to a small natural spring and pond bordering the cliffs of Sand Mountain below the cave entrance.

Hiking trails:

Two marked hiking trails roam the park. An old pioneer home from the early 1800's was moved to this site near the store.

Scenes

Waterfalls:

Several waterfalls and streams are inside the caverns.

Foliage:

Hardwoods, cedar and pine surround the park.

This bright red barn overlooks the pastures where White Fallow Deer, American Bison and a few goats graze. The goats are huddled under the tree (top right) near the park entrance.

Shoal Creek Falls

Description

This double waterfall is hidden just beside CR 240 near Guntersville Dam behind a country store. Owned by Marshall County but not developed as a park, the top of the falls can be seen from the bridge on CR 240. Park at the north side of the store where short trails lead to the waterfalls. Both the upper and lower falls drop about 10 feet each and are up to 40 to 50 feet wide, depending upon the amount of rainfall. The two falls are about 50 feet apart. This was the site of an old gristmill. The footings can be seen behind the store. The mill itself was destroyed quite some time ago.

Nearby Points of Interest

Guntersville Dam is three miles beyond the waterfalls. Lake Guntersville State Park is 12 miles east. Short Creek Falls is south of Guntersville State Park. Buck's Pocket State Park and High Falls County Park are 18 miles beyond Guntersville State Park. Ghost Creek Falls and Natural Bridge is just across the Tennessee River, but one must travel through Guntersville to reach it. Cathedral Caverns State Park is also located across the river. Monte Sano State Park and Madison County Nature Trail with its covered bridge replica are located northwest in Huntsville.

Location and Directions

From US 431 in Guntersville, take Ala. 69 south (west) 6.1 miles to CR 240. (Not marked; follow signs for Guntersville Dam). Turn right onto CR 240 and go 2.2 miles to the Guntersville Dam turnoff in Neighbor's Mill. Turn right toward the dam and stop immediately at the country store on the left. Park at the far side of the store. Several trails lead just a few steps to the falls.

From US 231 in Morgan City (8.9 miles south of the Tennessee River bridge south of Huntsville), take CR 240 east 10 miles to the Guntersville Dam turnoff in Neighbor's Mill. Turn left and stop at the store on the left. The falls are behind the store.

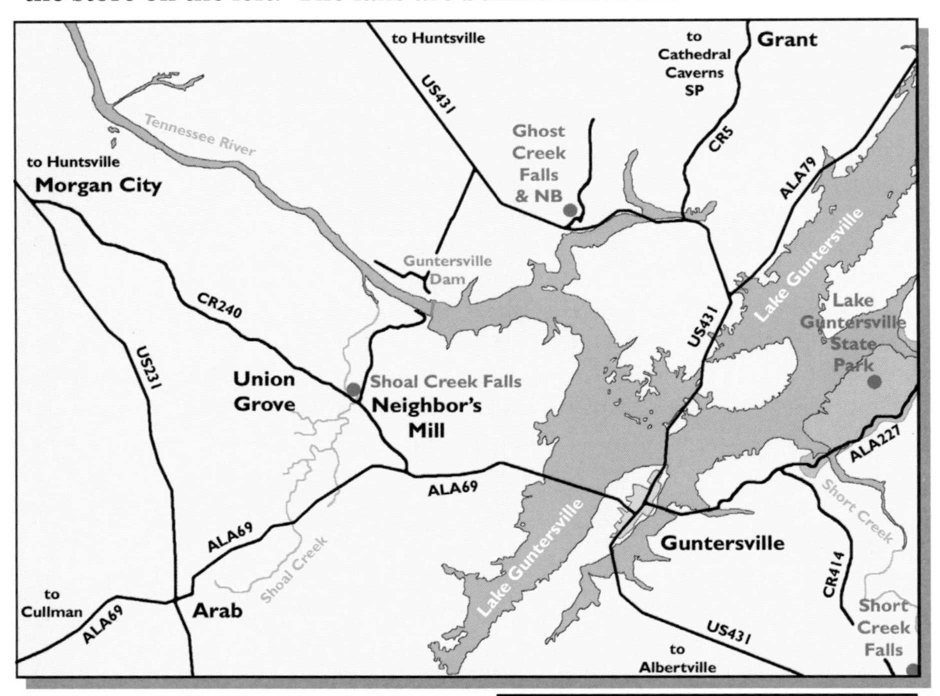

Facilities

Facilities:

Marshall County has never developed this area into a park. There is a privately owned country store adjacent the waterfalls.

Hiking trails:

Short moderate trails lead to the edge of both waterfalls.

Scenes

Waterfalls:

Each waterfall drops 10 feet and spans 40 or 50 feet. Several cascades are near the edge of the upper falls.

Creeks:

Shoal Creek continues downstream toward the Tennessee River, forming rapids around the boulders in the streambed below the falls.

***Upper and Lower Shoal Creek Falls*. The footings of an old mill remain at the left of the *Upper Falls* (above).**

Short Creek Falls

Description ★

Another hidden wonder of North Alabama, Short Creek Falls is located on private property, but the top of the falls can be seen from the bridge on CR 414. The falls are 150 feet wide and drop about 20 feet. An easy to moderate trail leads from a small pull off on the southwest side of the bridge, through a cornfield, a power line easement and the woods to the top of the falls. Being a large creek, water is usually flowing here. I rated this waterfall a one-star simply

***Short Creek Falls.* A portion escapes at the far end of the falls.**

because it's on private property. It would otherwise be rated four-stars. The waterfall is at an angle to the creek, so the best viewpoint is below and some distance away from the falls. If you decide to hike to the falls, refer to the Cautions Section in the front of this book. Please don't litter or damage the shrubbery.

Nearby Points of Interest

Lake Guntersville, Cathedral Caverns and Buck's Pocket State Parks, High Falls County Park with its natural bridge and Ghost Creek Falls and Natural Bridge are located nearby.

Location and Directions

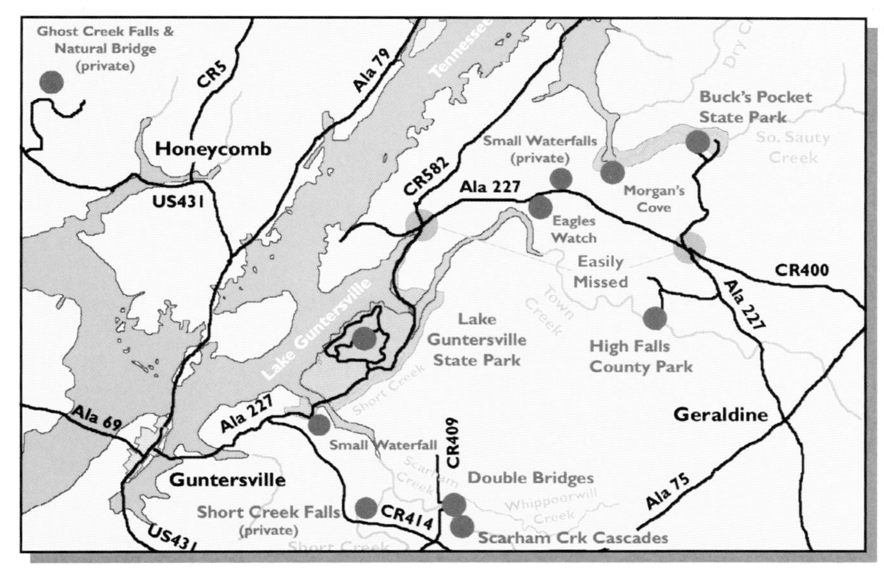

From US 431 in Guntersville, take Ala. 227 south (east) 4.3 miles, then turn right onto CR 414. Four miles ahead on CR 414 you'll cross the bridge over Short Creek. Look downstream to the left.

Area Map

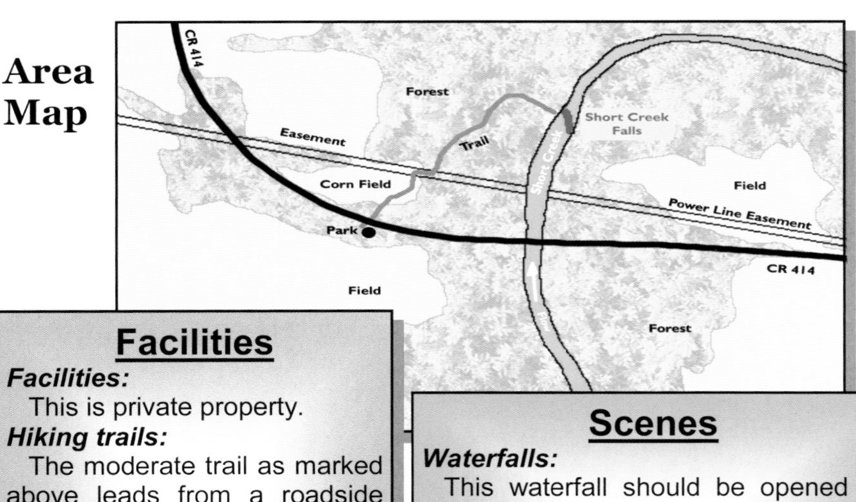

Facilities

Facilities:

This is private property.

Hiking trails:

The moderate trail as marked above leads from a roadside pull-off in the trees to the top of the waterfall, where you'll find a smaller creek flowing into Short Creek. Please be respectful of the area; do not litter or damage trees or shrubbery.

Scenes

Waterfalls:

This waterfall should be opened to the public! At 150 feet wide with a 20-foot fall, people would really enjoy seeing it.

Creeks:

Short Creek is only about 100 feet wide, but the falls are at an angle making them wider.

Talladega National Forest

Description 

Talladega National Forest covers two distinct areas in Alabama. This book only covers the northeast section around Talladega, managed by the Talladega and Shoal Creek Ranger Districts. Only the northern portion of the southwest section is shown on maps around Tuscaloosa and Moundville.

This northeast section of Talladega National Forest contains 217,000 acres of forested mountains at the southern extremity of the Appalachian Mountain Range. Most Forest Roads are dirt, but usually passable in smaller vehicles.

At the north end of the forest is Dugger Mountain, the second highest point in Alabama at 2,140 feet. To the east and south is the Choccolocco WMA. Here, Coleman Lake Recreation Area provides campgrounds, horse trails, swimming, fishing, picnicking and hiking. The nearby Pine Glen Area has additional picnic areas and horse trails. Just south of I-20, the *Talladega Scenic Drive* winds across mountain ridges for 20 miles until reaching Cheaha State Park, the highest point in Alabama at 2,407 above sea level. Several waterfalls are located near Mt. Cheaha, as is Chinnabee Lake.

Nearby Points of Interest

Talladega National Forest covers such an immense area, it depends on where you are in the forest. At the north extremity are Dugger Mountain Scenic Drive, Yellow Creek Falls and Little River Canyon Mouth Park near Leesburg. Cornwall Furnace is near Cedar Bluff. 20 miles south of I-20 is Cheaha State Park. In Oxford beside I-20 you'll find Coldwater Covered Bridge. To the east of Cheaha State Park, just south of Talladega is Waldo Covered Bridge and Old Mill Restaurant. Further west near Childersburg is DeSoto Caverns Park and Kymulga Grist Mill and Covered Bridge. To the southeast of the National Forest, you'll find Horseshoe Bend National Military Monument.

Location and Directions

From I-20, Exit 199, take Ala. 9 north one mile to US 78 in Heflin. From here, proceed as follows to your destination:

* To reach **Coleman Lake Recreation Area**, turn right and follow US 78 east to CR 61 and turn left.

The South Fork of Terrapin Creek as it flows under the bridge on Rabbittown Road (CR 55) during the drier month of June.

- To reach **Dugger Mountain Scenic Drive**, turn left onto US 78, pass the Talladega Scenic Drive signs and turn right onto Ala. 9 north.

* To reach **Cheaha State Park** or the **Talladega Scenic Drive**, turn left onto US 78, then turn right onto Ala. 281, the Talladega Scenic Drive. Ala. 281 leads 20 miles to Cheaha State Park.

Talladega National Forest north of I-20

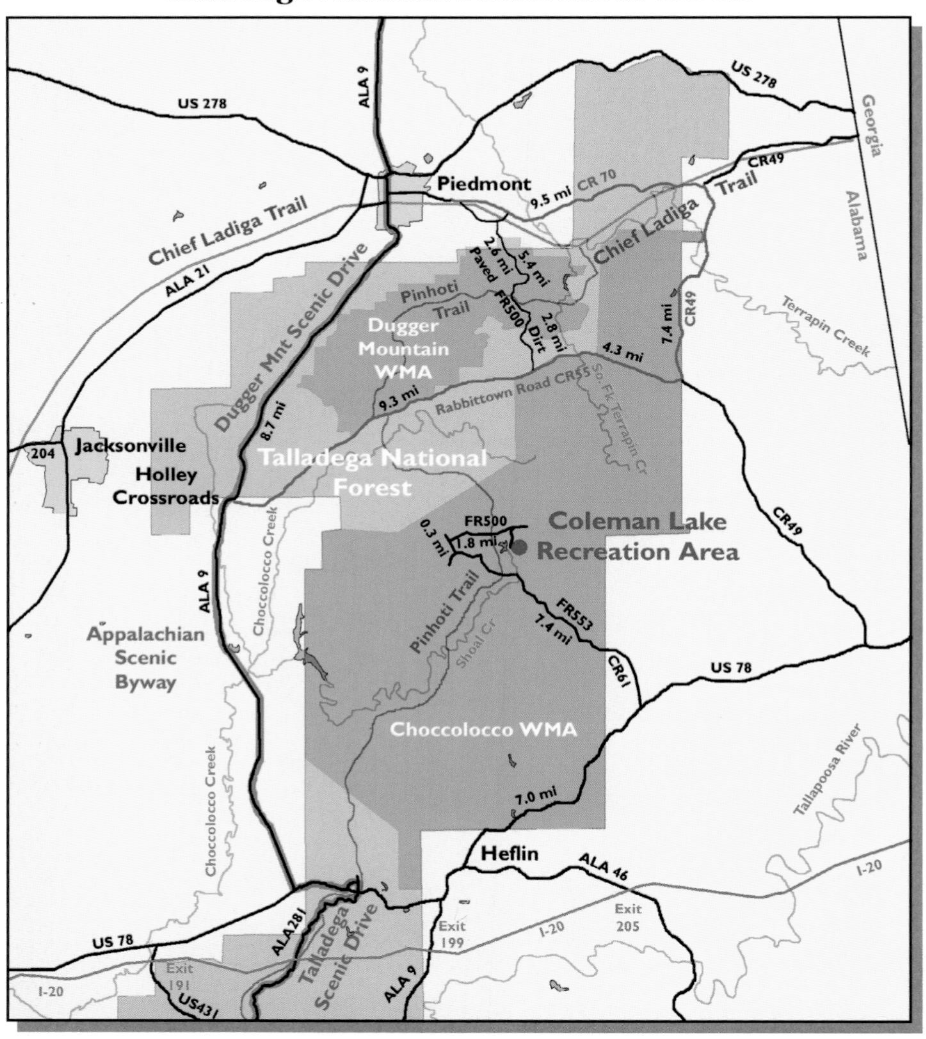

Talladega National Forest south of I-20

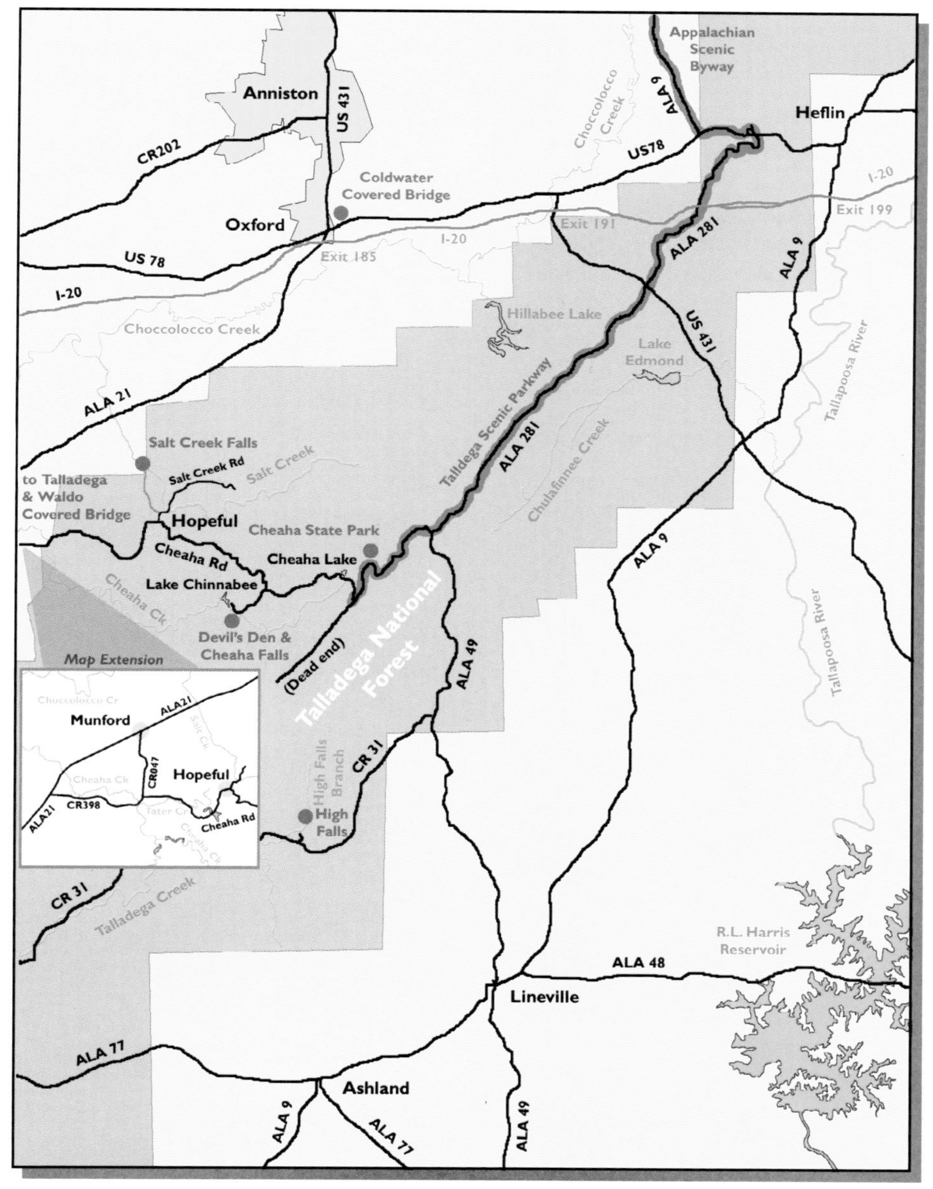

Scenes

Creeks:

Shoal Creek, just north of I-20 in the Choccolocco WMA, provides fishing and some canoeing activities.

Choccolocco Creek and **Terrapin Creek** both are popular for canoeing and kayaking activities.

Waterfalls:

All of these waterfalls are near the Cheaha State Park area.

Devil's Den Falls is a moderate 1/2-mile hike from the parking and picnic area at Chinnabee Lake, along the Chinnabee Silent Trail. Devil's Den is a small waterfall.

Cheaha Falls, a popular swimming area, is reached by hiking just beyond Devil's Den Falls. This waterfall drops about 10 feet and with the surrounding rocks and forest, is very scenic.

High Falls with a 15-foot drop, is located 15 miles south of Cheaha State Park. It requires an easy 1/4-mile hike to reach. Follow Ala. 281 north to Ala. 49 south to CR31 south.

Salt Creek Falls is outside Cheaha State Park, but inside the boundaries of Talladega National Forest. As far as I can tell, it is a beautiful waterfall dropping about 40 feet. The trail leads to the top of the falls and there is no easy way down to view them from below. However there is another small 3-foot waterfall just above the main waterfall that is worth the hike to view. BEWARE: the trail nearing the falls is very tough and dangerous. Steep inclines over rocks; be very careful. People have fallen here before resulting in drastic consequences. Refer to the cautions posted in the front of this book.

Foliage:

Many of the National Forest lands are harvested for pines, which returns funds to the encompassing counties. Various hardwoods and cedars are also protected.

Facilities

Lodge and Restaurant:

Cheaha State Park maintains the forest's only lodge, cabin and restaurant facilities.

Campgrounds:

The **Coleman Lake Recreation Area** provides camping around Coleman Lake. The campground contains 39 sites with water and electrical connections for tents and RV's. Two comfort stations are available. A dump station is also provided.

Cheaha State Park maintains 73 developed sites with 3 comfort stations.

Hiking trails:

The **Pinhoti Trail** system extends over 80 miles through the National Forest from Piedmont at the north to near Sylacauga at the southern boundary. In 1977, the Pinhoti was designated a *National Recreation Trail*.

Tannehill Historical State Park

Park Description ★★

One of the Tannehill furnaces. The small structure on the right is the blower house which provided air for the blast furnaces through the rusty, horizontal pipes.

This historical park encompasses 1,500 acres and many nineteenth century structures, some donated and moved to the park for preservation. Daniel Hillman first constructed a forge on this site in 1830 after finding rich deposits of iron ore beside Roupes Creek. Three tall sandstone furnaces still standing today were completed in 1863. These forges produced 70% of the Confederate military ordinance, about 20 tons per day. A dam constructed upstream on Roupes Creek fed water through a 285-foot canal to the blower house, where it was used to generate air pressure to fan the blast furnaces. Union soldiers under General James Wilson's command destroyed the iron works in 1865, just prior to General Lee's surrender.

Today, the park provides hiking and horse trails, campgrounds and rental cabins. An Iron & Steel Museum displays many artifacts from nineteenth century forging. A gristmill, blacksmith shop and pioneer farm are located on Mill Creek upstream from the furnaces at the far end of the park. A miniature train carries visitors between park sections.

Nearby Points of Interest

Two miles northeast of the park entrance on CR 97 is *Tannehill Valley Covered Bridge.* The bridge is now closed to traffic, but easily visible from CR 97 on the southeast side. Brierfield Ironworks Historical State Park is only 28 miles south. Oak Mountain State Park is 15 miles southeast of Birmingham following I-459 north, then I-65 south. Rickwood Caverns State Park is 41 miles from Tannehill following I-59 north, then I-65 north. Lake Lurleen State

Park and Moundville Archaeological Park are west near Tuscaloosa following I-59 south. Oxmoor Valley in Birmingham is part of Alabama's famous Robert Trent Jones Golf Trail.

Location and Directions

From I-20/59, Exit 100, take Tannehill Parkway south to CR 97 and turn right. The park entrance is immediately on the left. CR 97 changes to CR 18 at the county line.

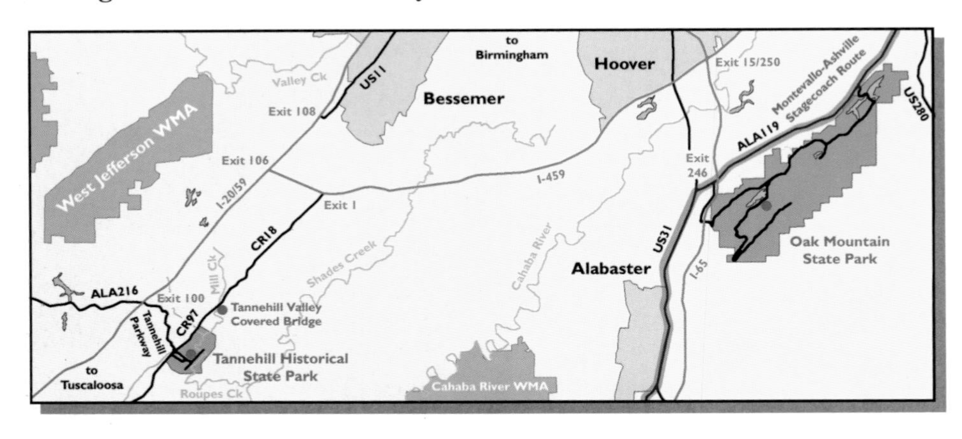

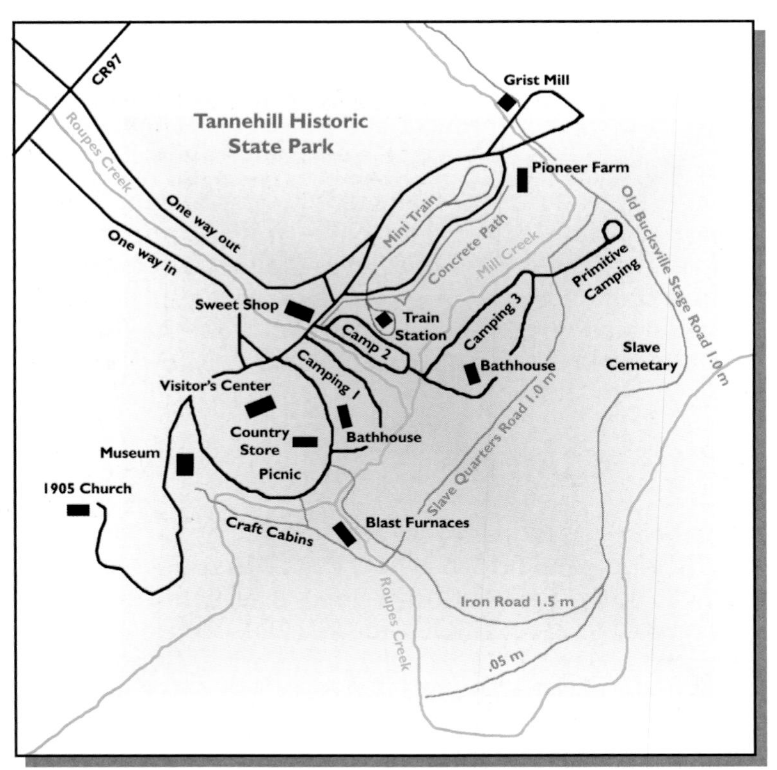

Park Map

Park Facilities

Cabins and Chalets:

The park maintains six cabins; five are restored rustic cabins available for six to eight persons. All cabins have a furnished kitchen, living room with a fireplace, bathroom, heat and air-conditioning. The cabins do not include TVs, radios or telephones.

Campgrounds:

One hundred-ninety five improved campsites along Roupes Creek and Mill Creek for tents, pop-ups or large RV's. Three comfort stations are located in the campgrounds. All sites have water and electrical connections, with a dump station available.

Visitors Center:

The Visitors Center and office provides information about the park. A nearby country store provides camping and picnicking supplies. A sweet shop provides additional treats. From spring to fall, several craft cabins provide interesting gift items.

Museum:

A large air-conditioned building houses many iron and steel artifacts forged during the 1800's and early 1900's. A nineteenth century cotton gin stands separately at the rear of the museum.

Picnic Areas:

The main picnic area is centrally located near the visitor center, country store and cabins.

Hiking trails:

Five miles of easy trails lead around the park, available for hikers or horseback riding. Trails lead to the furnaces, along Roupes Creek, between park sections and along several of the historic roads used to transport the processed iron ore.

Scenes

Furnaces:

Slaves constructed three large blast furnaces in the early 1860's using native sandstone blocks carved from the surrounding area. A 285-foot long canal was dug and lined with rock to funnel water from a dam upstream on Roupes Creek to the blower-house. Here, the water turned fans used to blow air into the blast furnaces.

Gristmill:

Located on Mill Creek, a mill-race channels water to the mill from a dam several hundred feet upstream.

Creeks:

Roupes Creek (also called Mud Creek) flows by the three historic blast furnaces. Small rapids upstream mark the location of the old dam, destroyed by floods in the late 1800's.

Mill Creek provided power for the gristmill.

Foliage:

Black walnut trees are found amidst the oak, cedar and pine. Walnuts were used for tanning (the process of making leather from rawhides).

South Caney Creek Falls **in Bankhead National Forest.**

Short Creek Falls **near Lake Guntersville State Park.**

Waterfall Locations

These are the major waterfalls of North Alabama. Some of these sites have more than one waterfall nearby. Bankhead National Forest for instance, has countless waterfalls, especially after heavy rains. Reaching falls in Bankhead will require hiking, except Kinlock Falls right beside FS 210. The largest falls are located in the northeast quadrant of Alabama. The other though smaller, are still beautiful. Most of these falls are near roadways and are reached with a short walk. A longer hike will lead to the others.

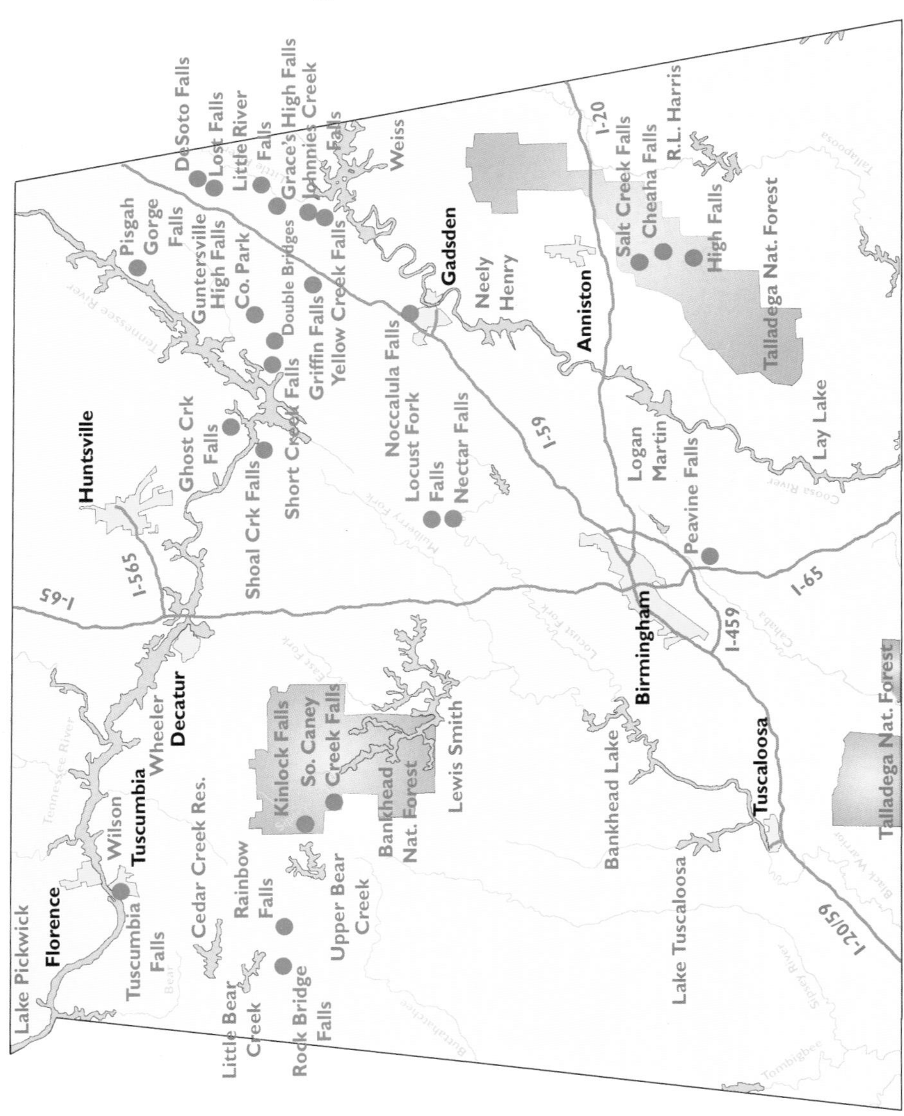

Wheeler National Wildlife Refuge

Description ★★★

Set aside in 1938, Wheeler NWR contains 34,500 acres along the Tennessee River between Huntsville and Decatur. The Refuge provides resting and feeding areas for 285 species of birds, 115 fishes, 74 reptiles and amphibians and 47 mammals. Several threatened and endangered species inhabit the Refuge. Canadian Geese use the Refuge as a wintering area. With 18,000 acres of water, the most popular activity in the Refuge is fishing, with wildlife observation, photography, hiking and hunting encouraged. Seven improved boat ramps are located on the north and south side of the river.

Sunset over Wheeler.

Nearby Points of Interest

Decatur is the closest city located just three miles west of the Visitor's Center. Point Mallard Water Park is also close, just five miles. Huntsville is about 40 miles northeast, where Monte Sano State Park sits atop Monte Sano Mountain, and Madison County Nature Trail sits on Green Mountain. The Space & Rocket Center is on I-565 in Huntsville. Joe Wheeler State Park is west across the Tennessee River.

Location and Directions

From I-65, take Exit 334. Follow Ala. 67 north (west) three miles to the Visitor's Center on the left.

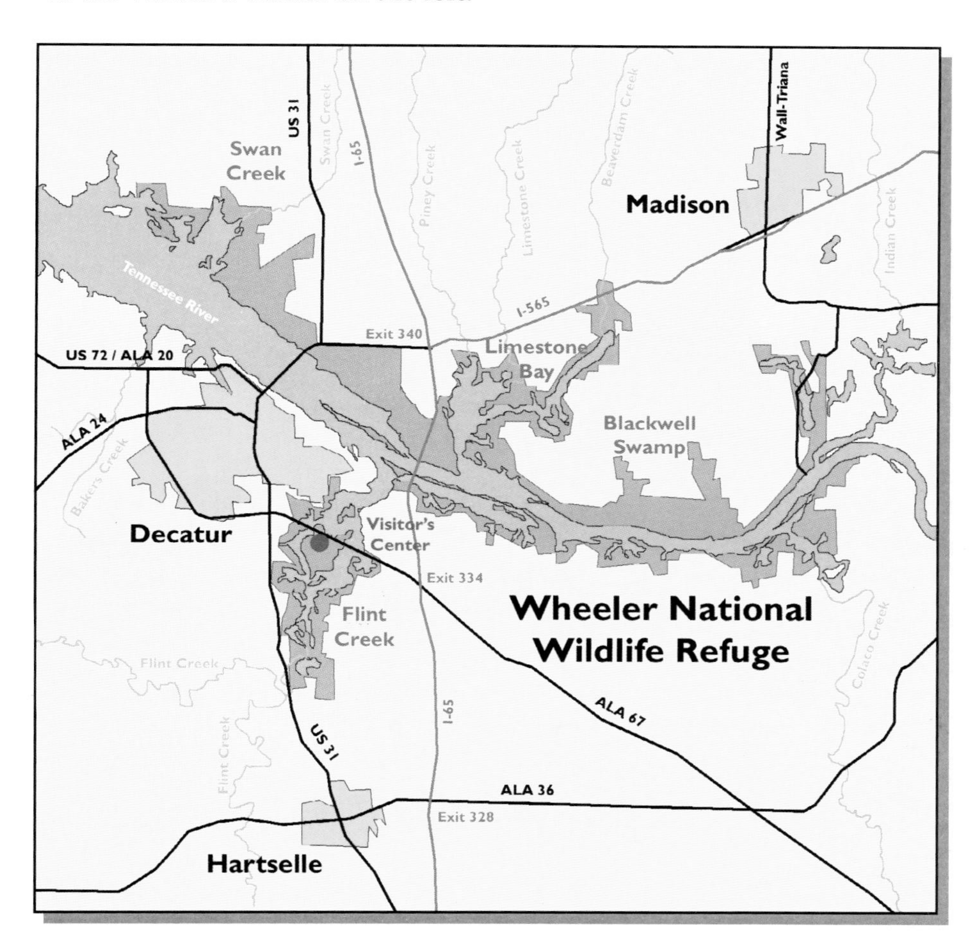

Facilities

Visitor's Center:

The only facility in the NWR is the Visitor's Center, which includes a Nature Center. There are no picnic, camping or lodging facilities. From the Visitor's Center it is a short, easy 0.3-mile hike to the wildlife observation platform overlooking fields and backwater. A great spot for viewing

Scenes

Creeks:

Being rather flat terrain in this area, Joe Wheeler Dam further west on the Tennessee River causes backwaters to fill all major creeks in the Refuge so they've become swamps or bays. This provides excellent habitat for animals and fishermen alike. Some areas are closed at times during

Light reflecting from drops of water on this lily pad made an interesting subject while waiting for the sunset.

waterfowl. The Visitor's Center hours are 10 am to 5 pm. From March 1st through September 30th, the Center is closed Monday and Tuesday.

Hiking trails:

Hiking trails are in several places around the Refuge. The most popular is the short easy path to the Observation Tower. Another popular trail is directly across Ala. 67 from the Visitor's Center. This easy trail leads 3/4 mile across the backwaters and around a small peninsula.

the year to provide isolation for the animals.

Flint Creek at the southwest border of the Refuge, provides a boat ramp at Hickory Hills.

Blackwell Swamp near the northeast border has some of Alabama's largest Tupelo Trees.

Limestone Bay is the largest bay in the Refuge. Arrowhead Landing boat ramp is on the west side of the bay. Fishing, hiking and biking are popular activities in this area.

Foliage:

Water lilies line the shorelines, with their blooms peaking in July. Redbud, cedar and pine are abundant. The Blackwell Swamp area contains some of Alabama's largest black tupelo trees.

William B. Bankhead National Forest

Description ★★★★★

First declared a National Forest in 1918 by President Woodrow Wilson, Bankhead National Forest encircles 180,000 acres of mostly untouched forests, gorges, cliffs, rivers and waterfalls. There are many Indian hieroglyphics in the soft sandstone and artifacts throughout the area. It is illegal to damage or remove them.

Centrally located in northwest Alabama between Florence, Huntsville, Birmingham and Tuscaloosa, the forest includes the Sipsey Wilderness Area and part of Lewis Smith Lake. The 25,000-acre Sipsey Wilderness Area is the third largest east of the Mississippi River and is home to hemlock trees up to 700 years old. The 21,000-acre Lewis Smith Lake has over 500 miles of shoreline. At least one-third of the lake is within the National Forest boundaries. The Sipsey Fork, popular for fishing and canoeing, is listed as a *National Wild and Scenic River*. With thousands of acres of water, numerous campgrounds and over 150 miles of trails for hiking, horseback riding and bicycling, the visitor has many choices of activities.

Nearby Points of Interest

The Warrior Mountain Trading Company is located in Wren just north of the National Forest on Ala. 33 at Ala. 36. Well known as the Gateway to Bankhead & Sipsey Wilderness, supplies and canoe rentals are available. Lake Shore Inn and Marina is a convenient location for those who prefer not to camp. Clarkson Covered Bridge is east near Cullman on US 278. Natural Bridge, Dismals Wonder Gardens and Rock Bridge Canyon are west of the forest. Rickwood Caverns State Park is southeast near I-65, while Joe Wheeler State Park is north on the Tennessee River.

South Caney Creek Falls is north of CR 2. Park on the roadside by the steel bar gate and hike past the gate 3/4 mile to the falls.

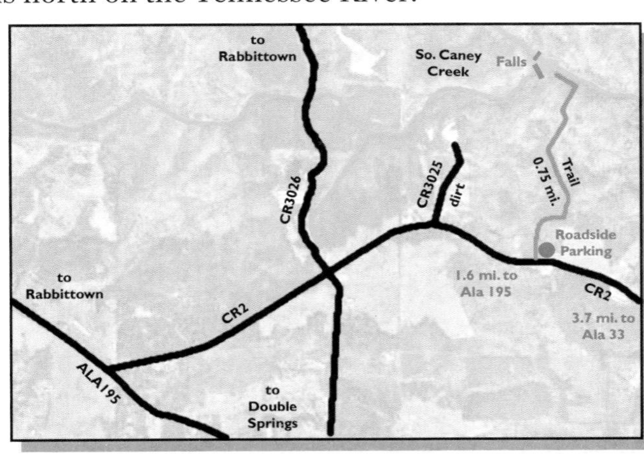

In mid-January, ice crystals form on this inverted tree at *South Caney Creek Falls*.

Location and Directions

This map reflects some of the major highways leading to Bankhead National Forest from the surrounding cities.

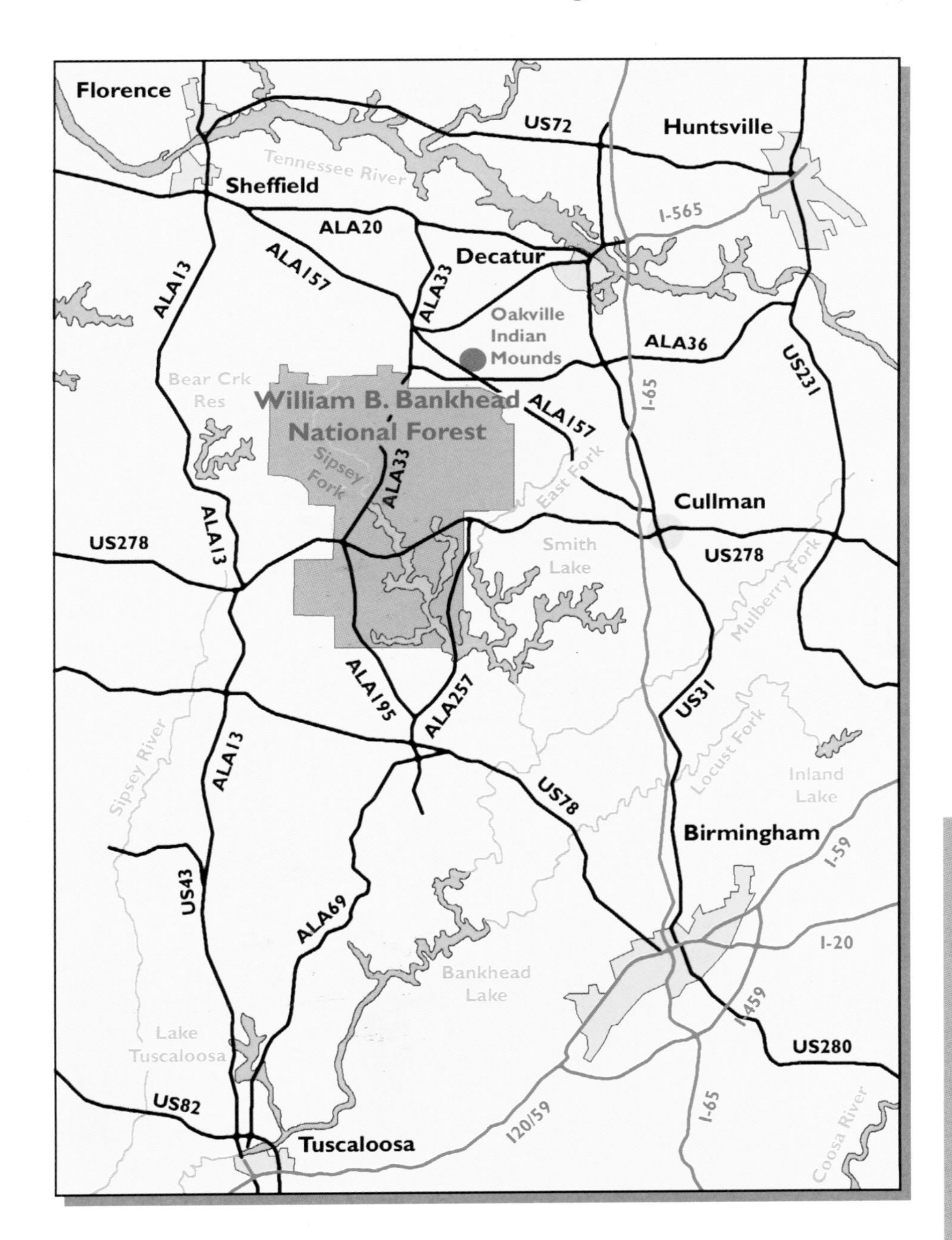

Area Map

Bankhead National Forest is so large, it is impossible to legibly detail all of the forest roads and trails on such a small map as this one. If you intend to spend time here, I recommend purchasing a Road and Recreational Map from one of the local shops, such as Warrior Mountain Trading Company at the north edge of the forest. All roads shown here are paved except FS 210 by Kinlock Falls.

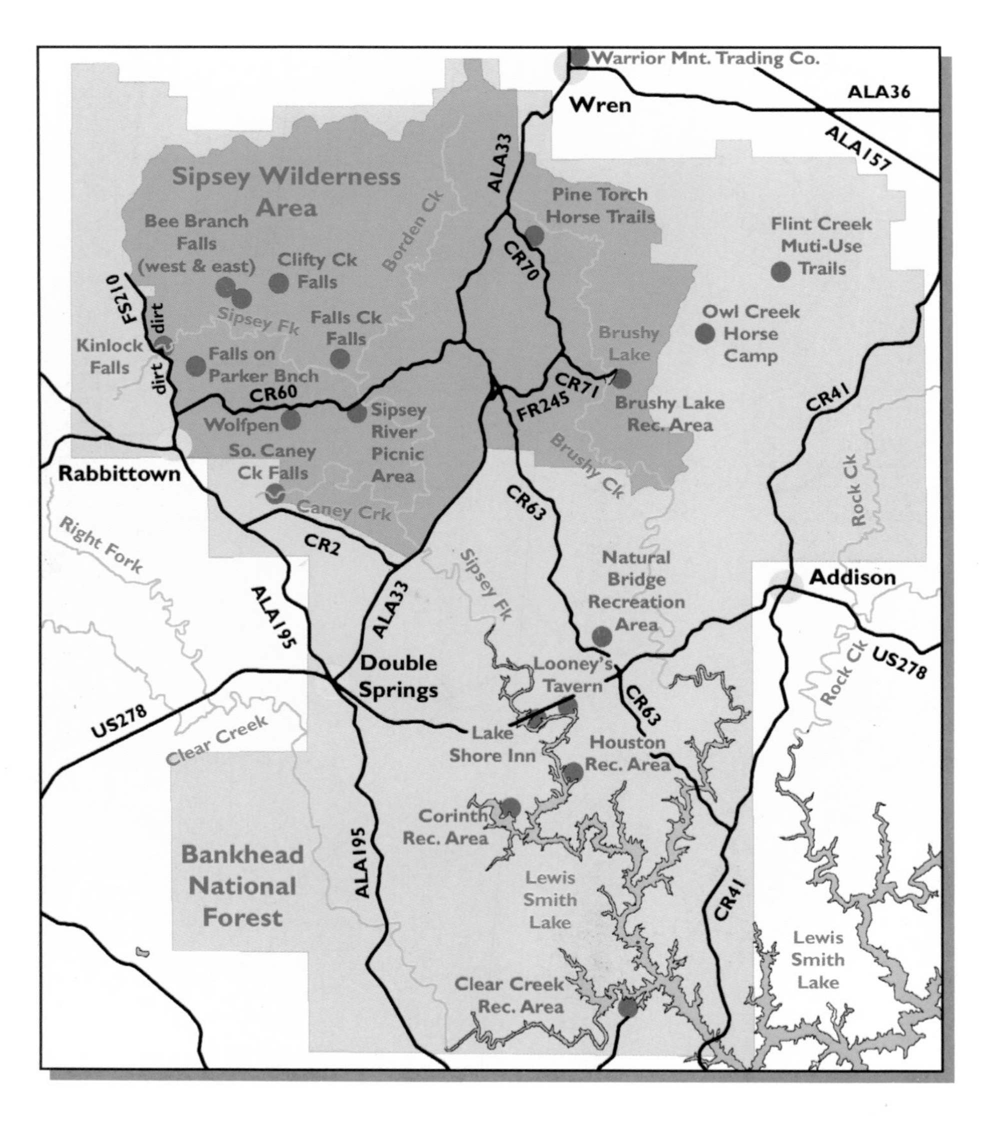

Park Facilities

Campgrounds, Trails & Picnic Areas:

There are several campgrounds within the National Forest. The Clear Creek and Corinth campgrounds are fully developed for tents or RV's with water, electric and sewer connections. Most of these campgrounds are open seasonally, April through October.

Clear Creek on Lewis Smith Lake is the largest and most popular recreation area with 102 developed campsites, comfort stations, playgrounds, picnic areas and a sand beach. The campground has gated access.

Corinth Recreation Area is on Lewis Smith Lake and has 52 developed sites with three comfort stations.

Houston Recreation Area is also on Lewis Smith Lake. It has 86 sites, a comfort station and dump station.

Brushy Lake Recreation Area is located in a remote area of the forest on 33-acre Brushy Lake. One minor comfort station is available for the 13 primitive campsites accommodating tents or small RV's. There are no water, electric or sewer connections.

Owl Creek Horse Camp offers primitive camping for trail riders with small RV's. Owl Creek has 30 miles of horse trails in the Black Warrior WMA. This WMA extends across the northeastern section of the National Forest, including the eastern portion of the Sipsey Wildlife Area.

Flint Creek Multi-Use Trails offer miles of trails for horseback riding, hiking and cycling.

Wolf Pen is a primitive hunter's camp.

Sipsey River Picnic Area by the Sipsey Fork on CR 60 includes tables along the riverbank. Several trails lead from here along the river north and south. The north trail leads to Falls Creek Falls.

Scenes

Waterfalls:

There are many waterfalls along the trails, many more than shown here. With the numerous cliffs and bluffs present, almost every trail in the Sipsey Wilderness Area will lead to several.

Kinlock Falls is located beside FS 210 in the northwest of the forest. More of a cascade, it drops 15 feet over a distance of 20 feet. A low bluff provides a magnificent viewpoint.

South Caney Creek Falls requires a hard 1-mile hike to reach, but its beauty and sereneness are unmatchable. Actually, two adjacent creeks fall over the 30-foot bluff side by side into the pool below. The sandy bottom pool casts a yellow-green tint to its shallow waters.

East and West Bee Branch Falls, Clifty Creek Falls and Falls Creek Falls all require longer hikes to reach.

Creeks:

The Sipsey River is listed as a *National Wild and Scenic River.* It is a popular destination for canoeists and fishermen.

Foliage:

The forests, being almost totally natural, contain a variety of plant life. The most spectacular are the hemlocks that grow abundantly throughout the area, some as old as 700 years. *Big Tree*, the state's record yellow poplar, grows in the Sipsey Wilderness Area north of CR 60 near the Sipsey Fork.

I hope you enjoy these images and
find this travel guide useful.
Comments? Send e-mail to
Robert@SchuffertStudios.Com
- Be safe! -